care
policy
renewal
sustainable
trusts
NGO
care social
NHS non-profits
environment
cohesion quality
management
leadership
grants
guard
em
development
housing
policy
reform
ethics
help
health
projects
government
public
community
charity innovation
human resources
voluntary actio
fundraising
cooperatives
racism diversity
well-being
poverty
volunteer
policy
NHS
education
inclusion
inputs
campaign
inequality
contracts
empower
public
care
neighbourhood
evaluation
health
outputs

Innovation and Change in Non-Profit Organisations

Case Studies in Survival, Sustainability and Success

Edited by Don Macdonald

Innovation and Change in Non-Profit Organisations
Case studies in survival, sustainability and success

Published by:
Pavilion Publishing and Media Ltd
Blue Sky Offices Shoreham
25 Cecil Pashley Way
Shoreham-by-Sea
West Sussex
BN43 5FF
Tel: 01273 434 943
Fax: 01273 227 308
Email: info@pavpub.com

Published 2019

ISBN: 978-1-912755-56-1

Pavilion is the leading training and development provider and publisher in the health, social care and allied fields, providing a range of innovative training solutions underpinned by sound research and professional values. We aim to put our customers first, through excellent customer service and value.

Editor: Don Macdonald
Production editor: Mike Benge, Pavilion Publishing and Media Ltd.
Cover design: Emma Dawe, Pavilion Publishing and Media Ltd.
Page layout and typesetting: Emma Dawe, Pavilion Publishing and Media Ltd.
Printing: Ashford Press

Innovation and Change in Non-Profit Organisations

Case Studies in Survival, Sustainability and Success

Edited by Don Macdonald with a foreword by Lord Victor Adebowale and contributions by Sarah Brennan, Chris Durkin, Kathryn Engelhardt-Cronk, Charles Fraser, Shaks Ghosh, Marchu Girma, Tommy Hutchinson, Sian Lockwood, Dr Chris O'Leary, Andy Shields and Dr Patrick Vernon.

This book is dedicated to
Dr Josephine Klein, Joan Tash and Harold Marchant,
my three community and youth work models.

Contents

About the authors

Don Macdonald (editor & contributor) has founded and managed charities, social enterprises and youth and community education projects in the UK for 40 years. He has also provided youth and community work training at different UK universities and coaching and management training, particularly to non-profit managers. Don provided consultancy, business planning and coaching for emerging social enterprises for a British Council project in Myanmar. He is chair of the LFJ charity and advises and mentors small and emerging social enterprises. BEP has published his book *21st Century Skills for Non-Profit Managers: A practical guide on leadership and management*. He also edited with Charles Oham and wrote with six other authors, another book, *Leading and Managing a Social Enterprise in Health and Social Care*.

Other contributors

Sarah Brennan OBE started as CEO at Young Minds, the UK's leading charity for children and young people's mental health in 2007 and retired in 2018. She now works as a consultant. She spent her earlier career in the non-profit sector and previously worked with young offenders and those at risk of offending as CEO of Motiv8 and at Centrepoint, where she was director of services and manager of Camberwell Foyer.

Chris Durkin is currently project manager for the D2N2 Social Work Teaching partnership, which covers Nottinghamshire and Derbyshire and also Principal Lecturer Social Work and Health (p/t) at Nottingham Trent University. He was previously associate professor at the University of Northampton, set up the Institute of Urban Affairs, was course leader for an MA in Social Innovation and was part of the senior management group and international academic lead in the School of Social Sciences. Chris has research interests in social entrepreneurship, social care, social innovation and community development. He co-edited with Robert Gunn *Social Entrepreneurship: A skills approach*, published by the Policy Press (2010 and 2017). He is a registered social worker.

Kathryn Engelhardt-Cronk is the founder/CEO at MissionBox, President of the MissionBox Philanthropic Fund in the USA and now the UK. She has over 25 years experience in non-profit services: first as a direct service provider with adults suffering from mental illness and later as an executive director of non-profits working in substance abuse treatment and child abuse prevention. She also served as VP of Community Impact for United Way. After seeing a critical non-profit need for service and outcomes reporting technology, Kathryn founded

Community TechKnowledge (CTK). In her role as CEO and co-designer of CTK software and services, she provides non-profits with tools to build their capacity, researching and writing relevant articles regularly. Several years after, CTK launched the CTK Foundation, which receives a portion of CTK profits to donate to non-profits across the world.

Charles Fraser CBE FRSA is the former CEO of St Mungo's (1994-2014). Having worked for St Mungo's as a hostel worker, resettlement manager and deputy director since 1980, Charles built up the organisation as the largest charity providing direct services for homeless people in the UK. With an operations background, he had a particular interest in resettlement, long-term unemployment, mental health and health inequalities. He participated in many boards and working groups, including the Ministerial Working Group on Equality in Mental Health; the National Health Inclusion Board; the London Mayor's Rough Sleeping Delivery Board; and the Big Lottery's programme tackling multiple needs. On three occasions he was recognised as one of London's 1,000 Most Influential People.

Shaks Ghosh is the CEO of Clore Social Leadership, where she writes regularly on relevant topics. She has a track record of service in the social sector, and wide experience of policy, housing, homelessness and youth unemployment issues. Her early career was in local government, housing associations, central government and the Indian NGO sector. Following 10 years as CEO of Crisis, she led the establishment of the Private Equity Foundation. She is passionate about social justice and is now focused on strengthening the sector.

Marchu Girma is a campaigner advocating for the rights of refugee and asylum seeking women. She works as the grassroots director for Women for Refugee Women and is passionate about empowering refugees and asylum seeking women to speak up about their experiences, and enabling them to use their voices for change. As part of her role at Women for Refugee Women, Marchu has co-authored research reports, delivered training, and helps to maintain refugee women's networks around the country. In 2017 Marchu was invited by UN Women to speak at their annual Commission on the Status of Women conference at the UN in New York.

Tommy Hutchinson is founder and CEO of i-genius, which promotes social entrepreneurship around the world, co-director of the Global Centre for Healthy Workplaces and a European Commission Expert on sustainability and innovation. He has worked in over 40 countries and established several social businesses. His previous career in the City of London included being an aerospace analyst, market intelligence and political adviser to NatWest Group. He is a visiting lecturer at several universities and honorary adviser to Hunan University. He has published several articles on aspects of the social economy and is co-author of *A Risky Business*. He is also working on other publications on social entrepreneurship.

Sian Lockwood OBE is the CEO of Community Catalysts, a CIC working through local partners across the UK to create an environment within which community social care and health enterprise can flourish. Sian blogs regularly about issues around health and social care. She has a long history of supporting community action to address social care and health issues and to create choice for people who need some support or care to live their lives.

Dr Chris O'Leary is deputy director of the Policy Evaluation and Research Unit at Manchester Metropolitan University. He is responsible for managing a number of research projects, providing leadership on the design and delivery of research and evaluation projects around public sector reform and its impact on social policy design, implementation and delivery. His research focuses on many aspects of public service reform, including outcome based commissioning (Payment by Results/Social Impact Bonds), commissioning and procurement, and the role of social innovation in driving reform. Chris has published numerous reports and papers along with chapters in a number of books.

Andy Shields is a consultant. Previously head of business development at 3SC, the social sector procurement organisation, Andy has also acted as head of business development at the Home Group and director of skills and learning at St Mungos, building up these services. He has also acted as an interim manager for a range of charities and non-profit organisations, working with service users from different client groups.

Dr Patrick Vernon OBE, a Clore and Winston Churchill Fellow, fellow at the Imperial War Museum and fellow of the Royal Historical Society, is currently Associate Director for Connected Communities at the Centre for Aging Better. He founded Every Generation Media and 100 Great Black Britons, providing education, publications and films on cultural and family history. Patrick was made Pioneer of the Nation for Cultural History by the Queen in 2003. In 2017 he was appointed editor for *Black History Month* magazine and in 2018 for the *Windrush Commemorative* magazine. Since 2010 he has led the campaign for Windrush Day and in 2018 started the campaign for a Windrush Generation amnesty, contributing to a government policy U-turn and the resignation of Home Secretary Amber Rudd. Patrick, awarded an OBE in 2012 for his work tackling health inequalities for UK ethnic minority communities, is patron of the ACCI mental health charity in Wolverhampton, Santé, a refugee project in Camden and was awarded an honorary Doctor of Letters by Wolverhampton University in 2018. In 2018 he was selected as one of the 1000 Evening Standard Progressive Londoners for his campaign for Windrush Day, and 2019 by the Independent Happy List for fundraising efforts regarding Windrush Justice Fund.

Foreword

This book gives voice to the expertise and views of activists and managers, who work or have worked on the front line in the community sector, achieving something substantial and becoming thought leaders. It examines relevant contemporary issues, currently affecting the non-profit sector, including racism, social enterprise, contracts and procurement, social housing, youth and community organising, sustainability, mental health, management skills, funding cuts, social innovation and self–help groups.

The content stimulates imaginative thinking, provides information and case studies, discusses the viability of a range of new strategies and forward thinking, outlining both utilitarian concepts and practical solutions, all based on solid experience at the coal face and reflective practice, as some research suggested that all the best new ideas in community care came from local projects.

From my own experience with Turning Point, Social Enterprise UK, Collaborate CIC and Urban Development, I understand at first hand both the pressures and potential of the non-profit sector. The challenges imposed by austerity have exacerbated the situation for people suffering in all walks of life from cuts in funding and services. In this depressing situation, the non-profit sector provides a beacon of hope.

Lord Victor Adebowale CBE

Introduction

By Don Macdonald

Rising levels of inequality and a growing demand for better services make the issues and challenges facing society and the non-profit sector more critical, both in the UK and the rest of the world. The population increases and becomes older, financial pressures curtail services, issues such as mental health and homelessness rise, and the environment continues to deteriorate. The UK government's imposition of 'austerity' has made things worse, particularly for the poorest 20% of society, while charities face increased demand for these services.

According to *The Guardian*'s economics editor, the government's austerity measures 'did much damage to the economy. It slowed a recovery still in its early stages and set Britain on a low-growth, weak-productivity path from which it has never really recovered'. According to the Institute for Fiscal Studies, the approach of Brexit has already compounded the problem with 'a consensus that the economy is about two per cent smaller today than it would have been had the referendum result gone the other way'.

The collapse of Carillion and care companies such as Southern Cross has showed the failures of the private sector, while the Grenfell Tower tragedy showed the failures of the public sector. Now there is a growing realisation that neither the market nor the state can meet the complex and fast changing needs of today's society, which requires innovation at a pace and scope beyond the public sector and at a quality beyond the private sector. This gap must be filled by the third sector, or as we are calling it, the non-profit sector.

The non-profit sector is absolutely vital to the fabric of UK society. There are around 170,000 registered charities, along with 100,000 non-profit organisations that are not registered. However there is a growing divide between small non-profits with low profile, high energy, real street credibility, and service user involvement, and the traditional UK large non-profits, with big reserves and highly paid chief executives. Big household names such as the Cancer Research, Save the Children and the Red Cross with incomes over £10m, make up less than one per cent of UK charities, but account for almost 50% of the sector's total income.

Context

The current context in which non-profit sector managers operate is very demanding, but still provides new opportunities along with the challenges. In the last 50 years (since the author started volunteering for a charity), the most important issues include the rise of feminism and women's rights, gay liberation, the push for diversity, the fact that human rights issues have become much higher profile, with disabled people and other minority groups demanding greater rights, while gaining greater access and support, all of which continue to be very critical.

The Windrush scandal highlighted the fundamental problems of racism still endemic in the UK, with the Home Office's 'hostile environment' permeating the Civil Service's decision-making. Diversity issues have become far more important, with the legalisation of homosexuality and, eventually, same sex marriage and gender identity changes. The UK population is growing apace, with both more children and an ageing population, with a consistent rise in non-native born residents, particularly European, in the last 10 years. In the UK, while Anglican Church attendance has declined, other 'Pentecostal' Christian churches and religions report increased attendances.

There is much less deference across the whole of society; service users' views are taken much more into account by non-profit organisations and government itself, with representation on organisation boards and government inquiries. Government has been obsessed with Brexit and so achieved little positive in civil society.

Standards of living had increased steadily over the 50 years prior to the 2008 recession, when the imposition of austerity in 2010 increased inequality. Enormous wealth gaps exist, along with poverty for certain groups, such as those suffering benefit cuts and the chaos of Universal Credit. The Brexit vote has highlighted the considerable divisions in Britain; with many people marginalised in the UK, communities have become fractured, hopelessness has increased and attitudes have become very polarised. Many people live in towns that have been neglected. 'Civil Society needs to work hard in these 'left-behind' places and doing so effectively is going to mean new models', according to Dan Corry[1].

Although vastly increased numbers now go to university, students inherit large amounts of debt. At the other end of the educational spectrum, the situation of certain young people has worsened, including children with special educational needs, excluded pupils or those who are not in

---

1   For more information, see www.pioneerspost.com/news-views/20181005/the-future-of-civil-society (accessed August 2019).

employment or education, the so-called NEETs. Family structures have changed, with more people living together and having children before marriage, which now occurs at an older age.

With financial deregulation, globalisation has increased, with a huge decline in UK heavy industries, a fall in manufacturing employment, a growth in service industries and an enormous increase in the power of multinational corporations. While there has been a growth in employment rights for those in work with contracts, this has been accompanied by a growth in zero hours' contracts, night working and part-time jobs, with fewer rights and benefits. It is the latter groups which have boosted the employment figures. There is much more international travel and a growth in international charities, which must be linked.

Homelessness for families and single people has increased enormously. Housing associations originally started off as charities, with a big boom in the 1960s, however the largest have now become heavily dependent on private finance and are involved in selling houses. There has also been an increase in councils transferring their housing stock to ALMOS (Arms' Length Management Organisations), like the organisation responsible for Grenfell Tower. Rogue private landlords, meanwhile, have been running riot, with the government unwilling to bring in proper legislation to tackle the issue. (The topic of housing requires a whole book in itself but we do have Charles Fraser writing about it.)

The rise of the contract culture and the introduction of privatisation over the last four decades has had a profound effect across many sectors, including probation and prison services, and its impact has been heavily criticised. It has led to an increase in private sector organisations delivering health and social care, community health services and unemployment support in the UK. This has been so profound that this has been described as 'a shadow state', with companies too pervasive to be allowed to fail unless they go downhill as fast and as far as Carillion.

Privatisation

Privatisation does not really work on two levels. First, the services provided by privatised industries are proving inadequate, such as the railways and probation and court services, and second, according to an IMF report, privatisation does not help the government's balance sheet but just creates, according to the *Financial Times*, a short-term 'fiscal illusion'. This report also states that the condition of the UK's finances is dangerous, one of the worst in the world and heavily exposed to recession and other risks.

Perhaps the most significant change of recent years is the arrival of the digital age and the rise social media, with immense changes in how we communicate, work and entertain ourselves. So it is rather unclear what will happen in the next five years, let alone the next 50 years. Brexit has shown the underpinning disillusion of so many people left behind by the economy, and this presents major challenges.

Opportunities

While the current situation for non-profit organisations is very pressurised, there are numerous opportunities opening up that might be exploited:

- With an aging population, and with the number of people aged 65 or over projected to continue to grow to nearly a quarter of the population by 2046, demand is increasing all the time for social care, increasing opportunities for innovative non-profit sectors, an example being technology for care.

- New types of organisations have developed, offering new ways of tackling social problems, for example online counselling, or Change.org.

- A great deal of self-help provision is being set up, empowering patients' groups, and minority and faith groups, often with a continuing involvement from idealistic young people but also new organisations like Citizens UK.

- New forms of funding, such as crowdfunding, encourage innovation.

- The 'Fourth Industrial Revolution' is bringing a great deal of new technology. One example is that online communication encourages a greater interchange of ideas, training and support, including across national boundaries, for example LinkedIn. Another is that large charities, such as Oxfam, can personalise responses to their donors by sending automatic emails thanking them for specific donations.

- Corporate Social Responsibility (CSR) is increasing in scope and influence. Commercial companies are now judged by the public on issues including their ethical treatment of staff (Nike 'slave wages'), sustainability and environmental footprints (BP), work practices (Uber), and payment of tax (Google, Amazon).

- New issues are being tackled, with a significant growth in medical charities and those protecting the environment.

- Movements such as Me Too and Black Lives Matters have seized the headlines, generated enormous support, and started to change societies.

Pressures

On the other hand there are numerous pressures on non-profit organisations:

- Government austerity and spending cuts continue, with the biggest ever squeeze in UK government grants hitting small non-profit organisations hardest. (See Chapter 12: Austerity.)

- Social problems (for example inequality, racial discrimination, youth unemployment, mental health issues and substance abuse) continue to increase, particularly because of cuts (see Chapters 6, 7, 8, 11 and 12).

- The Government is focused on Brexit and appears hamstrung with little real new innovation emerging from this quarter, apart from untested ideas such as Babylon, an online medical service.

- Charities have to pay staff the minimum wage (though some would argue they should have been doing this anyway) and council care home payments have been capped.

- There has been a huge increase in competitive tendering and commissioning. In these tenders, small non-profit organisations find it hard to compete, while large charities subsidise their contracts. In many cases, the results have led to non-profit organisations being undercut by other organisations, both private and non-profit, using fewer, less qualified and cheaper staff, or reducing service quality, with some organisations taking on contracts they cannot deliver properly and other private companies fiddling the results.

- Government, at all levels, has introduced policies of tendering out much bigger contracts, which excludes smaller non-profit organisations; even in tendering consortiums led by the private sector, many non-profit organisations complained they were just used as bid candy by private sector companies.

- Large UK charities in particular are currently being heavily criticised for a range of issues. Research for the UK Charity Commission and You Gov[2] reports that public trust and confidence in UK charities has fallen to the lowest level since 2005. This is based on criticism of high salaries for senior staff, fundraising methods such as excessive mailing and phone calls, and scandals, particularly over abuse.

Management

Management itself is a skill, but it is not an exact science as it involves working with people and coping with the unexpected. Bookshops now stock shelves of management books, though most are about private sector management – issues facing non-profit sector managers are very different.

2   UK Government https://www.civilsociety.co.uk/news/almost-half-of-people-surveyed-have-developed-trust-issues-about-charities.html (Accessed Jan 2019)

Non-profit organisations have become much more professional as I believe this book demonstrates. In fact, some think managerialism has gone too far in the sector. There has also been an enormous expansion of private companies supporting the charitable sector, in everything including IT, fundraising and HR.

There is no easily agreed bottom line in non-profit sector work, in the way that profit supplies this in the private sector. So there is often disagreement about objectives and methods, or a lack of agreement at all levels, which requires more consultation to achieve a consensus and proper understanding. Sometimes these disagreements are papered over, leaving a lack of clarity about objectives. An example of this is the way that the UK Anglican Church compromises on decisions about same sex marriage. Many experts believe that fudge and compromise are more prevalent in the non-profit sector.

Most non-profit organisations are competitive with their rivals, of any size or sector, for funding, influence and public attention. Small charities have recently been criticised in the UK for not merging or at least sharing more back office services. In my view this is only partially fair, as so many small local organisations fill a particular niche and meet specific needs.

Secular minority non-profit organisations in the UK have achieved a great deal locally, but not to the same extent nationally, compared to the influence developed by minority religious groups.

Management in the non-profit sector is subject to very different influences from the private sector; an example is that there are more stakeholders, such as donors and beneficiaries. In turn the media and social media also become involved and comments circulate. One significant group of stakeholders are the millions of volunteers in the non-profit sector, vastly more of whom are involved at all levels than in the public or private sectors, even though the influence of professionals prevails in the large non-profit organisations.

All UK governments since 2009 have tried to encourage social enterprise opt-outs from the NHS but this has proved relatively slow to take off, probably because of staff fears about pensions and job security. The emphasis in social finance on loans means that this option is avoided by most charities because of the risks involved. The much-trumpeted Social Value Act has proved to be rather ineffective (see Chapter 4 on procurement).

Cuts have hit small and medium non-profit organisations hardest. The financial squeeze on non-profit organisations has created enormous tension between managing 'flexibility, quality, and affordability', as Naomi Eisenstadt, a Scottish Government adviser, stated.

Non-profit sector management can be likened to a roller coaster ride, with all the highs and lows. Spending cuts have made things much worse for clients and service users, as these affect the most deprived in society. Austerity has hit the non-profit sector, hard with crucial choices having to be made on budgets regarding service users and staff, with centres and homes being closed, service users being moved and staff losing job. Leonard Cheshire Homes was in the news recently for implementing these closures[3], which follows the charity SCOPE introducing similar changes, closing nearly one third of its homes and planning to cut two thirds of its staff. Some homes are being sold to the private sector, so this provision could now follow old peoples' care which is dominated by the private sector and so liable to problems like the collapse of the UK's largest care home operator, Southern Cross Care, in 2011.

Influence

'In the last decades, the activity and influence of non-profit organisations in almost every country in the world have grown exponentially. Non-profits have become central to policy making, the promotion of civic action, and the delivery of new quasi-public services'[4]. However the pressures are now on the non-profit sector. The government has announced a new civil society strategy, presumably recognising that Cameron's Big Society has died, even if the original concept was valid. The Joseph Rowntree Trust and other trusts have mounted enquiries into Civil Society, presumably because of concerns about the future of the sector (these are discussed in the final chapter).

This book

This is not an academic book, nor does it pretend to be a comprehensive enquiry and there are several significant topics that we do not cover. We do however provide a range of views from the frontline of the non-profit sector. One of the strengths of this book is that we, the authors, are not afraid to disagree. Some of us believe that small is beautiful and that 'The small non-profit sector is absolutely vital to the fabric of UK society'. Other contributors believe that 'small is horrible' because small non-profit organisations are invariably '(a) pious (b) incompetent or (c) insolvent'.

I am using the term 'non-profit', although others would rather use voluntary or social sector. So this healthy disagreement will underpin our contributions.

3   The Guardian https://www.theguardian.com/society/2018/sep/26/leonard-cheshire-disability-charity-home-sell-off (Accessed Jan 2019)
4   John Casey http://dx.doi.org/10.18666/JNEL-2016-V6-I3-7583 (Accessed Jan 2019)

However, we are all agreed that non-profit organisations are operating in an ever-changing world with increasing pressures, hence the need for relevant information, ideas and skills, which this book tries to provide. Our book cannot cover every single aspect of the non-profit sector, but we highlight the points of view of specific activists and managers at the sharp end and point out some ways forward.

New community groups and grass-roots organisations are starting really exciting projects all over the world to tackle serious social issues and to encourage social innovation and self-help. This book describes how these could develop, with strategies to enable small and medium non-profit organisations to survive and evolve in demanding settings in a rapidly changing world. Each chapter is written by someone with deep experience in their specific field, able to share ideas and lessons that apply across the sector. The case studies are valuable to the sector, outlining the real challenges of contemporary non-profit management and innovation.

This book is practical, with analysis of previous experience and work sitting alongside new ideas for social innovation, community action and self-help, providing inspiration and practical advice for projects in different fields, enabling the reader to learn new skills, to reflect on their own experience and courses of action, and help plan, generate support and fundraise for new projects.

Acknowledgements

I would like to thank the authors for their hard work, all produced to quite short deadlines, and in particular Chris Durkin, who also helped me with my contributions. I would also like to thank those colleagues and friends who have put time into reading and commenting on my efforts, including Judy Edwards, Mike Locke, Paul Edwards and Charles Oham, and also to the non-profit managers who provided the content for my chapter on success and failure – Danny Maher (Ashford Place), Sue Measures (Sidings Community Centre), Richard Beard (Jericho Project) and Francesca Findlater (Bounceback). Darren Reed, Mike Benge, the editors and staff at Pavilion Publishing have been very helpful indeed. Finally the person who has, as always, put up with the most and provided the greatest backing – my wife and partner, Kate Macdonald.

Chapter One: 'Communities doing it for themselves – community responses to social care and health challenges'

By Sian Lockwood, OBE

Introduction

Health and social care systems across the world are facing unprecedented challenges as demand on services grows and resources tighten.

The world's population is ageing[1]. While this can bring great benefits (the majority of volunteers in the UK are drawn from newly-retired people), it also brings challenges. The fastest increase is in the numbers of people aged 85+[2], for example, and people in this group experience high levels of ill-health and disability with consequent growth in demand on public services. With the rise in life expectancy comes an increase in the likelihood of dementia, which one in three people born in the UK this year will develop in their lifetime[3].

Changes in family structures means that a high proportion of older people live alone, and of these many are lonely. Loneliness is one of the biggest challenges facing us in the UK. Over nine million people in the UK – almost a fifth of the population – say they are always or often lonely. Loneliness and social isolation are harmful to our health: lacking social connections is a comparable risk factor for early death as smoking 15 cigarettes a day, and is worse for us than well-known risk factors such as obesity and physical inactivity[4]. The government's recently launched cross-government loneliness

---

1   United Nations; accessed 19.10.18 http://www.un.org/en/sections/issues-depth/ageing/

2   Office for National Statistics; accessed 19.10.18 https://www.ons.gov.uk/peoplepopulationandcommunity/birthsdeathsandmarriages/ageing/articles/livinglongerhowourpopulationischangingandwhyitmatters/2018-08-13

3   Lewis, F: Estimation of future cases of dementia from those born in 2015 (July 2015); Consultation report for Alzheimer's Research UK

4   Campaign to end Loneliness accessed 19.10.18 https://www.campaigntoendloneliness.org/loneliness-research/

strategy[5] shines a spotlight on this, committing funding to support community and other initiatives that help tackle this issue.

Alongside this growth in demand for social care and health services, the public sector has been facing significant financial cutbacks and workforce challenges. Public services recognise that they cannot continue to do the same as they have been doing. There is therefore a renewed and urgent focus on prevention and the role that communities can play in promoting individual health and well-being, alongside a radical rethink of the role of public services in a changing world.

Government strategies for health and social care in England reflect this interest in the assets that communities have that can help people stay strong and well. These community assets are often seen in terms of community organisations or individuals that may be a resource for people in the health or social care system.

The Care Act (2014) gives local authorities in England the general responsibility for prevention, information and advice, and shaping the market of care and support services. The guidance accompanying the legislation explains that, 'in taking on this role, local authorities need to work with their communities and provide or arrange services that help to keep people well and independent. This should include identifying the local support and resources already available, and helping people to access them.'[6]

NHS England's Five Year Forward View, published in October 2014, sees communities as a source of volunteers to support the role of staff in health services:

'We need to engage with communities and citizens in new ways… Programmes like NHS Citizen point the way, but we also commit to four further actions to build on the energy and compassion that exists in communities across England. These are better support for carers; creating new options for health-related volunteering; designing easier ways for voluntary organisations to work alongside the NHS; and using the role of the NHS as an employer to achieve wider health goals.'[7]

---

5   UK Government accessed 19.10.18 https://www.gov.uk/government/publications/a-connected-society-a-strategy-for-tackling-loneliness

6   Care Act 2014 accessed 19.10.18http://www.legislation.gov.uk/ukpga/2014/23/contents/enacted

7   NHS England Five Year Forward View accessed 19.10.18 https://www.england.nhs.uk/wp-content/uploads/2014/10/5yfv-web.pdf

Promoting well-being in the community

Encouraging well-being in the community can improve health significantly. One initiative promoted by NHS England is 'social prescribing', which has grown rapidly. This model has developed in different ways in different areas, but in essence it is 'a means of enabling GPs and other frontline healthcare professionals to refer people to 'services' in their community instead of offering only medicalised solutions'[8]. It does what it says on the tin – referring people away from GP services to community groups that are seen as 'assets' that can be accessed by the health system to reduce or prevent demand.

Over the last few years, however, there has been a growing interest in strengths-based working and an increasing recognition of the vital importance of positive, mutually valued relationships and contribution to well-being. Public Health England, for example, published a guide to 'community-centred approaches'[9] in February 2018, which 'outlines how to create the conditions for community assets to thrive'. As it says:

> 'Community life, social connections and having a voice in local decisions are all factors that have a vital contribution to make to health and well-being. Community action is a necessary component of place-based approaches to reduce health inequalities, alongside and as part of healthy public policy and prevention services.'

There is an implicit assumption in many of the health and social care strategies that communities are passive partners in the drive towards better health and well-being for everyone. While there is certainly a nod towards co-design and consultation in some strategies, on the whole communities are variously described as assets to be exploited or areas to be 'developed', 'empowered' or 'activated'.

Communities doing it for themselves

Rather than being passive partners waiting to be 'activated', many communities are already 'doing it for themselves'. There is a rich vein of untapped gift and talent in local communities that will be a good resource for people in those neighbourhoods, with the right kind of help. A growing number of voluntary and community sector organisations have recognised this and are working to help communities act on the issues that affect them the most. These organisations use varying approaches, but they share the same commitment to helping communities and individuals understand and use their strengths to tackle the problems that matter most to them. All share the philosophy that underpins

---

8   NHS England accessed 19.10.18 https://www.england.nhs.uk/personalised-health-and-care/social-prescribing

9   Public Health England accessed 19.10.18 https://www.gov.uk/government/publications/health-and-wellbeing-a-guide-to-community-centred-approaches

Asset-Based Community Development. Some of the organisations using these approaches are listed in Think Local Act Personal's Six Innovations[10], such as our own Community Catalysts and Homeshare UK, but there are many more. Organisations working in this way are generous and naturally collaborative, actively looking for ways to work together and share learning.

Community Catalysts is a Community Interest Company launched in 2010 and working across the UK. We know that current approaches to care and health don't always work well for people and our aim is to find scalable community-rooted approaches that help people live the life they want. We know from our work in nearly 60 local authority areas over the last 10 years that every citizen and community has its assets and strengths. We help build capacity within communities and work through local partners to create an environment that allows people to use their gifts to help people who need care and support in ways that suit them, with real choice of attractive local options. We have a privileged role, seeing at first-hand what people and communities can do with just a little bit of the right kind of help.

Debenham village

Over the last 10 years we have met many inspiring communities and individuals who are, with or without professional advice and support, 'doing it for themselves'. One outstanding example is Debenham. Debenham is a large village in Suffolk, where, eight years ago, people came together to act on a common concern that their friends and neighbours with dementia were having to leave their community for care.

Over 100 people came to the first village meeting and agreed a long-term vision of extra-care facilities in the village. They appointed an action committee and mandated them not just to deliver their vision, but also, in the meantime, to 'just do something'. With very little financial support from statutory sources, they set up a range of activities and supports designed to help people stay at home for longer. I visited the village in 2012 and was amazed by the sheer number and variety of people involved and the creativity of their ideas and activities. The pop-up dementia-friendly restaurant and emergency weekend hotline stood out for me during that visit but there were many other initiatives, both small and large, that made a real difference to people's lives – for example, people really appreciated the local librarian's visit to the bi-weekly Carers Café, to help people access web-based information about dementia, and they were excited by the idea of a local homecare agency staffed by local people[11].

---

10 Think Local, Act Personal accessed 19.10.18 https://www.thinklocalactpersonal.org.uk/Latest/Six-innovations-in-social-care-/

11 JRF Report accessed 19.10.18 http://www.the-debenham-project.org.uk/downloads/articles/2012/121106report.pdf

The project has changed and adapted with local needs and the energies and skills of local people, but is still going strong six years later. It is still a community owned and led project but it has registered as a charity with trustees and paid staff. The action group (80+ strong) understands that each individual activity has a natural lifespan and that the gap left by the ending of one activity will, with the right kind of encouragement, be replaced by another. They also know that initiatives work when they are led by local people – well-meaning help from professionals can be the kiss of death to a new activity. As the co-ordinator of the action group says, 'professionals should only do what professionals can do – we'll do the rest and tell them when we need them'[12].

Role of local councils

Enabling communities to 'do it for themselves' requires public bodies to relinquish power and place their trust in the community. The infrastructure and motivation of a community can be easily damaged by well-intentioned activity that is top-down and lacks understanding of the community they intend to benefit. Some councils understand this well and are trying to find ways to work on a more equal and collaborative footing with local people and neighbourhoods. One example from our own experience is Wakefield Council, which contacted us in order to actively find ways of working more collaboratively with their communities.

The council commissioned us and another organisation, Inclusion North, to work intensively with two self-defined neighbourhoods, finding out what was already happening, understanding the positive forces that helped get things done in those neighbourhoods, what local people felt was needed and how the council could help them achieve their aims. We spent time getting to know those neighbourhoods and the people in them well before bringing people together to think about what mattered in the area and what could help the residents achieve their aims. Finally we brought people together with the council to help the council understand what local people thought was needed, what the council and other public bodies were doing that made it difficult for local people to sort this out themselves, and how the council could be more helpful.

This comparatively small project provided a window into a future for social care in which the relationship between public services and local people is very different. We and the council found:

■ that local people in the two neighbourhoods already had a really clear understanding of the challenges facing people in their communities and good ideas about possible solutions, but they didn't know who to talk to and how to make them happen

---

12 Debenham Project accessed 19.10.18 http://www.the-debenham-project.org.uk

■ public sector initiatives were often working in parallel or inadvertently cutting across each other

■ community initiatives were being inadvertently damaged by public sector activity that knew nothing about them or did not fully appreciate their value

■ national initiatives were not integrated with each other, let alone into those of local communities

■ there were a lot of untapped or misaligned resources in local businesses and local charitable organisations – one of the neighbourhoods, for example, had a number of small charities working in isolation from each other as well as a large business with a community fund worth £250,000, which it 'didn't know how to use'.

These neighbourhoods had plenty of internal and external resources, the problem was that they were being delivered in silos or were unseen and therefore unused. There were no mechanisms that allowed local people to be fully involved in deciding local priorities, shaping local solutions and directing the use of resources to help deliver them. It was clear to all those involved in the project that putting local people at the centre of decision making, with public bodies there to inform, support and work collaboratively with them, would lead to a much better use of scarce resources. Almost as transformative was the realisation that the resources provided by the state were just some of the resources in the neighbourhood (people, buildings, money). For example, small and large businesses had financial and volunteer resources which they did not know how to use. In one area, a pot of money worth £250,000 remained untouched as the business 'did not know how to engage with the community'.

The council used this new understanding to work with local people to design a better way of working together, in which resources (both in the community and the public sector) are more closely aligned and activities to address local challenges are identified by local people, and co-designed and co-delivered. Working with voluntary community and social enterprise (VCSE) sector partners and ward councillors, the council created mechanisms that enabled local people to identify priorities and shape solutions. These have led to a number of small grants programmes, designed to support individual community initiatives. Wakefield's recent success in gaining European funding to support the People Enabling Area Transformation (PEAT) project[13] demonstrates the strength of the collaborative relationship between the council and the voluntary and community sectors which has developed over the years since our small project.

---

13 The Peat Project, Wakefield accessed 19.10.18https://www.wakefieldfirst.com/the-peat-project-clld/

Case study: Pulp Friction

There has been a growth in the number of councils supporting the development of very small (micro) enterprises that offer care and support to people in their neighbourhoods. These organisations employ eight or fewer staff, with a significant minority delivering their service themselves.

Pulp Friction Smoothie Bar is a UK-based micro enterprise, launched in 2011, that works with young adults with learning disabilities to develop their social, independent and work-readiness skills. They provide opportunities and individual support for people to run pedal-powered smoothie bars at different community events.

Jill Carter runs the organisation with her daughter Jessie, who has learning disabilities. When Jessie was 17 she wanted a part-time job at the weekend, like a lot of her non-disabled friends. Jill felt it was unlikely that Jessie would be able gain employment locally so together they started looking for something that would interest Jessie and which could be supported by Jill.

They saw a smoothie bike at a local festival, and although Jessie cannot ride an ordinary bike, they thought that she might be able to manage something that was static. They spoke to a few of Jessie's friends and their families and in 2009 Jill supported them to make an application to the Youth Opportunity Fund for £1,800 to buy a smoothie bike for themselves. They were successful in their bid and the Pulp Friction Smoothie Bar project was born.

Initially Pulp Friction operated as a youth and community group recruiting non-disabled young adults to work alongside their regular members so that people began to build friendships and work as a team. Jill enrolled on a course for people interested in developing social enterprises run by a local non-profit network. As a result, and having identified viable income streams and recruited good volunteers, Jessie and Jill decided to set up Pulp Friction as a registered non-profit company and to this day it continues operating smoothly (forgive the pun).

http://pulpfrictionsmoothies.org.uk

Regulations

Communities trying to respond to local social care and health needs face additional challenges. The health and care sector is highly regulated, with regulations designed for medium-sized and large providers.

Two single mums with disabled children wanted to set up an agency to provide help in the home for other people in the same position on an estate in South Tyneside. They knew first-hand how stressful it can be to care for a disabled child, and they wanted to use the skills and knowledge that they had gained from caring for their own children to help other families. They wanted to be able to offer direct care to the disabled child to free parents to spend time with their non-disabled siblings – or simply to have a break – and so applied to register with the Care Quality Commission as a domiciliary care agency. This process was difficult for a very small organisation run by people who had no formal educational qualifications. One of the two founders had to register as the manager of the agency, and part of the registration process required them to have an appropriate qualification. The Skills for Care guide was a Level 5 Diploma in Leadership for Health and Social Care – a degree-level qualification. This felt to them wildly out of reach, and so sadly they decided to restrict their service to non-personal care, limiting the help that they could provide to families struggling to meet the needs of their disabled child and their siblings[14].

Barriers to new approaches

Councils often apply additional requirements that must be met by providers offering support to people eligible for public funding.

One community-led domiciliary care agency in the North West who successfully registered with the Care Quality Commission were principally used by people who paid for their support with their own money[15]. The barrier came, though, when they tried to widen their offer to include people with local-authority commissioned services, and they applied to be accepted onto the approved list. Domiciliary care agencies who wanted to be on the approved list had to install an electronic call monitoring system, a requirement that could not be varied just because the agency supported a very small number of clients (just eight families and with a planned maximum of 15). The cost was significant, but perhaps more importantly, the partners felt that the system skewed their working practices and damaged their ability to deliver good outcomes for people. The result was that people were denied access to a good service.

Another barrier to community-led care is the way money flows from public bodies to people who need some help and support. Public bodies have approved lists of providers from whom they will directly commission services, but even where people have a personal budget and take that budget as cash (a direct payment), there may still be rules preventing them from spending money as they wish. In addition, people may be deterred from taking direct payments because of the ingrained assumption that these are used to employ staff. But not everyone who needs services wants to become a direct employer, especially if their budget is too small for this; they lack the capacity to understand the issues and do not have a circle of people around them who can help; the right people are not available for them to employ; they find the responsibility of becoming an employer burdensome and are concerned about what happens if their personal assistant is sick or goes on holiday; or the approach has gone wrong for them in the past.

---

14 Unpublished Case Study from Community Catalysts
15 Unpublished Case Study from Community Catalysts

> ## Twitter comments from service users
>
> Twitter comments from service users provide providing a 'real time' commentary on the limitations and difficulties of using personal budgets when there is little choice apart from the choice to become an employer:
>
> '*.........really, how is the only choice between **** home care services & being an employer.'
>
> '* I love having a PA. But seriously, whoever thought up the idea of 'being an employer' to get direct payments needs spanking!'
>
> '* I need to set up payroll services, insurance & contracts & meet my advocate re DASS complaint. This really isn't an easy way to get support.'

Community-led enterprises also face a challenge to get information about their service to the people who may use it – and getting information from people about services they may need.

A small piece of research that we commissioned from Leeds Beckett University showed that most people get information through word-of-mouth or via trusted advisers. However, this information is inevitably limited by the knowledge of people offering word-of-mouth advice and by the risk-averse approach of many professional advisers. Local authority and other on-line 'directories' may be varied and downright confusing. In one London local authority, an analysis of the way people with personal health budgets found out about local services and groups, discovered 16 different directories, each with a slightly different focus and separate databases.

Councils that are keen to encourage community-led initiatives to provide care for other local people have long recognised the need to invest in the 'right kind of support', which will help people to safely navigate the wilderness of regulation, legislation and public procurement practices, and establish enterprises that deliver high quality and sustainable services that people want.

Somerset County Council

One notable example is Somerset County Council, which is responsible for a large, mainly rural country.

The home care market in Somerset, as across the whole UK, faces real challenges. Home care can only be successful when it attracts and retains compassionate staff, but current industry models are often unable to afford the time needed for dignity and companionship. Even when older people are adequately supported, they are often lonely, undervalued and disconnected from their communities.

Somerset County Council was concerned that people living in the most rural parts of the county could not access help to stay at home – it was simply uneconomic for some traditional care agencies to provide care in these remote rural areas. They therefore asked Community Catalysts to work with local partners (parish councils, GP surgeries, churches) to help local people set up enterprises that would provide the help and support that was unavailable from more traditional sources. Our local catalysts worked using the structures and positive energy that lies in every community, providing patient coaching and expert advice to the people he found who wanted to help their friends and neighbours by providing the care they needed to stay at home. Three years later there are nearly 300 enterprises, working in many different ways to support over 1,000 people to stay at home and remain connected to their communities[16].

Case study: Care 4 U

Sharon Walker has a lot of experience working in traditional care services. She took a career break to look after her mother-in-law and was profoundly affected by the experience of delivering person-centred care. Spurred on by this, and with support from Community Catalysts, she decided to set up Care4U in December 2015.

Care4U provides highly personalised flexible and consistent support to older people in and around Sharon's Somerset village. After 14 months running Care4U, she explains the difference it has made to the people she supports: 'I can organise my time so that people can get what they want at a time that suits them – it gives me the freedom to work around their family'.

The courage and trust shown by the council in the approach it took to the original challenge was vital to the success of this project. As well as commissioning some capacity-building help, the council trusted its people to make good choices by giving them direct payments and information about the range of enterprises in their neighbourhood.

Conclusion

These glimpses of communities doing it for themselves show people with passion and a desire to make a difference to their own lives and the lives of their neighbours and community. They show that the appetite for community enterprise and action is alive and well, needing just a little encouragement and support to make a big difference to people's lives. They show that you don't have to 'go big' to scale – many very small enterprises or activities can have just as much of an impact on an area as one or two big enterprises. They show that an approach that helps unlock people's imagination and talent and gives them the right kind of help allows many different flowers to bloom –

16 The Guardian accessed 19.10.18 https://www.theguardian.com/society/2017/apr/26/old-disabled-people-homecare-micro-providers-somerset

and stay blooming. They show the importance of 'place', and of understanding and engaging all the resources available in a neighbourhood. They also show a very different relationship with public bodies – one where the community is responsible for determining local priorities and shaping the solutions that will address those priorities; where public bodies trust local people to make good decisions and wait to be brought in to 'do those things only they can do'; where they help behind the scenes by making sure communities stay centre stage and are respected; that public activity is co-ordinated, good information is available and sources of money are identified and unblocked to help deliver community priorities.

Many areas can shine a spotlight on an example of the impact of this very different collaborative partnership between communities and public bodies – but these examples are patchy and disconnected. We need one or two (or three) brave areas to take all of this learning on board and demonstrate the creative power of local people who have the responsibility and resources needed to help people in their community live the best life they can, and where the public services... well... serve.

Chapter Two: Only wise and generous leadership can save us

By Shaks Ghosh

Introduction

Geoff Mulgan, CEO of NESTA and previously adviser to Prime Minister Blair, has a practical approach to leadership. Much about leadership, he says, is learned rather than innate. The wider the range of skills and behaviours you learn, knowing when to take control and when to enable, the easier you will find handling diverse situations. That's all!

Lord Victor Adebowale, CEO of Turning Point, has a more emotional and almost biblical definition. Leadership, he says, is about your relationships with your followers. Most leaders can impress in situations of comfort and certainty. But great leadership is about the personal courage and wisdom to lead followers through uncertainty and into new places.

Two very different definitions of leadership, and both deeply insightful for social leaders grappling with self-improvement. Many of us come to leadership development from a place of pain. We get 'sent on a course' by managers who need us to improve, we feel inadequate in the face of challenges, we are frustrated with our roles or want to advance our careers. But once we engage, there is no turning back. We are no longer 'accidental leaders'. We begin to understand that leadership is a lifelong journey and you're never done with the learning. I have come to see the curiosity that students of leadership have, the awareness about changing environments and the behaviour change that may be needed to succeed.

In my years at Clore Social, I have been privileged to observe closely many hundreds of social leaders, whom we trained and designated as Fellows. I will draw from this rich source to explain why I think social leadership could be a secret, untapped opportunity to transform the world we live in. Human ingenuity is our most abundant resource; social leadership should be the catalyst to unlock new ideas and energy for the next urgent phase of social change.

In the next section I attempt a definition of social leadership, and in Section Two I make the case that social leadership is a distinct subject, worthy of special attention. Section Three is about the need to respond to change, to modernise and democratise leadership. In Section Four, I ponder the challenges that the world faces and how the social sector is uniquely positioned to help, but only with wise, generous and socially minded leadership. In the fifth and final fifth section, I describe the strategies that I have witnessed Clore Fellows deploy, as they rise to some of these challenges. Today there are 300 Clore Social leaders in the UK, an incredible fighting force for justice, social change and community service. This chapter is a tribute to their leadership.

Defining social leadership

For 10 years, Clore Social has been at the forefront of developing leaders with social purpose. The content of the leadership programmes have evolved over time, but the principles and values have stood the test of time (see Figure 2.1). In essence, leadership can be broken down into three simple truths – The Self, The Context and The Follower.

Figure 2.1: Learning development model

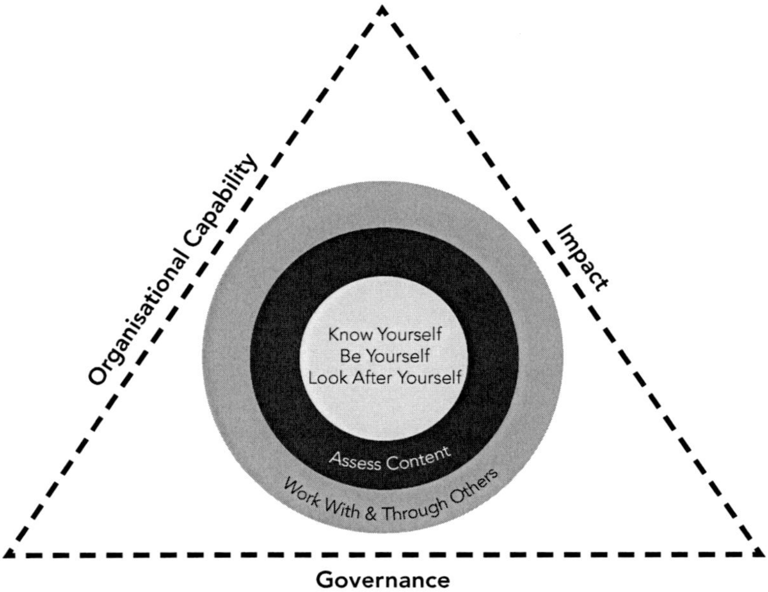

(Clore Social Leadership)

The Self

At the heart of the model lies the leader him or herself. Self-awareness, self-mastery and character building are the starting point for every good leader. Stephen Covey, in his *7 Habits of Highly Effective People* stresses the importance of deliberate behaviour-change. Develop, he says, the virtues of courage, focus, generosity, sincerity and fairness and you will be a better leader[1].

Changing behaviour is not easy, as everyone who has tried knows – most of us are set in patterns of behaviour that are hard to shake. Participants on Clore programmes are introduced early to two concepts: the Gift of Feedback and the extraordinary Power of Reflection – simple keys to greater self-awareness.

Self-care is another tell-tale sign of a good leader. Emotional tiredness and physical exhaustion are inevitably connected to leadership in the social sector. Most of us run small and fragile organisations and choose to put service before personal needs. All the more reason, then, to attend to the basic bodily needs of sleep, diet, exercise and friendship. Nobody needs a burnt-out leader.

The Context

Good leadership is situational i.e. it can only be judged in its context. A command and control style of leadership might be essential in our emergency services, but is hardly the best way of getting the creative juices of your creative teams flowing, for example. In a rapidly changing context, the successful leader is one who is quickly able to assess situations, understand context and adjust their behaviour accordingly.

Heifetz and Linsky, in their book *The Practice of Adaptive Leadership: Tools and tactics for changing your organisation and the world*[2], argue that leaders must move between technical leadership and adaptive leadership. Technical leadership is deployed where a situation is known and predictable, and where the leader has previous experience. Adaptive leadership is deployed in situations where the leader leads their followers in situations which are new, where behaviour change may be needed and where authority structures do not work.

---

1   Stephen Covey (1989; 2004) *The 7 Habits of Effective Leaders*. Free Press.

2   Heifetz RA, Grashow A & Linsky M (2009) *The Practice of Adaptive Leadership: Tools and tactics for changing your organisation and the world*. Boston, MA: Harvard Business Press.

Adaptive Leadership is rich with metaphors that bring alive the skills of adaptive leadership. The Harvard professors refer to spending as much time on the 'balcony as on the dance floor' – the importance of observing and seeing the whole picture, then intervening if necessary. I recognise in my own practice the lack of time on the balcony and my preference to be in the thick of the dance floor action. They urge us to 'walk the razor's edge', taking our followers to the brink of chaos without a plan! Those scary places encourage change, progress, the development of our people and the advancement of our cause. Theirs is not the leadership that endears; rather it is the bare-knuckle ride of courageous leadership. I highly recommended it.

The Follower

It seem obvious to say that there is no leadership without followership, but surprisingly few leaders stop to think about the followers. In our sector, we shy away from the language of leader/follower and few of us take time to consider the complexity of our human relationships. The really great Clore leaders never stop thinking about the people around them. About the deep moral issues, the small compromises, and ultimately the acceptance of human frailty. They celebrate small achievements, inspire through building trust and constant communication. These are skills that it takes one Clore programme to learn but a lifetime to perfect.

Is social leadership a distinct form of leadership?

The question I am asked most often is, how is social leadership is different from any other type of leadership?

Most importantly, the context within which social leaders operate is totally unique. The UK has the most incredible, growing and dynamic community sector – new charities are being registered every day, the social enterprise sector is finding innovative ways of looking at old problems and 98% of the British public engage with this sector each year. The sector is unique in its governance and regulation arrangements and is special in the relationship it has with the state.

Leading in this sector requires an awareness and critique of this unique context, and an ability to scan the changing landscape. Clore leaders will often talk about the constraints of charity regulation but they are also acutely aware of the 'special status' they have long had in the hearts of the British public. So leaders in our sector talk about the 'call', and the vocation to serve. Rarely motivated by wealth or power, most of our leaders are driven by a passion for their cause. Advocacy is in the DNA of the social leader.

In Section One I laid out the Clore leadership model – leaders must be responsive to their followers. They must understand, inspire and motivate the people who they lead, and good leaders are able to adjust their style while always remaining authentic. Our followers are often our beneficiaries – the people who use our services, the young, the vulnerable, the homeless and the disadvantaged. They are often our customers and the activists that champion our causes. Very many are in fact the volunteers that make our sector so unique – no other sector has a paid workforce of 800,000 and a volunteer force of 15 million! This alone makes social leadership a unique and challenging task, one that requires skill, ethical values and wisdom.

Heifetz and Linsky define two kinds of leadership challenges – technical and adaptive. Technical leadership requires authority and minimal change, followers are respectful and knowledgeable, solutions are obvious and products are standard. Adaptive challenges require a different leadership skill set – high risk appetite, agility, acute context sensing skills, the ability to 'walk on the razor's edge'. When we compare the social sector with the public and corporate sectors, the distinguishing features of our sector are size, fragmentation, service of people, social change and volunteering. Just about every challenge we face is complex, involving multiple stakeholders and multiple purposes. Added to this is the increasing speed of change and uncertainty. Everything we do points to the importance of adaptive leadership; a rare and difficult skillset to acquire.

Democratising leadership

In his Ted Talk, Marty Linsky says, 'I am not interested in leaders, only leadership'[3]. Powerful stuff. We have to awaken the leader in each one of us if we are to grapple with the social challenges of our time. This is particularly true of the social sector, where almost every one of our staff and volunteers has had the 'call' to step out and serve, to make the world a better place. This call is the hallmark of social leadership, and these are the leaders we must invest in. Helping them to achieve their true potential will release resources to improve the lives of vulnerable people.

One of the mantras that Clore Fellows often repeat is 'leaders grow leaders'. More and more commentators are observing a paradigm shift, were the meme is no longer leaders and followers but rather leaders leading leaders. Adaptive leadership is empowering and ultimately very democratic. It believes in the adaptability and resourcefulness of all human beings and encourages all to take responsibility.

---

3   Marty Linsky. Available at: https://www.youtube.com/watch?v=af-cSvnEExM (accessed March 2019).

Dispersed leadership models (sometimes called distributed leadership) make leaders at every level more visible, and are gaining popularity. Although they may have limitations in certain situations, it is always worth looking at how far we can extend the principles. (For an insightful series of blogs go to the Holacracy website[4].) The underpinning philosophy remains that flat structures are empowering and authority based leadership can discourage people to be their best. Dispersed leadership models are often more democratic, where leadership is exercised at every level from the CEO to the receptionist, and were it is done with skill and thoughtfulness.

Dr Eve Poole has a theory that, traditionally, leadership was about hierarchy, so it was very much the domain of CEOs and senior managers promoting the rather exclusive 'hero' model of leadership[5].This is reinforced by expensive business degrees from elite universities which are able to charge large sums to give leaders the patina and mystique of leadership. Young elite and mostly male leaders emerge with great CVs, command greater salaries and go on to control large budgets and work forces.

These business schools do not, however, teach character. My favourite read on leadership is *Road to Character* by David Brooks[6]. Courage, generosity, focus and inspirational leadership can all be learnt through reflection, receiving feedback, hanging out with the right people, practising behaviour change. These are the teachings we prioritise at Clore. Behaviour change requires time, reflection and practice rather than the gloss of an expensive business school degree. So bring on the revolution, says Eve Poole. Let's democratise leadership and ensure that every leader, no matter where they are in the hierarchy, is able to lead with skill and ethical values.

Women and leadership

Democratising leadership means two things. First, it means ensuring that everyone realises their leadership potential. Second, it means ensuring that leadership development is taken to the places that need it most.

Women hold up half the sky! I have found it interesting to ponder the differences between female leadership and feminist leadership. Where Sheryl Sandberg, COO of Facebook, urges us to play men at their own game and win, Mary Beard urges us to tear down the structures of male power. Sandberg insists women must 'lean in' and claim power. She urges us to change our behaviour, be great role models and 'fake it till we make it'[7].

---

4   Holacracy. Available at: https://www.holacracy.org/resources/ (accessed March 2019).

5   Dr Eve Poole – Leadersmithing. Available at: http://evepoole.com

6   David Brook (2015) *The Road to Character*. Random House.

7   Sheryl Sandberg (2013) *Lean In*. Random House.

Beard, the true feminist, maintains that the world is coded for men, and women can never succeed in this paradigm[8]. Beard's analysis is radical, political and based on women organising together.

Whether it is feminist leadership or female leadership, we must build confidence and open pathways for women to move into leadership positions. Women must do this for each other.

What are the leadership challenges in the social sector?

Releasing untapped resources

Economists and environmentalists tell us that the Earth's resources are running out. Here in the UK, our social welfare is creaking under the burdens of austerity and demography. Everywhere in the social sector leaders are tightening their belts, preparing for a future of growing need and diminishing resources. Tackling these challenges requires wisdom, resilience and great motivational skill.

For many of us, living with wealth and health inequalities is intolerable. In the absence of state support, we must find new resources to meet the needs of the communities left behind. It is my belief that the untapped resources will come from three sources:

1. Wells of human ingenuity and invention.
2. Even greater compassion and generosity.
3. Powerful collaborations.

Nobody can look at the social sector and be in any doubt that there are rich seams of untapped resources. It will be for the next generation of leaders to release them and put them to work in the fight against poverty and injustice.

Wrestling with size and fragility

Clore leaders often describe their biggest challenge as 'achieving lift-off'. Apart from survival (see Chapter Nine), the main problem with small and tiny organisations is their inability to keep up with rapid change. Leaders are continually putting out fires, and their chronically under-invested companies are unable to resource their back offices.

---

8   Mary Beard (2017) *Women & Power: A manifesto*. Profile Books.

Many CEOs of smaller charities envy the resources of the larger organisations, and it is true that economies of scale and the ability to employ experts can sometimes make management easier. But leading in the full spotlight of the media and always being held to high moral standards can be tough for large charity CEOs. The CEO's task is never easy and the personal toll is often difficult to bear.

Board leadership: the Achilles' heel of the sector

Wikipedia describes an Achilles' heel as 'a weakness despite overall strength which can lead to downfall'. This is how I see our boards and trustees. Governance is the leadership issue that is most CEO's Achilles' heel. Boards that are out of touch lack the right skills and whose meeting cycles are not compatible with the fast moving environment.

Board leadership is under severe scrutiny. Even where the right skill set is present, Boards find it hard to manage their collective behaviour in a way which suits their organisation. For if personal leadership is a struggle, collective leadership is an even more difficult task. But without a concerted effort to tackle this area of leadership, our sector will continue to struggle. Resources are limited, training is of dubious quality and seems like nobody's priority. We are fans of Julia Unwin's 5 S's of board leadership, because it is a behavioural model rather than a treatise on governance – stretch, support, scrutiny, strategy and stewardship[9]. (See also Clore Social's Board Leadership – Practical Guide for the Social Sector[10].)

Moral challenges and rebuilding public trust

The Charity Commission has sounded the alarm bells about the reduction in public trust in charities. Fundraising from individuals requires leaders to have high profiles and claim great things for their organisations – these leaders not only suffer the daily stress of the media glare, but also the unforgiving spotlight when things go wrong. And like the big banks before them, these cases cast a pall over the whole sector, and their embattled CEOs hold in th eir hands the reputation of the entire not-for-profit industry.

Social leaders face a continual series of moral issues – who to serve and who not to; conflicts between fundraising and ethics; fairness in dismissal and redundancies... the list is endless. However much we wish for clear choices between right and wrong, too often we are called on to choose between right and right. Claire Foster-Gilbert urges us to think about unclear moral decisions

---

9   Julia Unwin. Available at: http://www.gettingonboard.org/news/4585134114/The-five-Ss-in-governance/10242909 (accessed March 2019).

10   Clore Social Leadership. *Board Leadership: A practical guide for the social sector*. Clore Social Leadership. Available at: https://www.cloresocialleadership.org.uk/assets/resources/Board-Leadership-A-Practical-Guide-for-the-Social-Sector.pdf (accessed March 2019).

in three ways: goal based morality, which rests on the idea that actions are right if their outcomes are right; duty based morality, which considers the content/execution of an action, irrespective of the outcome: right based morality, which respects the right of a stakeholder to act autonomously[11].

Soft skills are the new hard skills

Many CEOs face a long list of day-to-day challenges – fundraising, communicating, being better than the competition, marketing, digital transformation – this list goes on. Too often the priority becomes developing hard skills. However, CEOs are short changing their organisations if they don't encourage soft skills too. The emotionally mature organisation is better able to weather change and get the best of its people. Soft skills are the new hard skills, and I would encourage leaders to take time to build the skills of self-awareness, resilience and courage.

Getting the right people on the bus

Optimism and good humour are the pit props of good leadership. And yet most leaders will also admit that their greatest stress comes from managing people, whether it is their volunteers, staff, beneficiaries, families, bosses or boards.

I admire the leaders who build their organisations around the right people. Slavishly adhering to job descriptions, knowledge and experience might be the right way in a repetitive and technical situation, but the best staff for the social sector are those who are passionate about what they do and curious to learn. Jim Collins, in his excellent book *Good to Great*, talks about 'getting the right people on the bus'[12]. The people with the right attitudes, the people who will share your vision and values.

My experience is that once you have the right people on the bus, it truly frees you up as a leader. The right people enable you to focus on *leading* more than *managing*. With the right kind of autonomy they will figure out how to achieve the company's goals. I have found Daniel Pink's AMP rule works – autonomy, mastery and purpose[13]. Pink's work has shown that rewards and bonuses in wealthier economies are much less significant as motivators than the individual's desire to excel and master their work. It's an easy formula to remember and implement, but it only works when you have the right people on the bus!

---

11 Claire Foster-Gilbert (2017) *The Moral Heart of Public Service*. Jessica Kingsley Publishers,

12 Jim Collins (2011). *Good to Great*.

13 Daniel Pink. *The Puzzle of Motivation*. Available at: https://www.ted.com/talks/dan_pink_on_motivation?language=en (accessed March 2019).

Strategy loops, not lines

No thinking on social leadership can be complete without a comment on change management and change strategy. Change management has been a constant for all of my working life, during which the social sector has seen incredible changes – organisations in transition, companies outgrowing their infrastructures, charities modernising and professionalising. While change will continue, the pace at which it happens will quicken, and the strategies we adopt to manage it will need to evolve. Business gurus talk about the 'death of strategy' and our need to learn 'agile' ways of planning change.

About half way through my time as Crisis CEO, we knew a major change programme was needed. The senior team disappeared into our planning bunker, we announced a major repositioning of the charity, systematically closing services and diverting funds into new ones. The organisation was rebranded, reskilled and completely re-set. The process took a full six months, during which the business of the organisation was almost at a standstill.

I'd never do it like that again, and indeed today that sort of change programme today would be unthinkable. Today I never stop managing change, and see it as a continual and evolutionary process. Donald Sull from MIT/Sloane talks about replacing linear strategic planning with four iterative loops which are run in quick and continual succession: making sense, making choices, making things happen and making revisions[14]. In other words, you have to rebuild the bus and drive the bus all at the same time. This needs wise leadership indeed…

How Clore Social helps leaders navigate choppy waters

In this chapter I have shown that social leadership is uniquely rewarding but also uniquely difficult. The vocation the social leaders have for social change, the lack of clear career pathways, the nature and culture of their organisations and the unrelenting pace of social change create an incredibly stressful environment. Many are blessed with an unstinting sense of responsibility for their fellow human beings. Where would the sector be without them?

Clore Social has for the last ten years developed and engaged with many incredible leaders. The Clore Social Development Model and the Clore Social Capability Framework (see below) are the principles upon which the programme is based. In this section I have set out some of the key principles that the programme is based on.

---

14 Donald N Sull. MIT/Sloan review. *Closing the Gap between Strategy and Execution.* Available at: http://donsull.com/wp-content/uploads/2013/07/closing-the-gap-FINAL-pdf-JUL-07.pdf (accessed March 2019).

The Clore Leadership Capability Framework

No leader is complete, and all leaders must work on a range of skills.
The Capability Framework is a complex and comprehensive guide for social
leaders to consider the diverse skills they need.

Figure 2.2: Clore Social Leadership Capability Framework

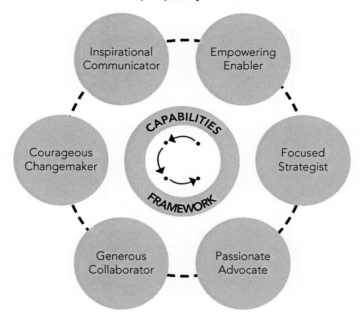

Practice not knowledge makes you a good leader

Clore Social Leaders know that leadership is about having multiple strings
to your bow and being able to adapt your behaviour and flex your style.
They know that behaviour change and leadership practice is about just that
– practise. Continuous practise. It is not about knowledge or charisma.

Remember to start with why

Simon Sinek's 'Start with Why'[15] is one of the very first provocations used
on Clore Social programmes, and continues to be an inspiration to most
Clore Social leaders. Most of us entered the social sector clearly knowing
why – a desire for social change or social service. But many of us lose
touch with this, and get caught up in the struggles of a leader's life. Clore
Social leaders never forget why!

---

15 Simon Sinek. *Start with Why*. Available at: https://www.youtube.com/
    watch?v=u4ZoJKF_VuA (accessed March 2019).

The gift of feedback... the art of listening... the power of reflection... the magic of curiosity

Ask a Clore Social Fellow what they learnt on their immersive leadership programme, and few will talk about good governance or implementing strategy. They are more likely to talk about their struggles with giving and receiving feedback, how they have calmed the 'chattering mind' and how they continually challenge their own behaviour. Clore Social Fellows prize most highly the qualities of listening and curiosity, feedback and reflection[16].

Leadership is a mind-set

At Clore Social we believe that everyone is a leader and leadership can be learnt by all. Leadership development is as simple as listening well, being generous, empowering others and developing a peer network. It makes leadership a mind-set that can be cultivated and mastered. It is not an elite activity connected with power.

The wisdom of Clore Social Fellows

To conclude this chapter, I want to share some of the mantras of Clore Social Fellows, who over the years have developed their own language of leadership. Unfailingly optimistic and mutually supportive, they have inspired a whole generation of great social leaders.

Clore is for a moment, fellowship is for life

Clore Social Fellows, years after they have completed the Fellowship, will say that they learnt most from their peers. As they mature and take greater responsibility, these are the wise and solid networks that they learn from and lean on for years to come.

Leadership is a lifelong learning journey

Social leaders know they live in a fast-changing world where they must keep 'sharpening the saw'[17]. They know the journey is uneven and they will need regular pit-stops to refresh and reconnect. They understand that character building is never finished.

What would you do if you were 10 times braver?

This is a great question that Clore Social Fellows throw at each other when they are faced with practical dilemmas. Social change makers sit up and remember their calling.

---

16   See Chapter 5 for more on reflective practice.

17   Stephen Covey (1989; 2004) *The 7 Habits of Effective Leaders*. Free Press.

The function of leadership is to produce more leaders, not more followers

Clore Social Fellows know that in the fast-paced world, you need the people around you to be smart, self-motivated and responsible. In other words, you need them to be leaders. Today, our best leaders are growing leaders, ensuring that they pass on the skills they have gained, mentoring and supporting people outside their organisations, encouraging independent thinking and action.

Dedication

I dedicate this chapter to Clore Social Fellows everywhere, beacons of generous and courageous leadership, changing the world everywhere, every day.

Chapter Three: Thinking differently and adapting to change

By Chris Durkin & Tommy Hutchinson

'Change? Why do we need Change? Aren't things bad enough as it is?'
Queen Victoria

Summary

Social entrepreneurs have been grappling with change throughout history – sometimes forced upon them by various external factors, sometimes initiated by themselves in pursuit of innovation and efficiency. This chapter identifies several areas where change is a pressing reality for contemporary social businesses. The areas addressed have implications for policy makers and stakeholders.

Setting social business in an historical context

The industrial revolution in Britain changed many things, driving people to move to the towns due to the rise of factories and mechanical production. This rapid industrialisation broke down old societal structures and caused a sharp rise in both poverty and wealth. This period also saw people begin to ask fundamental questions about how society is organised. Charles Booth, working in London, and Seebohm Rowntree, researching in York, shone a light on levels of poverty in 19th Century England that challenged societal conventions. Other social reformers began to initiate change. Reformers such as Florence Nightingale, the founder of the nursing profession, or Benjamin Waugh, credited with setting up the NSPCC and the Cadbury brothers in Birmingham designed and developed the village of Bourneville. These pioneers began by thinking differently in order to address social inequalities by putting in place new institutions to provide long-term solutions or to alleviate the most extreme cases of poverty.

The late 1990s and early 2000s have often been seen as an age of social enterprise, and the wider Third Sector has been seen as a deliverer of services. This period also saw public sector contracts being awarded to large private sector infrastructure organisations like G4S, Serco and Capita.

These companies were able to fulfil state requirements while tolerating a level of risk unsuitable for businesses, which possess smaller balances. From such contracts, social enterprises, as sub-contractors, were often excluded or were left with 'crumbs from the rich man's table'.

The time of writing this chapter coincided with the anniversary of the collapse of Lehman Brothers Holdings Inc., which filed for bankruptcy in September 2008 leading to a major international financial crash that sent economic tidal waves round the world. This produced a period of grave uncertainty and raised significant questions about the operations of the capitalist system. Although ten years later much of the financial sector appears to have returned to 'business as usual', banks are required to hold greater reserves to prevent a similar recurrence. Martin Wolf of the *Financial Times* noted, 'The chief aim of post-crisis policymaking was rescue', and 'this prevented collapse' but 'the financial system is much as before… Policymakers have barely questioned the relative roles of government and markets.'[1]

Although the main levers of the financial sector may not have changed much, there are real stirrings and movements taking place. Such revision is not new. We can trace back over history, movements from the rise of the co-operative movement, the setting-up of trade unions through to anti-racist movements. Issues such as homelessness led to the setting up of Shelter or Erin Pizzey starting the first Women's Refuge in Chiswick, London. Many drivers of such initiatives were as a direct result of market failure or the failure of the state to deliver.

Globalisation has arguably brought many benefits, both economic and cultural, but it has also contributed to greater uncertainty and caused ruptures in conventional social, political and environmental models. Climate change, UK's Brexit, austerity and the election of populists including Donald Trump are prominent examples of some recent events. One could argue that this was all part of an economic system readjusting itself to what Joseph Schumpeter called the 'the perennial gale of creative destruction'[2]. Rapid technological change and the growth of artificial intelligence, for instance, is beginning to change the way we work and could potentially 'wipe out' many existing jobs and change lives. The report on climate change published by the UN Intergovernmental Panel on October 8th 2018[3] shows how pressing the issue has become and the urgent need to

1   Wolf M (2018) 'Why so little has changed since the financial crash'. *Financial Times* 4th September.

2   Alm R & Cox WM (2019) *Creative Destruction* [online]. Available at: www.econlib.org/library/Enc/CreativeDestruction.html (accessed March 2019).

3   IPCC (2018) *Summary for Policymakers of Special Report on Global Warming of 1.5°C approved by governments* [online]. Available at: www.ipcc.ch/2018/10/08/summary-for-policymakers-of-ipcc-special-report-on-global-warming-of-1-5c-approved-by-governments/ (accessed March 2019).

alter both lifestyles and the fundamental means of energy production and conservation. Tweaking is no longer an option!

Some have used the term VUCA (volatility, uncertainty, complexity, and ambiguity) to describe the world in which we now operate. Others use the analogy of 'choppy waters' to illustrate the way in which organisations can be buffeted by a hostile environment, causing problems particularly for cash-strapped small voluntary and community sector organisations.

Social businesses have developed from an idea, at a particular time, in response to an identified need, and are operating within a context or wider social economic system. Many are systemic, caused in large part by massive external forces such as government policies and cuts in government funding or demographic changes. For true entrepreneurs, change represents both a challenge and an opportunity. Often these are localised, such as responses to providing education provision to specific communities, for example, a local pre-school, or even 'free schools' (for example, School 21, in Stratford, East London). As we look to the future, we can begin to see what the forces might be that will determine the shape of society in the future.

Any list of significant macro factors is likely to include:

■ Climate change, bringing with it a host of problems affecting health, food provision, migration, urbanisation, and even war. 'Most wars in the future will be caused by water' (Bill Clinton).

■ Technological advances, including artificial intelligence affecting individuals in areas such as health, privacy and the workplace.

■ The concentration of economic power and rising inequality.

■ Disconnections between people and those in power leading to a rise in political 'populism', in part aided by more open forms of communication. Whether this trend will be for the short term or long is as yet unclear.

How countries respond to these challenges is partly shaped by their local economic and political conditions. The UK is one of the most centrally organised countries in the world. This has a bearing on a range of policies including commissioning policies. Public sector commissioning policies disadvantage small social businesses by 'increasingly favouring economies of scale'[4]. Education is such an area where an increasing number of schools are run by private enterprises – quasi-private academy trusts,

4   Dayson C, Baker L & Rees J, with Batty E, Bennett E, Damm C, Coule T, Patmore B, Garforth H, Hennessy C, Turner K, Jacklin-Jarvis C & Terry V (2018) *The Value of Small: In-depth research into the distinctive contribution, value and experiences of small & medium-sized charities in England and Wales* [online]. Available at: www4.shu.ac.uk/research/cresr/sites/shu.ac.uk/files/value-of-small-final.pdf (accessed March 2019).

which are governmentally regulated but are ultimately run by private companies. Austerity has decimated local government funding and made it difficult to provide more than the basic requirements, leaving little room for experimenting with social initiatives at a local level. Local communities, meanwhile, are also being severely affected by changes in areas such as technology and the manner in which people shop. The impact on city centres is potentially disastrous. Big tech companies like Amazon, Airbnb and Uber are changing the landscape, forcing many companies in the retail sector out of business.

How social businesses respond to these challenges

However, social businesses can and do respond to these challenges in a range of ways. Earlier on in the chapter we introduced the notion of VUCA to explain the world today. Bill George, Harvard Business School, illustrates related challenges for leaders with what he calls VUCA 2:

Figure 3.1: Vuca 2[5]

VUCA	VUCA 2
Volatile	Vision
Uncertainty	Understanding
Complexity	Courage
Ambiguity	Adaptability

Vision: Every organisation needs to have a vision of its purpose, taking into account the needs of stakeholders. There is a real danger for small social businesses that 'mission creep' can occur, with the organisation moving away from its original purpose. This is not to say that organisations should not adapt and change, but that change must have a purpose linked to the mission of the organisation. Social businesses are especially vulnerable to mission creep as they typically serve two purposes: one is the social reason for its existence, and the other is the financial imperative to survive. The Kids Company is a sad example of an organisation that ceased trading in 2015 due to the CEO and trustees losing sight of its financial imperative.

Understanding: Understanding the purpose of the organisation is critical, as is comprehending the markets and communities one works and lives in. However complex the problems an organisation faces might be, it is vital

---

5   George B (2017) *VUCA 2.0: A strategy for steady leadership in an unsteady world* [online]. Available at: https://www.forbes.com/sites/hbsworkingknowledge/2017/02/17/vuca-2-0-a-strategy-for-steady-leadership-in-an-unsteady-world/#589eccd213d8 (accessed March 2019).

to maintain a deep understanding of both the nature of those problems and, most importantly, the needs and tastes of the customers or users of the business, as these are likely to change. Design thinking is an excellent approach that is being used by many to address some of these complex issues because at its core is empathy[6].

Courage: Leaders need to have the courage to make difficult decisions – if things are not working or the environment is changing around them, they need to recognise the need to change. The American writer Alvin Toffler's comments are pertinent here:

> *'The illiterate of the 21st century will not be those who cannot read and write, but those who cannot learn, unlearn, and relearn.'*

Unless businesses are willing to learn and have the courage to change, they are likely to slowly wither and decline.

Adaptability: This is an extension of the previous point. Unless organisations adapt and change to new opportunities and challenges, they will not survive. Exercises in scenario planning are a useful tool for helping leaders evaluate the ability of their organisations to adapt and react to challenging situations. They can be effectively deployed in role-playing exercises where leaders or teams of employees (or volunteers) get to test their judgement and decision-making against a series of challenging hypotheses. The hypotheses or scenarios can be both opportunistic and hostile; for instance, how to take advantage of a merger opportunity or crises manage a damaging media story. As well as processes around decision-making, such scenarios provide leaders with valuable insights into organisational behaviour, group dynamics and even relationships with stakeholders.

Revamping communities

All social businesses develop from an idea and at a particular time in response to an identified need, and they operate within a context or wider social economic system. We now want to focus on how communities are adapting to change – cause, nature and impact.

Large swathes of Britain's city suburbs, towns and villages are deprived and isolated. Typically, they suffer from unemployment, a high proportion of welfare claimants, an ageing population (in part brought about from a 'brain drain' of younger residents), and a low level of amenities such as shops and community spaces. In many cases, social problems brought about

---

6   See for example, Dam R & Siang T (2018) *Design Thinking: new innovative thinking for new problems* [online]. Available at: www.interaction-design.org/literature/article/design-thinking-new-innovative-thinking-for-new-problems (accessed March 2019).

by crime, drugs and the breakdown of families are common. This is not a recent phenomenon – after the Second World War, there was a pressing need for new housing to replace what was lost to German bombing. This led many areas, like Dagenham for example, being rebuilt with large numbers of housing units, however imperfectly constructed, but little thought was given to the construction of other amenities such as shops, cafes and community centres, which go to making a harmonious and happy environment. Today, such areas are among the most impoverished, with high numbers on benefits and limited activities for the old and young to do.

Woodberry Down Estate in North London, in contrast, is an exceptional example of regeneration taking care to design with the active engagement of the local community. Originally built shortly after the Second World War following the opening of Manor House underground station, the estate combined plentiful housing of varying styles with practical facilities such as the first NHS community centre, which brought various provisions and treatments previously accessible only from a traditional hospital. However, the area then became run down and suffered from a variety of social problems including drug taking and petty crime in the 1980s.

Since 2009 the estate has undergone a significant programme of modernisation. Old housing stock was replaced with high quality apartments, many overlooking the two reservoirs, which double as a nature reserve for migrating birds that was reopened by Sir David Attenborough, complete with walkways and café converted from a derelict coal store. A high-quality community centre was opened and operated by the Manor House Development Trust[7], a charitable social enterprise, providing a library, meeting rooms and space for yoga and dance sessions. This provides space for the community as well as a place where other social enterprises have been able to develop, offering employment opportunities for residents[8]. Privately owned restaurants and a 24-hour gym also operate in the vicinity.

The estate at Woodberry Down blends quality transport and housing with community amenities and immediate access to nature, including two parks. Crucially, the local population was engaged at all stages of its development, from formal consultation right down to the artwork and design of the open playing spaces. Such facilities do not run well if left alone. They need careful, intelligent interventions and the encouragement of local people to use them to develop community businesses, along with ample engagement with sport and art activities.

---

7   Manor House Development Trust: www.mhdt.org.uk/.

8   Mannion L (2017) *SE100 Impact Champion: Manor House Development Trust, Pioneers Post* [online]. Available at: www.pioneerspost.com/videos/20170320/se100-impact-champion-manor-house-development-trust (accessed March 2019).

Such areas that mix private and social ventures can be transformed by some straightforward policy initiatives complemented by basic funding from both central and local government, and the involvement of private enterprises. With intelligent ecosystem support in place to create social businesses, revival of many deprived areas is possible. Such an approach requires three basic infrastructure elements to attract and sustain social entrepreneurship. The first is a regular public transport services (bus or train). The second is a post office enabling local businesses to conduct basic banking. The third is high-quality broadband internet connection. These three basic provisions enable small firms, including sole traders working from home, to be viable.

Interventions that are relatively straightforward to implement have a better chance of being replicated elsewhere. Such an approach, served by relatively small levels of public funding, can help retain or attract new people to live in the community (or prevent departures), and generally bring prosperity and life back to the area.

In contrast to the large-scale regeneration project taking place in London, Alston Moor, an isolated town in rural Cumbria, is an illustration of a community that began to use social businesses as a way of developing their own services. Many businesses had closed and in response the community came together to set up their own community owned co-operative in order to install and ultimately run their own Wi-Fi company called Cybermoor, which now delivers internet connection to this and some other communities. This was in part paid for through a government grant and rectified a major problem in the area: poor Wi-Fi. Alston Moor was thus designated as the UK's first Social Enterprise Town in 2013[9], with the sector having 'a combined annual turnover of around £1.5M…' and employing '…around 50 people, with a further 250 volunteers also contributing to the running of the various enterprises'[10].

The Bromley-by-Bow Centre in London provides another example of the impact that local initiatives can have. The centre has developed from a small community project into a charity that combines an extensive neighbourhood hub with a medical practice and a community research project. In this example, Bromley-by-Bow has had to develop through partnerships, navigating the difficult waters of negotiation, partnership formation and development with some organisations much larger than they are. What was crucial here is that planners understood the area and

9   Buckland H & Murillo D (2015) *Antenna for Social Innovation: The quest for precision: The search for a common framework and recent examples of successful social innovations.* Barcelona: ESADE. Instituto de Innovación Social. Available at: www.slideshare.net/ESADE/antenna-for-social-innovation-the-quest-for-precision (accessed March 2019)

10 *Alston Moor: History of social enterprises in Alston Moor* [online]. Available at: www.socialenterprise.org.uk/alston-moor (accessed March 2019).

the people that lived there. Bromley-by-Bow can also be viewed as an anchor organisation, which in its evidence to the House of Lords, Locality, a national network supporting community organisations, observed:

'In increasingly uncertain times, the role that community anchor organisations play is more important than ever. They stimulate active citizenship and civic participation through volunteering and community organising, and act as a catalyst for community cohesion, bringing together diverse groups to work together for the local neighbourhood. Community anchors build and harness a huge amount of social capital in their local communities...'[11]

The Bromley-by-Bow Centre is an example of a community anchor, a relatively small-scale project operating out of one neighbourhood. It is an interesting case, albeit a large organisation compared to most social businesses, which have few if any employees and low turnover. If we look at charities as one form of a social business, we see that most charities are small.

'There are currently 167,000 registered charities in England and Wales. Organisations with an annual income of less than £100,000 make up almost three quarters (73%) of the sector, while the largest charities, with an annual income of £5m or above, make up just 1% of the sector. However, the largest charities account for 72% of the income for the sector.'[12]

The issue of scale is difficult for many social businesses. Many do not want to increase in size, preferring to concentrate on what they do best.

A slightly different approach that is increasingly gaining traction is the idea of 'local wealth building', which focuses on the existing wealth of a local area. A good example of this approach was adopted in the city of Preston[13] where anchor organisations came together 'to collectively change cultures and behaviours so that greater economic, social and environmental benefit is derived for the Preston economy and its residents[14]. Local wealth building – or community wealth building

11 Authority of the House of Lords (2017) *'Stronger Charities for a Stronger Society' House of Lords Select Committee on Charities Report of Session 2016–17 HL Paper 133* [online] Available at: https://publications.parliament.uk/pa/ld201617/ldselect/ldchar/133/133.pdf (accessed March 2019).

12 Ibid

13 See also Chakrabortty A (2018) In 2011 Preston hit rock bottom. Then it took back control. *The Guardian* 31 January. Available at: www.theguardian.com/commentisfree/2018/jan/31/preston-hit-rock-bottom-took-back-control (accessed March 2019).

14 Todd M (2017) Local Wealth Building: Harnessing the potential of anchor institutions in Preston [online]. Available at: https://cles.org.uk/blog/local-wealth-building-harnessing-the-potential-of-anchor-institutions-in-preston/ (accessed March 2019).

– is regarded as a promising new approach that is becoming more mainstream. Community wealth building is defined as:

'... a place-based approach to economic regeneration which empowers local government and enables communities to create and retain wealth locally.'[15]

As was the case in Bromley-by-Bow, the importance of community anchors is crucial. However, operating on a city-wide basis across the whole of an urban area, the scale was different and required the project to work with seven local anchor institutions focusing on such things as the city's commissioning and procurement strategies. As a response, they broke 'contracts into lots to enable smaller organisations to be supported to bid'[16], something that was very much 'against the grain' of normal commissioning and procurement practices but that enabled local smaller businesses to compete, thus ensuring that a greater amount of wealth remained local. The project 'looked at redirecting the £1.2bn total annual spending power of these anchors to local businesses. Preston City Council has since spent an additional £4m locally, from 14% of its budget in 2012 to 28% in 2016.'[17]

Small social organisations do not operate in isolation. They are part of wider socio-economic systems sometimes spanning the globe, and at the same time, by their very nature, they are connected and rooted in communities. One example of this international scale was the establishment of the social enterprise Divine Chocolate in the 1990s, which brought together NGOs from the UK with farmers from Ghana to form a company that is now competing with the traditional large multinational companies. This demonstrates the importance of partnership and collaboration[18], as well as the importance of stakeholders and co-creation in developing an organisation.

It is important to choose the right structure for any organisation and some do not use a social enterprise or social business model. Many adopt a charitable approach instead, and complement their charitable activities with trading

15 Birley A (2017) *6 steps to build Community Wealth Using what we already have to generate local economic growth co-operatively* [online]. Available at: https://party.coop/publication/6-steps-to-build-community-wealth/ (accessed March 2019).

16 Todd M (2017) Local Wealth Building: Harnessing the potential of anchor institutions in Preston [online]. Available at: https://cles.org.uk/blog/local-wealth-building-harnessing-the-potential-of-anchor-institutions-in-preston/ (accessed March 2019).

17 Sheffield H (2017) The Preston model: UK takes lessons in recovery from rust-belt Cleveland. *The Guardian* 11 April. Available at: www.theguardian.com/cities/2017/apr/11/preston-cleveland-model-lessons-recovery-rust-belt (accessed March 2019).

18 Dayson C, Baker L & Rees J, with Batty E, Bennett E, Damm C, Coule T, Patmore B, Garforth H, Hennessy C, Turner K, Jacklin-Jarvis C & Terry V (2018) *The Value of Small: In-depth research into the distinctive contribution, value and experiences of small & medium-sized charities in England and Wales* [online]. Available at: www4.shu.ac.uk/research/cresr/sites/shu.ac.uk/files/value-of-small-final.pdf (accessed March 2019)..

services, sometimes arranged as a separate legal entity such as a community interest company, a company limited by guarantee or a fully trading commercial company limited by shares. There are many reasons why charities do not adopt a social business function. These broadly fit into four categories

1. **Not appropriate to the vision or brand**

   The Maytree Sanctuary for the Suicidal[19] is a charity based at Finsbury Park in North London, providing respite accommodation for severely depressed individuals. Charities like this, which rely on donations, may struggle to provide trading services without harming their brand. Providing a trading service may simply not appear appropriate, although some services might be separate and distinct, such as those that provide training. Many charities have developed trading arms or have employed private companies to raise money for them on the high street, which, in the eyes of some, has affected people's perception of them, especially where vulnerable individuals are targeted to sign up for long-term direct debit donations, or where charities have adopted sophisticated marketing techniques.

2. **Mission creep**

   A charity may fear that creating an income generating trading arm with the necessary obligation to ensure it is successful may cause the organisation as a whole to lose focus on its core purpose. This might be due to management and employees being distracted by generating income, or by the perception of the stakeholders (beneficiaries and donors).

3. **Management complexities**

   Managing a small charity inevitably carries with it a range of administrative burdens including fulfilling the regulatory requirements of the charity commission. Adding an extra trading function, requiring its own legal entity, accounts, taxation, and possibly even employment conditions (including pension arrangements), may prove overwhelming. Such requirements add an additional burden on management and can even lead to internal divisions, especially if there are differences in employment conditions or if one part of the organisation – such as that which generates income – appears to have a higher status among management and peers.

4. **Achieving critical competitive scale**

   As any social business leader will testify, running a successful venture is usually a full-time job and its long-term survival is often reliant on growth and achieving a sufficient scale. This is especially so where a business seeks to win government funding or to compete in the public procurement market. Government officials are traditionally risk adverse and prone only to award contracts to businesses which enjoy a strong balance sheet. Under competitive tendering, many social businesses whose management is already engaged in activities more central to the charity's mission will struggle to gain the necessary growth to enable the trading arms to compete.

19 For more information, see: http://www.maytree.org.uk/

Drivers of change

Broadly speaking, there are two forms of change. That which is initiated by people themselves – usually to solve a problem or to improve a situation – and that which is imposed upon people from the outside. While the first such change is generally regarded as positive, sometimes creative and even fun, the second is usually viewed less favourably. External change, however, can also be positive – the latest phone or app, for instance. Other external forms of change, however, can be challenging. They can affect an organisation's income or cause it to lose valuable employees or assets.

One example of significant change was that the coalition government of 2008 cut back all specialist youth employment provision, while introducing programmes for adults with completely new referral and achievement criteria, which made programmes harder to deliver. Many non-profit organisations providing employment support lost out significantly, with several closing and others winding up their provision. Also, court rulings about equality of pay or sleep-in payments for residential staff can increase costs enormously for organisations, like MENCAP, providing residential services.

On the other hand, there can even be positive external changes, such as large legacies left to non-profit organisations. In 2018 Oxfam received an unexpected £41 million legacy, while the research charity LifeArc received £1bn from the sale of a cancer drug royalties in 2019.

These forms of external change are difficult for both large and small organisations, and how they react can determine the success and sustainability of the enterprise's future.

So, let us look at how organisations commonly respond to such external changes and the implications of such responses. To illustrate this, let us use the example of a struggling community business and look at what options might be open to them.

Option one – cut the pay roll: Cut the payroll, stop recruiting, lay off existing employees, and shift the remainder to short term or insecure contracts. Such a response is common in many businesses because it is immediate, easy to measure, and does not automatically lead to a loss of services. It is rare, however, that such actions can be undertaken without a significant loss of motivation and commitment from the employees and all too often this causes serious internal divisions, as staff are distracted, worried, desperately defending their positions within the organisation.

Option two – cut the service: Similar to cutting the payroll, such an approach is easy to measure, but it runs the danger of harming the beneficiaries and/or the reputation of the business. A community café that is closed most of the time can quickly cease to be a meaningful service. Its customers may become confused as to when it is open or go elsewhere to somewhere that is.

Option three – grow your way out of trouble: Aggressively seeking new income streams that are in line with the purpose of the business; extending the service by opening longer; investing in the quality of the food or drinks to attract more sales; offering sales promotions to attract new customers; investing through regeneration of capital or finance to open an additional outlet in another part of town. Such an approach often generates greater internal creativity and even excitement, yet, if misjudged, can leave the business even more exposed, whether financially or in quality provision.

Option four – greater focus: Carefully analyse what the organisation does best and prioritise it. Our café, for example, might trim its menu and focus on fewer, better-quality – concentrating on what they are good at.

Option five – change management: Alter bad practice. Too often bad practice is located at the top, among management or the boss. A lack of management skills, empathy, ability to understand one's role, with an unwillingness to change, are just some of the problems found in struggling businesses. Often this can be addressed by greater self-awareness and personal honesty with some reskilling outside advice or consultancy. Without good management, few businesses will survive, and will certainly not fulfil their potential.

Option six – reinvent: In the case of our café, a total overhaul of the menu and décor, clarification of roles, introducing new systems, and a team working together for each other with a clear focus on delivering quality service to its customers or beneficiaries. This is not an easy solution; it takes brave and intelligent thinking… and usually a little luck, but it is often essential if a business is in steep decline. A revamp focusing on the needs of customers or service users is not a guarantee of success, but without it continual decline and eventual insolvency is more likely than not to occur. Paradoxically, it can be the most difficult, yet easiest of the options available.

Conclusion

Albert Einstein once said, 'We cannot solve our problems with the same thinking we used when we created them'. However, what we mustn't do is rush head long into trying to change things without understanding the context and the environment in which the business operates, the stakeholders, and above all, the customers or beneficiaries of our business. In this chapter, we have looked at the historical development of social businesses, the uncertain times that they are operating in and the need to develop new leadership skills. We have also looked at the importance of partnerships and the significance communities play in the lives of social businesses, and finally we have examined the drivers of change along with the responses that businesses might turn to. Paradoxically, change can destroy a business, and yet without it, most businesses will be destroyed.

Chapter Four: Procurement and commissioning in the non-profit sector

By Dr Chris O'Leary and Don Macdonald

Vital role of non-profit organisations

The UK's non-profit sector 'touches almost every facet of civil society' according to a House of Lords Committee[1], and is a significant and growing part of the economy. There are some 170,000 charities in the UK, with a total annual income of between £45 billion and £75 billion[2]. The sector is key to the delivery of a significant and growing part of public services in the UK with between a third and half of charities' annual income coming from contracts procured by central and local government. While the income generated from voluntary contributions and investments has barely changed over the past 20 years, earned income has increased significantly, from around £10 billion in 2000 to around £15 billion in 2016[3].

But this earned income from government contracts is concentrated in a small number of large charities. And there is evidence to suggest that the scope, scale and value of contracts is increasing, which further excludes the majority of charities from bidding for this work as contract size is growing and small charities do not have the capacity to compete, let alone win (see the case study in Chapter Nine on p143). There are a significant number of well-documented barriers faced by many UK charities in public sector procurement. But there are also significant opportunities. Far from being a dry, bureaucratic process, public sector procurement can and should be a means by which innovation is encouraged, charities and social enterprises can flourish, and real improvements can be made in the quality and cost effectiveness of public services.

1   House of Lords (2017) Stronger charities for a stronger society: Select Committee on Charities, Report Session 2016-2017, HL Paper 133, House of Lords, UK: London. Accessed 4/10/18 https://publications.parliament.uk/pa/ld201617/ldselect/ldchar/133/133.pdf

2   Keen, A and Audickas, L (2017) Charities and the voluntary sector: statistics, Briefing paper SN05428, House of Commons Library, UK: London. Accessed 4/10/18 https://researchbriefings.parliament.uk/ResearchBriefing/Summary/SN05428#fullreport

3   NCVO (2018) UK Civil Society Almanac 2018, NCVO, UK: London. Accessed 1/10/18 https://data.ncvo.org.uk/

This chapter explores the role of procurement in the funding and work of the non-profit sector. It examines the opportunities and barriers that procurement presents for charities, and its role in encouraging innovation. We then set out a number of recommendations – for charities and social enterprises, for procurement teams, and for policy makers more generally – for improving the procurement process for the non-profit sector and encouraging innovation and service quality.

Public sector procurement and the non-profit sector

Over the past 30 years, government has emerged as a significant source of funding for charities, through the procurement of public services[4]. Having risen significantly in the period up to 2008, funding has remained largely unchanged since then, but is still the second largest source of funding for the sector. In the UK, this growth in government procurement of charities' services has occurred alongside an overall growth in resources, an increase in the size and scope of the sector, an increase in the policy impact of the sector, and the delivery of better and more services to people and communities in need. This has also gone together with a reduction in grants from both local and central government.

But there are stark differences within the sector in terms of earned income generated from government procurement of services. Research by the National Council for Voluntary Organisations[5] suggests that a small number of large charities have been very effective at securing government contracts. (In fact, research by the Charity Finance Group suggests that large charities are subsidising their public sector contracts by 11%, with a loss made on average by 11 charities with income above £50m[6].) However, smaller and medium sized charities continue to rely on grants from trusts, individual donations, gifts, memberships and sales/services to individuals.

So while overall resources to the sector have increased, the proportion of this income that goes to smaller charities has fallen (from 5.4% to 3.5% for charities with an annual income of less than £100k[7]). Figure 4.1 illustrates the differences in income source by size of charity.

4   Han, J (2017) Social marketization and policy influence of Third Sector organisations: evidence from the UK, Voluntas, 28:1209-1225

5   NCVO (2018) UK Civil Society Almanac 2018, NCVO, UK: London. Accessed 1/10/18 https://data.ncvo.org.uk/

6   O'Brien, A (2016) Whither value? Voluntary organisations and the delivery of public services, CFG Policy Discussion Paper Series, Charities Finance Group, UK: London. Accessed 10/9/18 https://study.sagepub.com/sites/default/files/discussionpaperpublicservices.pdf

7   CSJ (2013) Something's got to give: the state of Britain's voluntary and community sector, Centre for Social Justice, UK: London

Figure 4.1: Income sources for UK charities by size of organisation (adapted from NCVO, 2018)

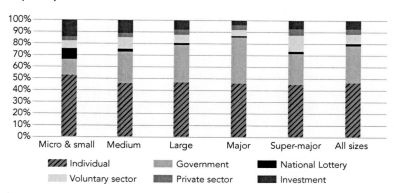

There are also significant differences in government funding as a proportion of all funding by the sector within which the charity operates. Charities in employment and training, social services and playgroups receive the highest proportions of funding from government, at 48%, 46% and 44% respectively. Those that receive the lowest proportion are grant-making foundations (4%), research, religion and environment (each at 11%), and Parent Teacher Associations (12%). Figure 4.2 provides a breakdown of funding source by sector. (Data are from the NCVO's 2018 Civil Society Almanac, based on data for the 2014/15 financial year.)

Figure 4.2: Funding sources for UK charities, by sector (adapted from NCVO, 2018)

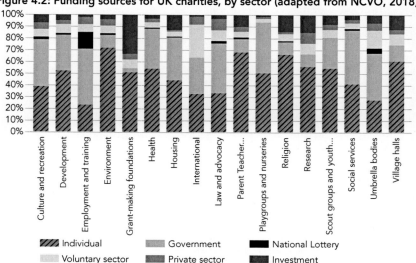

The backbone of the non-profit sector is small and medium-sized voluntary charities and voluntary organisations. The Lloyds Bank Foundation for England and Wales contends that such organisations are created by local people in response to local issues, and as such are both trusted and have the expertise and knowledge to work effectively[8]. They are focused on local and community needs. These organisations rely a great deal on the input of volunteers, who are often both a way to finance social investment but also a means of building social and human capital[9], and are therefore mission critical. But the lack of professional staff, bid-writing expertise, previous relevant experience and wider resources relative to larger organisations, means that these smaller charities lack the resources to engage successfully with government procurement processes[10].

Change in size and scope of government funding

Government funding has not just grown in size, it has also fundamentally changed in nature. There have been a number of shifts in the scope of this funding, each of which disadvantages smaller non-profit organisations. First, there has been a move away from grants and towards procurement of services[11]. Grants to charities are being replaced by contracts, which are often put out to competitive tender, and large charities and social enterprises are better placed to bid for and win these contracts. They are better placed because the process of bidding for and managing public sector contracts requires dedicated resources, often requiring scale. Overly bureaucratic procurement rules actively discourage small companies and charities from bidding for government contracts.

But larger charities are also better placed because of the way in which government scales and specifies contracts. Public contracts are growing in size, value and geographical coverage. This has resulted in a shift in government funding from smaller, more local charities, towards bigger organisations. This move towards larger contracts has seen small and medium-sized charities lose up to 44% of their income from public bodies. These contracts are increasingly awarded to a small number of large organisations because public sector commissioners believe that large organisations with extensive track records of

8   Lloyds Bank Foundation (2016) Commissioning in crisis: how contracting and procurement processes threaten small charities, Lloyds Bank Foundation, UK: London

9   O'Leary, C, Baines, S, Bailey, G, McNeill, T, Csoba, J and Sipis, F (2018) Innovation and social investment programmes in Europe. *European Policy Analysis* 4(2) pp294-312.

10 Aitken, M and Harris, M (2017). The 'hollowing' out of smaller Third Sector organisations? Voluntary Sector Review, 8:3, pp333-42

11 House of Lords (2017) Stronger charities for a stronger society: Select Committee on Charities, Report Session 2016-2017, HL Paper 133, House of Lords, UK: London. Accessed 4/10/18 https://publications.parliament.uk/pa/ld201617/ldselect/ldchar/133/133.pdf

public sector work are less risky choices than small companies and charities[12]. In reality, rather than avoiding risk, these 'mega' contracts are in fact more risky in the longer term, as we have seen from the collapse of Carillion, Transforming Rehabilitation (probation outsourcing), and the scandals over claiming and mismanagement on offender tagging by G4S and Serco. The National Audit Office warned that poor oversight had left the government exposed to widespread fraud and overcharging by these companies[13].

Secondly, there is an increasing move towards outcome-based commissioning or funding arrangements, such as Payment by Results (PbR) or Social Impact Bonds. Cundy[14], the DCLG[15], the Compact Voice[16], and Ward *et al*[17] all argue that the high upfront costs of bidding and managing PbR contracts discourage or prevent smaller and/or local third sector organisations from bidding for PbR related work. Jessica Cundy, in her research for Barnardo's on the experiences of third sector organisations in the commissioning of family services, states that the upfront costs of bidding are a major barrier to third sector organisations presented by PbR. Similarly, the Compact Voice reports that 'PbR contracts often require a significant amount of upfront capital and can involve a degree of risk that precludes the involvement of many smaller voluntary organisations, even if they are the most appropriate provider of the service'.

Part of the risk associated with PbR contracts is that of deferred payment; that a proportion of funding is provided after work has been completed, and only when outcomes have been achieved. To illustrate this, Cundy quotes a survey response by one non-profit organisation who stated, 'we couldn't survive on a PbR contract because we simply couldn't afford to pay our rent and our salaries. We don't have the money that's required in reserve for 6 months or a year.'

Finally, and perhaps driving the changes outlined above, there has been a centralisation of funding over the past ten years. Local government funding

---

12 O'Leary, C (2018a) The lesson to be learnt from Carillion is that we need more private sector and charities involved in delivering public services, not fewer, MetroPolis blog,, Manchester Metropolitan University. UK: Manchester. Accessed 1/10/18 https://mcrmetropolis.uk/blog/the-lesson-to-be-learnt-from-carillion-is-that-we-need-more-private-sector-and-charities-involved-in-delivering-public-services-not-fewer/

13 NAO (2013) The Ministry of Justice's electronic monitoring contracts, HC 737, Session 2013-14, National Audit Office, UK: London

14 Cundy, J (2016) Commissioning for better outcomes: understanding local authority and voluntary sector experiences of family services commissioning in England. Barnardo's. UK: London

15 DCLG (2014) Supporting People Payment by Results pilots. Final evaluation. Department of Communities and Local Government. UK: London

16 Compact Voice (2016) Annual survey of Compacts. Compact Voice. UK: London. Accessed 1/10/18 http://www.compactvoice.org.uk/sites/default/files/imgupload/compact_voice_annual_survey_2015_final.pdf

17 Ward, E, Sample, E, and Roberts, M (2010) Testing the waters. Druglink, 25(6), pp.11-1

of the non-profit sector – both through grants and through the procurement of services – has fallen in real terms and as a proportion of overall government funding. This means that in 2014/15, central government overtook local government as the main source of government funding[18]. Central government will of course be less knowledgeable and supportive of smaller local non-profit organisations.

Procurement for innovation

Using public procurement to stimulate innovation is high on the policy agenda[19]. For example, the Organisation for Economic Cooperation and Development[20], the European Commission[21], the UK Government (2017) and the Local Government Association (2017) have each set out calls for, and strategies to, encourage the use of public sector procurement to foster innovation.

Innovation is a broad and multifaceted concept. It can be associated with newness and discontinuity, often associated with the private sector and with technology and manufacturing[22]. For the non-profit sector, it is the *social* innovation agenda that is key, broadly aligned in themes of processes of social change, sustainable development, the services sector[23] and of creating social value. The non-profit sector is, and has always been, key to social innovation and social value. This started with the extraordinary upsurge in social enterprise and innovation that accompanied the UK's industrial revolution[24], through *Building the Future Together*[25], which set the tone for Labour's engagement with the non-profit sector between 1997 and 2010, and the 'Big Society' and

18 Keen, A and Audickas, L (2017) Charities and the voluntary sector: statistics, Briefing paper SN05428, House of Commons Library, UK: London. Accessed 4/10/18 https://researchbriefings.parliament.uk/ResearchBriefing/Summary/SN05428#fullreport

19 Uyarra, E and Flanaghan, K (2010) Understanding the innovation impacts of public procurement, European Planning Studies, 18 (1), pp123-143

20 OECD (2017) Public Procurement for Innovation: Good Practices and Strategies, OECD Public Governance Reviews, OECD Publishing, France: Paris

21 European Commission (2018) Innovation procurement, European Commission, Belgium: Brussels. Accessed on 1/10/18 https://ec.europa.eu/info/policies/public-procurement/support-tools-public-buyers/innovation-procurement_en

22 Chew, C and Lyon, F (2012) Innovation and social enterprise activity in Third Sector organisations, working paper 83, Third Sector Research Centre, University of Birmingham, UK: Birmingham

23 Edwards-Schachter, M and Wallace, M (2017) 'Shaken, but not stirred': Sixty years of defining social innovation, Technological Forecasting and Social Change, 119: C, pp64-79

24 Mulgan, G. (2006) 'The process of social innovation. Innovations: technology, governance, globalization', MIT Press Journals, 1(2), pp.145–162

25 Labour Party (1997) Building the Future Together: Labour Party's Policies for partnership between Government and the Voluntary Sector, Labour Party. UK: London. Haugh, H and Kitson, M (2007) The Third Way and the third sector: Labour's economic policy and the social economy, Cambridge Journal of Economics 2007, 31, 973–994

'Shared Society' of recent Conservative government policies. Charities – and particularly smaller, locally focused charities – are uniquely placed to respond in new and different ways to the needs and expectations of individuals, families and communities. Yet it is recognised that both government policies and organisational structure/culture significantly impact on innovation in non-profit organisations[26].

Two recent examples illustrate this – the Public Services (Social Value) Act (2012) and the use of outcome-based Payment by Results by UK governments since 2008.

The Social Value Act requires public bodies to consider securing improvements in economic, social and environmental well-being – ie. 'social value' – when they procure goods and services above a certain value. Several reports and reviews, however, have found that the act is not working as thoroughly and consistently as it should. The Local Government Association, for example, found some positive changes in procurement culture and approaches, but concluded that 'the encouragement of innovative suppliers has not been well integrated into the social value imperative even though the Act was intended to encourage a more holistic approach to commissioning'[27]. And the government's own review of the act, found that it:

> '...has therefore proved popular and effective amongst those actively using it. However, this points to one of the early findings of this review: that despite its growing awareness amongst public bodies, the incorporation of social value in actual procurements appears to be relatively low when considered against the number and value of procurement across the whole public sector.'

Indeed, some 40% of NHS commissioners are not using the act to consider tender proposals properly[28] and 66% of councils have not fully embraced it because of insufficient resources, risk aversion, and poor procurement practices[29]. Indeed, the Public Administration and

26 Osborne, S, Chew, C and McLaughlin, K (2008). The once and future pioneers? The innovative capacity of voluntary organisations and the provision of public services: A longitudinal approach, Public Management Review, 10:1, pp51-70

27 LGA (2017) Encouraging innovation in local government procurement, Local Government Association, UK: London

28 Butler, J and Redding, D (2017) Healthy commissioning: how the Social Value Act is being used by Clinical Commissioning Groups, Social Enterprise UK and National Voices, UK: London. Accessed 14/10/18 https://www.nationalvoices.org.uk/publications/our-publications/healthy-commissioning-how-social-value-act-being-used-clinical

29 Jones, N and Yeo, A (2017) Community business and the Social Value Act, Research Institute Report No.8, Power to Change, UK: London. Accessed on 4/10/18 https://www.powertochange.org.uk/wp-content/uploads/2017/08/Report-8-Community-Business-Social-Value-Act-1.pdf

Constitutional Affairs Committee in its recent report on the Carillion Collapse suggested that government is too preoccupied with contract cost at the expense of service quality[30].

A key objective of outcome-based Payment by Results (PbR) was to incentivise innovation by influencing both commissioners' and providers' behaviour. PbR was intended to change their focus: towards the outcomes achieved by providers and away from specifying service delivery models and monitoring inputs and outputs, so that 'the choice of method to achieve those objectives is transferred from the commissioner the provider'[31]. For providers, the flexibility and choice of how and what interventions were delivered to meet the desired outcomes, coupled with financial incentives for meeting those outcomes, was intended to generate creativity and innovation in service delivery approaches. But evidence from several evaluations provides a mixed picture of the extent to which the use of PbR has in fact encouraged innovation.

What needs to change?

There are several calls from organisations within and outside the non-profit sector for changes to public sector procurement in relation to charities. These calls identify that the current system does not work, and advocate changes to the Social Value Act and to the wider process of public sector procurement. There are three key reasons why such changes are necessary.

First, they are needed in terms of the management of risk by government and other commissioners. One of the assumptions driving the increased size and scale of government contracts is that bigger organisations make less risky contractors. But this has resulted in a concentration of contracts in the hands of an ever decreasing group of large organisations. Rather than reduce risk, this actually increases risks, as we saw with the collapse of Carillion in 2018 or the outsourcing messes involving Capita[32], Atos[33], Clearsprings[34], Maximus[35], HES[36] and others. Changing

---

30 Public Administration and Constitutional Affairs Committee. Accessed on 19.10.18. https://www.parliament.uk/business/committees/committees-a-z/commons-select/public-administration-and-constitutional-affairs-committee/news-parliament-2017/carillion-outsourcing-report-published-17-19

31 Frontier Economics and the Colebrooke Centre (2014) Payment by Results in Children's Centres evaluation. Department for Education, UK: London

32 Practice Index Accessed 5.10.18 https://practiceindex.co.uk/gp/blog/news-lost-letters-scandal-capita-contract-led-warehousing

33 BBC. Accessed on 5.10.18 https://www.bbc.co.uk/news/uk-43058789

34 John Harris Accessed 5.10.18 https://www.theguardian.com/society/2018/jan/10/rats-mould-and-broken-furniture-the-scandal-of-the-uks-refugee-housing

35 Guardian Accessed 5.10.18 https://www.theguardian.com/society/2016/jan/08/maximus-miss-fitness-to-work-test-targets-despite-spiralling-costs

36 Health Business Accessed on 5.10.18 http://www.healthbusinessuk.net/news/09102018/hes-stripped-nhs-contracts-following-waste-scandal

the procurement rules to enable more – and more diverse – providers will spread the risks and reduce the potential impact if one contractor goes bust.

Second, while larger contractors might bring economies of scale in terms of costs, procuring small and medium-sized charities is likely to generate higher levels of social value, because they are generally more embedded in and responsive to the needs of local communities. By procuring services for smaller, local charities, public sector commissioners can help support local economies, contribute to the development of human and social capital, and make a wider contribution to local communities.

Finally, the collaboration and competition generated through creating and sustaining a plurality of providers is key to ensuring innovation in the way that public services are designed and delivered, and how they engage with service users and wider communities. Public sector commissioners have a role as market markers. By investing in civil society organisation, especially local, small and medium-sized charities, central and local government can support existing non-profit organisations and develop new organisations at the local level.

Recommendations for non-profit organisations

Some argue that charities should withdraw from outsourcing[37]; however, while this may be viable for large, high-profile charities with other substantial sources of income, it is not an option for smaller charities without their own fundraising and publicity teams. Small charities and social enterprises need to be careful in their approach to bidding for tenders.

If you are such an organisation, you need to be prepared to:

■ **Collaborate.** Work with other organisations, including those that deliver similar services. Join non-profit networks (such as 3SC, the third sector consortium[38]), work in closer partnership or even merge with other non-profit organisations as a means of growing and generating sufficient resources to bid for government contracts. But make sure you are not being used just as 'bid candy' by large organisations, particularly private sector ones, who may want to allocate you the hardest to achieve parts of any contract.

---

37 Evans, K (2018) What charities can learn from the collapse of Carillion, Civil Society UK. Accessed on 1/10/18 www.civilsociety.co.uk/voices/kathy-evans-who-wants-to-be-a-carillion-heir.html
38 3SC Accessed on 17.10.18 http://www.3sc.org/

■ **Be strategic.** Build up your services slowly but surely; even mergers can cause problems. And don't put all of your eggs in one basket – spread your exposure by having a mix of funding streams.

■ **Be savvy.** Check out who has held the contract previously and, if possible, talk to them about their experiences and find if they are bidding again. Find out who else is bidding. Clearly, if there are large numbers of strong competitors, your chances will be reduced severely. Do not waste your time bidding for contracts that you have no chance of gaining because you lack the expertise, track record or financial backing.

■ **Be realistic.** Make sure that you have not agreed to deliver something your organisation cannot achieve. An example might be that your organisation contracts to recruit and find work for large numbers of a target group, such as offenders, when you lack the right links, referral structures or expertise to recruit them, train them or place them in jobs.

The NCVO also has comprehensive advice on its Knowhow site[39]. This gives the following advice on tendering:

1. Ensure you understand the specification fully.

2. Consider the operational impact at all stages (can you deliver?).

3. Analyse the time commitment required.

4. Weigh up the risks and opportunities.

Recommendations for government and local government

The Social Value Act is a good step in the right direction, but it needs to be significantly and radically strengthened. This is a key recommendation of both a recent government review[40] and of the NCVO[41], which has called on government to require public sector commissioners to 'account for' rather than merely 'consider' social value when they commission public services. NCVO believes this would be a significant step forward in terms of encouraging better outcomes for communities – hopefully the government will agree when it concludes its forthcoming second review of the act[42].

---

39 NCVO (undated) How to decide whether to respond to a tender opportunity, KnowHow website. Accessed on 1/10/18 https://knowhownon-profit.org/how-to/how-to-decide-whether-to-respond-to-a-tender-opportunity

40 HMG (2018) Government announces major changes to rebuild trust after Carillion: 25 June 2018, Press Release dated 25/6/18. Accessed 1/10/18 www.gov.uk/government/news/government-announces-major-changes-to-rebuild-trust-after-carillion-25-june-2018

41 Etherington, S NCVO. Accessed 17.10.18 https://www.ncvo.org.uk/about-us/media-centre/press-releases/799-ncvo-responds-to-review-of-social-value-act

42 Winyard, P NCVO. Accessed on 17.10.18 https://blogs.ncvo.org.uk/2017/02/09/review-of-the-social-value-act

Embrace your role as market makers and as social value enablers, but review your procurement processes and procedures and make changes to encourage and support smaller and more local charities in your procurement processes. In particular, avoid putting all of your eggs in one basket, and embrace the fact that social innovation is often built on the experience from previous failure (not all new ideas will work out initially).

Government response

After the Carillion collapse and pressure from the non-profit sector, the government responded. The Cabinet Office Minister David Lidington announced a series of measures designed to improve the health of public service commissioning[43]. These included commitments to:

- strengthen the application of the Social Value Act to central government departments, so that major procurements must have social value 'explicitly evaluated' as part of the process, rather than simply 'considered', and require regular reporting on the use of the act

- require public service suppliers to create 'living wills', namely, contingency plans for services to continue in case of corporate failure

- issue new guidelines and principles to commissioners to encourage building mixed markets of suppliers

- require the largest government suppliers to provide greater levels of transparency, namely by publishing KPI's such as response rates and customer feedback, as well as data on the way they are addressing social issues such as workforce diversity, modern slavery and the gender pay gap

- provide supplier management training to 30,000 contract managers and social value training to commissioners.

Conclusion

Innovation often comes from the non-profit sector and this needs to be encouraged. A great deal of concern has been expressed about the tendering process by a range of organisations and committees, including the NCVO, committees in both the House of Lords and Commons, and the Lloyds Foundation. They have all published reports and this has generated a general mood that something needs to be done. The government has committed itself to some reform, as outlined above, but the proof will be

43 HMG (2018) Government announces major changes to rebuild trust after Carillion: 25 June 2018, Press Release dated 25/6/18. Accessed 1/10/18 www.gov.uk/government/news/government-announces-major-changes-to-rebuild-trust-after-carillion-25-june-2018

if local councils and other public commissioners, who are of course short of funding, are actually prepared to change from low cost contracting in favour of procuring services at a reasonable price from local charities and social enterprises to provide greater social value.

Chapter Five: Service improvement in small non-profit organisations

By Don Macdonald

Introduction

The pressures on non-profit organisations are enormous and have increased significantly since the government's policy of 'austerity' was introduced, due to greater competition for funding, at the same time as greater demands being made for service quality. Evaluation and monitoring are now essential in the non-profit sector, with the development of new impact evaluation methods and funders requiring evaluation to be built in and described as part of the bidding process. Quality accreditation is also being strongly encouraged by commissioners and funders, while there are legal requirements to follow, for instance for safeguarding of children and vulnerable adults. Many small non-profits lack the expertise and resources to initiate and implement the right measures to the level required. Also, to initiate and implement these systems, it is essential that staff understand and support them wholeheartedly. It is equally important to maintain and improve the standards of service delivery through high quality supervision, learning and professional development for staff, thus improving services continually while at the same time supporting staff.

To maintain a high standard of services, a 2017 Lloyds Foundation report[1] emphasised the need to promote well-being among staff, ensuring that any quality systems improve staff well-being rather than decrease it. Thus, managers are presented with a range of complex decisions, at times bewildering, in order to design, introduce and oversee the most appropriate and coherent system for meeting different objectives.

This chapter describes cost-effective and practical methods to initiate, develop and deliver high-quality services, listing useful publications that go into more detail about key aspects of evaluation, performance management and quality accreditation. The key elements are:

---

1   Lloyd's Bank Foundation accessed 18.12.18 https://www.lloydsbankfoundation.org.uk/
     Facing-Forward-2017.pdf

■ research into good practice

■ improving organisational quality

■ quality accreditation

■ monitoring and evaluation.

Continuous improvement

To ensure that high-quality services are delivered, managers should make certain that continuous improvements happen throughout the organisation. These should be supported by two underpinning fundamentals: high level management skills (see Chapter Two) and the production of an organisational strategy or business plan outlining the operational context, funding, contracts and resources for improvement and location. This must outline a viable strategy, covering the finances in detail, with fully worked-out three year budgets and cash flows with resources for business planning listed in Appendix 2.

This chapter will take these two fundamentals as covered and focus on the range of approaches that will be needed, including high-quality management, comprehensive supervision, proper staff development and in-service training, sound reflective practice and evaluation.

It is impossible to manage and evaluate a non-profit properly just by measuring numbers; it is essential to use more sophisticated methods, co-opting staff and gaining their support, with their involvement built in at an early stage, with feedback and input taken into account.

Research good practice

The first step in initiating a new high-quality service must be to research the most effective work methods for the proposed target group in order to design the most appropriate service. This is crucial as there are examples of new methods of work being widely adopted but singularly failing. William MacAskill, in his book *Doing Good Better*, argues that most programmes don't really achieve anything[2]. MacAskill said, 'The best estimate we have is that about 75 per cent of social programmes, when tested, were found to have no impact at all.' This figure is disputed by others, but even if it is only 50% right, it is still important to consider fully the potential impact in planning new programmes.

---

2   Will MacAskill accessed 18.12.18 https://www.effectivealtruism.org/doing-good-better

One recent example highlighted by William MacAskill was Scared Straight, a US initiative set up to stop young offenders from ending up in prison by getting them to spend time with inmates, which was adopted in hundreds of US prisons. However, MacAskill states that although re-offending rates fell among those taking part, studies indicated that re-offending rates would have fallen further if the programme had never been run.

Sources of good practice

Obviously it is critical to talk to existing projects during the planning stage. But it is also important to research in detail the key components of the service being planned, effective work methods and the outcomes expected from research into good practice.

The non-profit sector is very diverse, but an enormous amount of specialist experience and expertise can be drawn on to inform planning. For example, Barnardo's publish a range of papers on work with children and young people, such as those leaving care, those with mental health and many other topics. Most are free. The Youth Justice Board publishes papers on effective practice with young offenders. Social Care Online provides the UK's largest database of information and research on all aspects of social care and social work (see Appendix 2 for details of these three). There are also networks offering help and information on rural projects, community energy and many more specialisms, along with the NCVO and local voluntary action associations (see Appendix 2).

Theory of change

One way to ensure that your programme is soundly based is to create a framework known as the Theory of Change (TOC). Developed by the Aspen Institute[3] and then refined by NPC and other organisations, this defines long-term goals and changes that the organisation seeks to achieve and then works backwards to identify critical success factors necessary to achieve long-term goals. The table below shows a TOC mapping exercise, outlining the various outcomes, outputs and activities necessary to achieve long-term goals.

---

3   Aspen Institute accessed 18.12.18 https://happyhealthynon-profit.wordpress.com/

Figure 5.1: Theory of Change showing the mapping of a reduction in an offending project				
Activities	Inputs	Outputs	Outcomes after programme	Long-term wider impact
Action planning, information & advice, one-to-one counselling, positive change courses & skills training for 100 offenders & ex-offenders from one region.	Programme attended by 90% of participants for 75% of sessions.	75% of participants complete positive change course & achieve a skills qualification.	75% of completers progress into work, further education or self-employment, with a 65% reduction in reported offending.	Lower levels of offending, greater levels of employment, better health and well-being in the wider community.

Maintaining organisational quality

Designing a good programme in theory is still only a start. Recruiting good staff and setting up effective delivery systems is also important. One crucial dimension in managing quality is the size of the organisation. In small organisations, a skilled manager can support, supervise and encourage staff directly, while at the same time monitoring and improving service quality. However in larger organisations it becomes necessary to appoint team leaders, middle managers and quality officers, while setting up reporting and support systems, which in turn must be managed and evaluated. All of this creates opportunities for miscommunication and conflicts to arise. Good systems are needed to gather feedback from customers, improve the delivery of services and demonstrate value for money to commissioners and funders.

It is also important to take into account which services are being provided. If 24-hour care is being provided for a high-risk group of service users, for example, then this will be statutorily inspected and regulated, while higher staff ratios and more health and safety measures will be required than in, say, a day care or training service for a less high-risk user group.

Possible tensions can also arise over achieving different objectives, particularly within target-driven projects where there can be a conflict between providing quality services to fewer numbers of clients or achieving larger output numbers as required by a contract (An example is the meals on wheels case study in Chapter Nine.).

Delivering high quality levels

The first task for a manager new to an organisation is to assess the capabilities, strengths and weaknesses of their organisation in order to find out what is working and what isn't, what the prospects are for different services, which staff perform well, which work methods produce good results and what quality, monitoring and evaluation systems are in place. It may be that the organisation is doing well and only needs fine-tuning. If it needs a major change of management, this is a project in itself and the quicker this is done the less painful for everyone concerned. Managers new to an organisation invariably have a honeymoon period in which to implement changes.

Learning for staff

A culture of learning should be encouraged across the whole organisation so that objectivity is valued, experiences and issues are discussed, analysed and learned from, and new strategies and innovation are introduced. In other words, the process leads to a culture of self-improvement from top to bottom. This does require proper planning along with a consistent lead from the manager, but, as with all change, this can still be met with resistance from within the organisation, forces such as 'time pressures, organisational politics, non-supportive supervisors/colleagues, confusion over the process'[4]. Thus, a great deal of thought and hard work is required to initiate and implement this process in full.

Training

A significant level of training is essential in order to induct and train new staff, impart knowledge about new measures, such as laws, and describe new ventures. Training can provide a useful opportunity for communication with your peers and colleagues. My experience as both a trainer and a trainee has led me to the strong belief that training is best delivered with others in a similar situation: training with much more experienced people can be confusing, while training with much less experienced people is unstimulating.

However, a great deal of training unfortunately can become 'sheep-dipping', processing large numbers quickly and superficially, particularly using online courses, where involvement can be shallow. Research shows adults learn between six and seven times more through practice and feedback than lectures. So this approach is needed.

The prominent New Zealand club rugby team the Crusaders, have a motto: 'Tell me and I will forget. Show me and I will remember. Involve me and I will understand.'

---

4   Laura Bierema, 1997 accessed 18.12.18 http://www.leeds.ac.uk/educol/documents/000000203.htm

Supervision

In all non-profits, where staff work with people, particularly clients with complex needs, regular supervision should be provided by the line manager, particularly to new or inexperienced staff. As one consultant stated, this process involves 'clearly communicating to every member of staff the aims and objectives most directly relevant to them, enabling them to think for themselves about how they can make their best contribution, then supporting and developing them, both professionally and personally, so that they can optimise that contribution'[5].

The amount and intensity of supervision can reduce as staff gain experience and demonstrate they are coping with work. However this should increase if needed to tackle demanding issues such as abusive or violent behaviour. Some organisations even pay for skilled external supervisors.

Proper supervision should provide 'a safe and confidential environment for staff to reflect on and discuss their work and their personal and professional responses to their work. The focus is on supporting staff in their personal and professional development and in reflecting on their practice'[6].

Staff development

Staff development reviews or appraisal systems are often criticised as a waste of time. This can be true if the actual development reviews or appraisals are carried out superficially, if managers are not skilled enough, or if systems are developed without the involvement of staff. A high standard of staff development should follow naturally from good practice in supervision. In fact, staff development reviews were cited by three-quarters of social organisations as being crucial in improving the quality of services, and more important than quality marks[7].

Reflective practice

Reflective practice and supervision can be more relevant than training, as they require participants to examine closely and reflect more carefully on their work, skills, objectives and situation.

---

5   Gill Taylor accessed 18.12.18 https://www.thirdsector.co.uk/gill-taylor-why-need-performance-management-framework/management/article/1432099

6   CQC 2013 accessed 18.12.18 https://www.cqc.org.uk/sites/default/files/documents/20130625_800734_v1_00_supporting_information-effective_clinical_supervision_for_publication.pdf

7   Big Lottery Fund accessed 18.12.18 https://www.biglotteryfund.org.uk/research/making-the-most-of-funding/quality-assurance

Reflective practice can be defined as the process of reflecting on your experiences and your work, so gaining new insights and improving your performance. Reflective practice is required for professional development in certain professions.

The process is particularly important for those organisations who work with vulnerable people with complex needs, as staff have to hope for progress and change, yet results can often be negligible or even depressing, while clients can take out their feelings on staff, all of which in turn creates stress among staff. Non-profit staff are vulnerable to burnout because of the combination of scarce resources and clients with high needs.

Reflective learning in a group enables learning to be shared across the organisation, while providing support and developing team work. There are similarities with the quality improvement circles introduced in some companies.

'There is a robust evidence base demonstrating that teams who regularly meet to reflect on their practice are more effective than those who do not. Furthermore, literature indicates that effective teams achieve better outcomes for their client group.'[8]

To be properly effective, reflective practice needs to be given proper emphasis and arranged regularly. It can also be carried out on an individual basis, including keeping a reflective journal or learning diary, but this really constitutes supervision or coaching. (I am defining supervision as one-to-one sessions focusing on work with service users, while coaching focuses on skills in leadership, management and other areas.)

Organising reflective practice

To be effective, any system of reflective practice needs to be taken seriously and to pervade the whole organisation. Many team meetings include a space for this as a regular item on their agendas, so that issues and experiences can be shared, understood and learnt from on a confidential basis. If the process is given sufficient emphasis and support, often with an outside facilitator running the session, reflective practice will contribute to the right decisions being made, encouraging problem solving and critical thinking skills, resulting in a higher quality of care being offered and staff stress being reduced. (Some organisations call these sessions group supervision.)

---

8   Michael A. West, Lynn Markiewicz accessed 18.12.18 https://www.wiley.com/en-gb/
     Building+Team+Based+Working:+A+Practical+Guide+to+Organisational+
     Transformation-p-97814051115

Oelofsen's research on the effect of reflective practice groups in organisations found these sessions helped 'practitioners become more confident, practice more thoughtfully and reflectively'[9] and found:

'...the group support from colleagues and the input from the facilitator is useful in managing stress. The potential benefits are immense: better decision making, better and more humane care, increased staff well-being and engagement, and, perhaps also, fewer incidents and complaints.'

Reflective practice groups are also useful for managers in a different way, enabling them to reflect on their own management effectiveness, consider their team's performance, develop objective views on the performance of their own organisation and staff, share insights with other managers, learn new skills and strategies and reduce their own and (hopefully) their teams' stress. Some social service departments organise them for senior front-line managers.

Supporting and up-skilling yourself as a manager

For a non-profit manager, the current situation is very challenging. As the manager, you are probably the most important resource in the organisation. It is critical that you ensure your skills are continually updated, that you receive the right support and that you are equipped to make the right decisions to get your organisation going and sustaining its services.

In small organisations managers have to multitask. As a result it is very easy to be diverted from the most important tasks. It is essential for managers to prioritise their work load regularly and consistently in order to achieve their own and the organisation's objectives.

Coaching assists this process as it is individualised, adapting to the coachee's specific needs and situation. The process should enable participants to clarify their own ideas and to build and implement strategies. Good coaching will be challenging, rigorous and time efficient – coachees examine their most pressing concerns and focus on their own needs and potential, rather than wasting time on irrelevant topics or listening to irrelevant presentations.

It is surprising that coaching is not more popular; only around one third of CEOs in the US have used it, although 100% say they would like it. Apparently coaching used to be seen as remedial, whereas now coaching indicates that 'one's company considers one worth an investment'[10].

---

9   Dr N Oelofsen 20.9.12 HSJ accessed 20.7.19 https://www.hsj.co.uk/workforce/the-importance-of-reflective-practices/5048994.article

10 Nadine Page, Erik de Haan accessed 18.12.18 https://thepsychologist.bps.org.uk/volume-27/edition-8/does-executive-coaching-work

Coaching and reflective learning are very similar, in that your own and your team's performance provides the basis for reflecting on your own work. These reflections are then reviewed, experience is interpreted, new concepts are developed and an action plan is drawn up, in which you test and experiment, and in turn reflect and observe again, thereby continually improving your own and your organisation's competence and skills.

While reflective practice and coaching will improve the performance of both the team and the individual, other measures are still required to monitor and evaluate the work, which I cover below.

Quality accreditation

Quality marks are becoming increasingly popular: in a survey of voluntary organisations by NCVO/OPM, 58% stated that they held one or more quality marks[11]. One benefit of holding quality marks is that many funders and commissioners prefer organisations to have external quality accreditation when they are bidding for tenders and procurement. One rationale was that this is a way of 'managing risk, particularly in service areas where expert knowledge may be lacking in the commissioning team'.

Although commissioners require minimum quality levels, sometimes too much emphasis can be placed on writing organisational quality policies and completing evaluation returns rather than generating good practice. It is critical to ensure that not too much effort is spent setting up and managing any time-consuming quality systems to the detriment of other essential work.

As the NCVO/OPM report stated, 'Even the most popular quality standards are a marginal activity when compared with other methods of improving the quality of a VCO or its services', such as service user or staff feedback.

However, there is as an increasing and often bewildering number of different quality and accreditation systems available to non-profit organisations – the NCVO/OPM survey found over 130 were in use. A list of the most relevant is provided in Appendix 1, including some generic ones, some oriented toward specialist services (e.g. restorative justice) or part of your services (e.g. volunteers).

Serious criticisms can be made about the relevance of some quality systems. One of the most popular commercial quality standards, ISO 9001, has been described as expensive, resource intensive, too focused on processes rather than outcomes and not appropriate for the non-profit sector.

---

11 NCVO/OPM/Big Lottery accessed 18.12.18 https://www.biglotteryfund.org.uk/research/making-the-most-of-funding/quality-assurance/

Another standard, Investors in People (IIP), concentrates mainly on HR processes. It is well-thought of by many and was viewed as useful in the NCVO/OPM Quality Survey. However, a substantial review of IIP stated that the process had 'the potential to result in skewed company decision making and result in poor allocation of internal resources' and should be changed radically[12]. Clearly taking on the IIP process is difficult to justify for very small social organisations with limited resources.

Some quality tools, such as the performance measurement tool Outcomes Star involve service users in their operation, helping service users assess and measure their own progress, including soft outcomes.

Benchmarking is also being used to compare performance in particular spheres such as fundraising[13] or digital readiness[14], while the London Benchmarking Group for homeless charities compares outcomes, client survey data and housing management performance[15].

Social auditing

Social auditing has also become fashionable, providing a tool to measure whether your organisation meets standards of operating sustainably and making a difference. Social Return on Investment (SROI) is another tool, mostly used in social enterprises to 'measure outcomes in order to quantify the social value organisations are creating'. The SROI calculations should produce figures outlining both the social and financial benefits of a specific project. Again, this can be difficult for small organisations to implement but an example is provided by Step by Step (see Appendix 2 for details of SROI and this example).

Choosing your quality system

Choosing a quality system is difficult. Each quality standard has different requirements, costs and time commitments, while some carry more weight in specific sectors. Most small non-profit organisations do not have HR or standards departments, so invariably this becomes another job for the manager and any implementation therefore needs to be carefully assessed against other priorities, including staff time – the scarcest resource in a small organisation.

---

12   ISHCM accessed 18.12.18 http://www.valuentis.com/Publications/Books/ISHCM_IiP_EvalStudy_030406.pdf

13   UK Fundraising accessed 18.12.18 https://fundraising.co.uk/2018/01/11/new-benchmarking-service-launches-charity-sector/#.W1WeMdJKjn0

14   Voluntary Sector Digital Maturity Matrix (NCVO) accessed 18.12.18 http://digitalmaturity.co.uk/

15   St Mungos accessed 18.12.18 https://www.mungos.org/work-with-us/commitment-to-quality/

So, sensible choices must be made, based on the following questions:

- Are there particular quality systems that are the standard across the service you are providing? (e.g. Matrix, for careers advice.)

- What quality systems are deployed by similar organisations and do they have any advice?

- Are any quality systems mentioned in the bidding documents by funders and commissioners?

- What are the financial and resource costs of the quality system you are considering compared to similar systems?

- What resources does your organisation have for introducing quality systems with regard to staff and organisational expertise?

- How much training will your staff need to introduce any complex new systems?

Monitoring and evaluation

CES describes monitoring and evaluation and quality assurance as two distinct, if complementary and overlapping, processes. In quality assurance, agreed external standards form the criteria against which judgements are made; in evaluation, the criteria may be set with individual terms of reference or they may emerge through the evaluation process itself. Effective monitoring and evaluation is required to provide information for quality assurance, while any findings should be used to improve performance. A key aspect of evaluation is to make judgements about the performance of a project or intervention, and to make any necessary changes and improvements required.

A report by NCVO on evaluation emphasised the need for 'practical methods' and 'light analytical methods'[16]. There has been a move towards a focus on 'benefits for users' rather than just head counts, with 95% of non-profits in one survey stating that they use service user satisfaction and other feedback methods to improve the quality of their service or the running of their organisation.

As bidding for funds has become more competitive, so requirements for and expectations of effective evaluation have increased. Increasing numbers of funders favour, or even require, the inclusion of impact evaluation and effective monitoring systems. Output related funded projects, such as Social Impact Bonds (SIB), require hard evidence to be collected of outputs and verified for payment.

---

16 CES (Now NCVO) accessed 18.12.18 http://www.poolecvs.org.uk/documents/
cesresearchreportaccountabilityandlearning320328.pdf

Some websites, such as Charity Navigators and Givewell in the US and Giving What We Can in the UK, evaluate charities on their effectiveness and value for money, then publicise the results (see Appendix 2). One commentator writes that the latter two websites 'tend to recommend small healthcare charities serving the developing world', because they believe that the evaluations of their services demonstrate that they provide the best value[17].

MacAskill states that, in order to rate the effectiveness of charity programmes, you should ask five questions:

1. What does the charity do?
2. How cost effective is each programme?
3. How robust is the evidence behind each programme?
4. How well is each programme implemented?
5. Does the charity need additional funds?[18]

If you manage a small non-profit where you are responsible for organising evaluation yourself, or are commissioning a consultant, you must ensure that effective systems are put in place for monitoring and evaluation, while co-opting the support of your staff and service users. Great care must be taken in selecting and implementing any evaluation systems as they consume a great deal of time and resources.

Self-evaluation

Self-evaluation is a reflective process, namely: 'a project evaluation that is carried out or commissioned by those running the project'[19] and 'a form of evaluation whereby the project itself seeks to understand and assess the value of its work. The project is the judge.'

However this process still requires the setting up of effective evaluation systems, objective data collection and monitoring, followed by stringent analysis, so a valid strategy must be drawn up and implemented. (It is being encouraged by the Big Lottery.)

Street League, a youth charity, argue for greater honesty and transparency over charities' achievements, believing there should be a straightforward and simple framework which all charities could adopt (see Appendix 2

---

17 SA Mathieson accessed 18.12.18 https://www.theguardian.com/voluntary-sector-network/2013/jun/11/charity-evaluators-assess-charities

18 Will MacAskill accessed 18.12.18 https://www.effectivealtruism.org/doing-good-better

19 Big Lottery accessed 18.12.18 https://www.biglotteryfund.org.uk/-/media/Files/.../self_evaluation_guidance.pdf

for details). Street League believe that, if charities followed three rules, transparency should follow. Street League's rules are that:

1. *We will never over claim what we do*
2. *All percentages are backed up by absolute numbers to avoid being misleading*
3. *All our outcomes are backed by auditable evidence.*

They claim that hundreds of organisations have agreed to comply with these rules.

Choosing your impact evaluation system

Evaluation is effective only when an effective monitoring system is in place (see below), but to evaluate properly you need to consider and answer these questions:

■ What is the context in which you are operating with regard to services and service users?

■ Are there any agencies you are trying to influence and what impact are you trying to make with your evaluation?

■ What key indicators of good performance exist in your specialism? For example, for employment training projects, one key outcome is entry into work.

■ Are there any statutory regulations or inspection regimes that you should follow? For example, regulations from Ofsted, CQC?

■ What systems are being used by similar organisations?

■ What requirements or contracts do any funders and commissioners have of your organisation for monitoring and evaluation?

■ What resources does your organisation have for monitoring with regard to staffing, software and hardware?

■ How much training will your staff need to introduce any complex new systems?

■ What audience are you trying to reach with your evaluation results – funders, commissioners, policy-makers or public opinion?

Impact and targets

Of course, some contracts with statutory agencies will clearly define the targets for you. You must still ensure that your staff complete any documentation and gather evidence to prove you have reached these targets. It is important that staff, trustees and other key stakeholders are consulted in developing evaluation systems in order to bring ideas that are crucial for the success of the project. If you can produce a thorough evaluation, it is also useful for publicising your organisation's work and effectiveness.

With trusts, you will sometimes be asked to define your own targets, so make sure that any that you propose are both realistic (so that you can achieve them) but challenging (so that they are attractive to the trust). As part of their grant, some trusts will allocate specific funds for non-profits to employ an independent consultant to evaluate the project they are funding or conduct their own evaluations, both of which can be useful to the project.

However it is also possible to organise something worthwhile to demonstrate your organisation's impact and effectiveness, particularly if you do not overburden your organisation with a cumbersome evaluation system that consumes large amounts of scarce resources. Luckily there is a great deal of help available from organisations such as NCVO, trusts such as Esmee Fairbairn and others. (See Appendix 2.)

When evaluating the effectiveness of your programmes, you should consider whether participants would have succeeded anyway without your provision and whether your programmes provided real added value. Value for money should be considered – the National Citizen Service was criticised for poor value for money[20] as well as for not trying to evaluate the long term effects of their programme.

IT systems

Unless your organisation's service user base is tiny, you will almost certainly need software to record and analyse any data collected. It can be sufficient to use either a spread sheet or a Customer Relationship Manager database and there are free versions of these available (see Appendix 2). Microsoft and Google also provide some free software to charities.

An IT database manager with long experience in the non-profit sector told the author that, in his opinion, the key aspect of good database management is organising the charity's targets and reports correctly. If the data has been collected accurately in the first place, this data can always be rigorously evaluated later. It is essential to gather participants' agreement to collect their data and to follow any other legal requirements, including data laws such as GDPR.

20   Third Sector accessed 18.12.18 https://www.thirdsector.co.uk/cost-national-citizen-service-unjustified-says-mps-report/policy-and-politics/article/1427327

Monitoring and data

Monitoring is the systematic collection and analysis of information about the delivery of services, examining the quality of the services and answering questions about the programme's performance from funders and other agencies.

Monitoring systems should be designed and implemented from the planning phase of a non-profit organisation, though, for specific programmes, commissioners and funders may impose their own monitoring requirements. Any data collected must be measurable and objective – using phrases such as 'distance travelled' is too woolly, while irrelevant data is just burdensome.

At a minimum you need to record the following data:

■ Numbers and profile of users (ethnic origin, gender, age, residence, background regarding service provided e.g. employment status for job-finding projects).

■ Inputs, against targets, namely actual services provided to different clients (e.g. reaching the right service users, delivering courses and/or providing information and/or support).

■ Outputs: quantifiable objective targets that have been achieved (e.g. qualifications, numbers of people trained or service users advised).

■ Outcomes: changes that have occurred as a result of the programme, with supporting evidence. For example, if the outcome is progress into employment, the evidence is a job offer letter; if the outcome is better literacy, the evidence an improved test score.

■ Feedback and self-assessment from clients, stakeholders and partner agencies.

Evaluation

Evaluation is the process of critically examining information and data collected by monitoring, and it is effective only where a good monitoring system is operating. It is generally accepted that a key aspect of evaluation is to make judgements about the performance of a project or service and to recommend any necessary changes and improvements required.

Evaluation requires the ability to make qualitative or quantitative judgements, to set out reasoned arguments and to criticise constructively. There must also be some form of planning to design solutions if a project is failing. Projects have often succeeded when their service delivery has been changed after an initial evaluation has taken place. Therefore, the objective of an evaluation process is to discover what has really happened, to measure outcomes against targets, and, if necessary, to take corrective measures if targets are not being met. It may also identify any future needs for the project.

One issue is that some objectives are unsuitable or contradictory to an organisation's goals. School performance, for example, is usually measured by exam results, but schools have recently been trying to improve their exam performances by excluding large numbers of under-performing pupils before their exams. Likewise, until very recently hospital performance was adversely measured on the numbers of caesareans carried out, a metric that has now been changed.

Soft outcomes

With some projects it may only be possible to measure soft outcomes, such as increased confidence or skills, rather than hard outcomes such as job entry. Evidence for soft outcomes could come from feedback from staff or teachers, or example. A community organisation could argue that a crime prevention programme had been effective but would still need to provide evidence, for example a feedback from residents' groups or the police stating that a neighbourhood is now safer.

The area of soft outcomes can pose issues. One management mantra states that 'if it can't be measured, it can't be managed'. That may be true in a widget-making factory, but it is misleading for services for people. One reason is that the measurement of soft outcomes is still not very sophisticated, particularly in small non-profits without research and evaluation teams.

The Outcomes Star is an example of involving service users in assessing and documenting their own progress. Triangle, a social consulting company, worked with St Mungo's to develop this system in 2003. With their key workers, clients rate their own progress in different areas of their lives. Triangle have also adapted the Outcome Star for use with other vulnerable client groups, including young people[21].

Final thoughts

Non-profit companies can be harder to manage than private companies because there is not always universal agreement about objectives, as there is in companies where profit provides the bottom line. Also there are more stakeholders and their views are more important.

---

21 The Outcomes Star www.outcomesstar.org.uk is described in more detail in my chapter on evaluation with Charles Oham in '21st Century Skills for Non Profit Managers.' published by BEP https://tinyurl.com/yagppste

One experienced consultant expressed his concern to the author that many non-profit organisations spent too much time on implementing quality systems instead of concentrating on generating income. Another concern, expressed by Professor Jerry Z Muller, is that the obsession with managing performance through statistical analysis is detrimental, as it encourages poor decision making while undervaluing professional acumen and hindering innovation[22].

One of the fundamental aspects of community groups is their informal approach, but in the current climate, more formal systems such as evaluation are clearly required. Small and medium organisations need to plan carefully how they approach quality, service improvement and evaluation. As Muller says, 'The problem is not measurement, but excessive measurement and inappropriate measurement – not metrics, but metric fixation'. With good planning and assistance, it is possible to design and implement systems that provide added value, while still valuing professional knowledge and encouraging creative problem-solving.

22   Muller, Jerry Z 'The Tyranny of Metrics' (Princeton University Press, 2018),

Appendix 1: Quality accreditation

Quality accreditation	
This is only a partial list	
Organisation-based	ISO 9001 https://www.iso.org/home.html EFQM http://www.efqm.org/
Charity standard & volunteering	PQASSO https://www.ncvo.org.uk/practical-support/quality-and-standards/pqasso Volunteer management (IIV) https://iiv.investinginvolunteers.org.uk/
Social enterprise	B Corporation (mostly USA) https://bcorporation.net/about-b-corps Social Enterprise Quality Mark https://www.socialenterprisemark.org.uk
Client groups	Age Concern CQS https://www.ageuk.org.uk/merton/about-us/organisational-quality-standards Two Ticks Disability http://creativediversitynetwork.com/two-ticks-disability-scheme London Youth http://londonyouth.org/what-we-do/quality-assurance/
Specialist services	Advice Quality Standard http://advicequalitystandard.org.uk Careers Advice (Matrix) http://matrixstandard.com/ Restorative Justice https://restorativejustice.org.uk/restorative-service-quality-mark

Appendix 2: Useful non-profit networks and resources

- NCVO Knowhow https://knowhow.ncvo.org.uk

- Charity Retail Association http:/www.charityretail.org.uk

- Reuse Network http://www.frn.org.uk

- Sporta for sports & leisure trusts http://www.sporta.org/

- INCA for community broadband http://www.inca.coop/

- Plunkett Foundation for rural projects and co-operatives http://www.plunkett.co.uk

- Community Catalysts, supporting micro social enterprises involved in social care http://www.communitycatalysts.co.uk

- Community Energy Centre for Sustainable Energy https://www.cse.org.uk/local-energy/funding-your-project

- Locality https://locality.org.uk/services-tools/resources/resources-for-community-organisations/

- Resource Centre https://www.resourcecentre.org.uk/information

- Esmee Fairbairn https://esmeefairbairn.org.uk/useful-sector-resources#evaluation

Other Resources

- My previous book has a more detailed description of business planning processes. Macdonald D (2017) 21st Century Skills for Non-Profit Managers. BEP. See https://www.businessexpertpress.com/books/21st-century-skills-for-non-profit-managers-a-practical-guide-on-leadership-and-management/

- Manchester Community Council publish a business plan template https://www.manchestercommunitycentral.org/sites/manchestercommunitycentral.co.uk/files/Business%20Plan%20Template_0.doc

- A model for reflective practice https://docplayer.net/24158150-A-model-for-reflective-practice-and-peer-supervision-groups-howard-edmunds-june-2012.html

- Barnardo's papers on work with children & young people http://www. barnardos.org.uk/what_we_do/policy_research_unit/research_and_ publications/mental_health_policy_research.htm

- Youth Justice Board papers on effective practice with young offenders https://yjresourcehub.uk/effective-practice.html

- Social Care Online database on all aspects of social care and social work https://www.scie-socialcareonline.org.uk

- Social Auditing http://www.socialauditnetwork.org.uk/getting-started/ what-is-social-accounting-and-audit

- Social Return on Investment (SROI) https://neweconomics.org/2009/05/ guide-social-return-investment

- Step by Step https://www.stepbystep.org.uk/media/downloads/844-sroi-report.pdf

- Street League's Transparency Rules https://www.streetleague.co.uk/ transparency

- Software Small Charities Coalition http://www.smallcharities.org.uk/ resources-databases/ https://www.quora.com/What-is-the-best-open-source-CRM-for-a-small-non-profit

- Charity Navigators https://www.charitynavigator.org/

- Givewell https://www.givewell.org/charities/top-charities

- Giving What We Can https://www.givingwhatwecan.org

Appendix 3:
Case study – St Mungo's
Quality Systems

St Mungo's is a large charity and housing association for homeless people, substance abusers and other people with complex needs, providing beds and support to 2,700 people, along with training centres and outreach services supporting 5,000 people and housing support for 5,000 ex-offenders (see Chapter 6). Since 1969 it has operated in London and across South and West England. It has an annual turnover of £85 million, 75% from different government departments (including Housing Benefit), employs 1,400 staff and deploys 900 volunteers.

Its quality systems include:

■ A continuous improvement and quality audit programme, conducted by a dedicated team, which identifies good practice, high-risk settings and areas for improvement.

■ Involvement with and feedback from staff – managers meetings, team meetings, staff union, diversity staff groups, supervision and reflective practice for staff and managers.

■ The EFQM Excellence Model, which assesses both organisational processes and outcomes (ISO 9001 just assesses processes).

■ Benchmarking on outcomes with peer organisations (client satisfaction, rehousing, costs etc.) and other KPIs (starting work, participation in training/education).

■ Involvement with and feedback from clients via various structures including the staff Client Involvement Team; Outside In Project which involves clients in giving feedback; clients' representation on the St Mungos Board of Trustees; progression routes for former clients as volunteers, apprentices etc.

■ The Homes and Communities Agency regulates their work as a housing association, and the Care Quality Commission regulates and inspects their care homes.

■ The Charity Commission regulates their work as a charity and the Fundraising Regulator oversees their fundraising.

■ Contracts for hostels and other services are also overseen by the relevant funding agencies and local authorities.

Chapter Six:
The development of front line service delivery

By Charles Fraser (Former CEO of St Mungo's)

Introduction

I have been asked to reflect on my time working for, and leading, St Mungo's – with particular reference to two questions: first, to what was our success attributable? And second, what lessons, if any, might be derived from it for the voluntary sector more broadly? Even though these are generalisable questions, they are easier to answer if set in context – which is why the background is important. Chronology also provides a helpful prism through which to view and comprehend the nature of our success.

St Mungo's was established in 1969 as the St Mungo Community Trust. The name 'St Mungo' was the nickname of Kentigern, a 6th century bishop of Glasgow and patron saint of wandering Celts, and was chosen because many of London's street homeless at the time came from Glasgow and the name resonated with them. The St Mungo Community did not refer to the community at large – it was a self-referencing community (and an unauthorised spin-off of The Simon Community).

The 1970s

St Mungo's was initially established as a soup-run: in an early edition of 'World in Action', the founder-director Jim Horne is shown explaining to new volunteers how they should work – 'always seek out those on the periphery of the crowd' – an important and enduring tenet for St Mungo's. It quickly obtained a short-life house in Home Road, Battersea, from the GLC (Greater London Council). This three-bedroomed mid-terrace rapidly came to accommodate as many as 23 men nightly, brought in from the soup-run.

Although St Mungo's always saw the benefits of small, shared housing projects, it decided to focus on a volume response to the sheer number of people on the streets, and in 1970 opened the Old Marmite Factory in Vauxhall as a night-shelter. Jim Horne had real charisma, and successfully cultivated the media and political contacts, as well as stimulating charitable donations. As a consequence, in 1974 St Mungo's was offered the Old

Charing Cross Hospital, consisting of 550 bed spaces spread over three projects (a homeless hostel, rooms in the nurses' wing, and a students' hostel), as well as Lennox Buildings, a block of flats on Vauxhall Cross. In order to attract and channel capital funding, St Mungo's set up a housing association as a sister organisation (ironically, it was this rather than the Trust which continued and expanded St Mungo's work, and which came to be known as 'St Mungo's'). The condition of both properties was poor, but their scale catapulted St Mungo's into being the largest of the 'new-kids-on-the-block' in the homelessness sector.

In the 1970s the government funded a research programme into the effectiveness of programmes tackling destitution, in which St Mungo's featured prominently[1]. Over the years, homelessness organisations have commissioned or conducted research into a wide variety of specific issues, but these have generally covered issues that backed up their particular approach to homelessness: there has been little serious overall research into homelessness (with the honourable exceptions of Madeleine Drake in the 1980s and, more recently, Prof Fitzpatrick). Unfortunately, the sector has not used research findings well enough to inform service delivery.

The 1970s saw St Mungo's consolidate its position, therefore, but it also saw the emergence of ideological differences between homelessness organisations: some saw homelessness as the expression of an individual psychopathology; others saw it as the consequence of structural socio-economic inequalities in wider society. Sometimes the sector expended more energy on ideological in-fighting than on holding the government of the day to account and securing real change.

In 1979 the manager of St Mungo's night-shelter in Bondway, Vauxhall, made a unilateral declaration of independence and, following financial investigations, Jim Horne found himself in the Old Bailey in 1980 on charges of false accounting. The trial was stopped on the first day, but the fallout had a profound impact for St Mungo's, not least through the resulting separation of the trust from the housing association. The future of the latter was in the balance, but ultimately it was backed by the authorities, in large part because closure would have caused a surge in visible homelessness in central London.

The 1980s

In 1980 the government announced a Hostels Initiative, intended to increase the availability of temporary housing for single homeless people (and 'adjacent' client groups, such as ex-offenders, people with mental illness and those with learning difficulties). This did not mean large hostels – indeed, this

---

1   *Helping Destitute Men* (1980) John Leach and John Wing. Tavistock.

was the period when the benefits of large institutions were being examined very critically. Institutions were held to be by definition deleterious, despite the fact that the most comprehensive research into homelessness in the 1980s – 'Single and Homeless'[2] – was categorical that size was much less important than facilities and management style. Simultaneously, however, St Mungo's was served notice on the Old Charing Cross Hospital by its owner, the Metropolitan Police. We were faced with the need to obtain replacement buildings rapidly, but there was never the slightest prospect of obtaining buildings of anything like the same capacity in central London.

The corollary to 'small is beautiful' was this 'large is horrible' ideology: 30 beds was the magic threshold beyond which a project became an 'institution'. This yardstick was embraced by the Housing Corporation, our regulator and capital funder, which over many years demonstrated its inability to understand single homelessness. When we found a (much smaller) replacement hostel for Charing Cross around the corner in Covent Garden, with a capacity of just 120 beds, we were informed superciliously that we would have to replace it with hostels of no more than 30 beds within five years (which betrayed an ignorance of the realities of planning permission, as well as of the additional revenue costs which this would entail). We agreed, pointing out that we would be reliant on them for the capital and revenue implications of this requirement – and, predictably, they never raised it again.

Before we reached that stage, however, we had to decant Charing Cross. Our staffing levels were very sparse – about 12 operational staff to provide 24/7 cover for 550 people – and the work was by necessity a containment job. We had already branched out into resettlement because of a fatal fire in our block of flats in Vauxhall. (The GLC, as the fire authority, was going to prosecute the landlord, until it discovered that this was the GLC's housing department. Ranks were closed and the decision was taken to just close the building). With the unexpected closure of Charing Cross too, our embryonic resettlement 'team' (one person) was expanded. Resettlement was a relatively new discipline, and the few existing rehousing experts in London provided us with generous help to develop our own expertise. Despite having only a replacement capacity of 190, we were able to rehouse all 550 residents of Charing Cross – nobody had to go back to the streets.

This decanting was a huge learning process for St Mungo's: self-evidently, those who were easiest to resettle were rehoused first, which made us realise for just how many people in the hostel the primary problem was simply a lack of housing. Nevertheless, the majority did have additional support needs, commonly alcohol dependency, marginal productivity, and acute social isolation. There was much talk at the time of the voluntary

---

2   Drake M, O'Brien M, Biebuyck T (1982) *Single and Homeless*. HMSO, London.

sector's 'network of provision' – and rather less about the sector's selectiveness. Our repeated experience of other organisations told us that small projects would exclude the single homeless with whom we worked.

This was because their needs were not neatly packaged, so to speak. We had many people with, for example, the kind of mental health problems that would have made them eligible for admission to specialist provision. But if they also drank, that would serve to disqualify them. People with multiple needs were thus neglected by both the state and by most of the voluntary sector. This was recognised by John Leach and John Wing:

'People exposed to one type of disadvantage tend to accumulate others, notably because they become stigmatized and lose status. The emphasis on 'single solutions' has led to a multiplicity of agencies, each dealing with one type of disadvantage, and thus to the possibility that multiply disadvantaged people will fail to receive adequate help from any of them.'[3]

This was a prescient finding.

Resettlement

The 1980s was the decade when the progressive voluntary sector discovered resettlement – helping people to move on from hostels and settle in the community. This raised interesting questions about whether the range of provision was adequate (it wasn't), and what precisely was meant by 'the community'. Certainly in the sense of a mutually caring wrap-around, it no longer existed.

Resettlement presented the sector with challenges to its traditional mind-sets: staff had to assume that their residents' stays would be temporary, and therefore had to add the skill of assessment to their basic role of sympathetic support worker. Identifying needs (and trying to find a service that could and would meet them) required discipline in working methods and record-keeping. It also meant, perhaps crucially, that staff could no longer satisfy their own 'need to be needed' through their residents' neediness.

Successful voluntary agencies were those which, like St Mungo's, sought to help people become as independent as they could be. We were still committed, however, to providing long-term care for those who had nowhere else to go. One of our mantras at this time was: **'Support for those who can, care for those who can't'**.

The strategic question which the closure of Charing Cross posed to us was: do we rehouse the residents or replace the facility? We did both, but many subsequent closure programmes in England saw the residents rehoused, and then new projects opened for markedly different client groups, always easier to manage. Camberwell Reception Centre, run by the Department

---

3   *Helping Destitute Men* John Leach and John Wing, Tavistock 1980, p.43

of Health & Social Security (DHSS) and reputed to be the second-largest hostel in Europe, was closed. A significant programme of capital and revenue investment did replace most of the capacity, but the direct-access element was never fully replaced. This tendency was repeated in other sectors: one only has to look at the closure of the psychiatric hospitals, which saw a plummeting in the options for in-patient treatment, because the orthodoxy held that it wouldn't be needed on anything like the same scale as previously, thanks to the increasing effectiveness of drug regimes – a mistake of analysis which not only made 'Care in the Community' a dirty term for the general public, but which also contributed to the random killing of Jonathan Zito by Christopher Clunis, which in turn helped lay the groundwork for the Homeless Mentally-Ill Initiative.

One effect of this increased selectiveness by many organisations was that those which were still willing to work with people on the basis of need found themselves working almost exclusively with extremely vulnerable people. It was commonplace for charities to claim to funders that 'we work with those nobody else will work with', a claim which was at best disingenuous and at worst downright bogus, bar for two agencies in London, one of which was St Mungo's. We were very clear: when it came to improving pure housing stock, we would willingly go 'up-market' in terms of the quality of accommodation, but absolutely not go 'up-market' in terms of *whom* we would house. A guiding principle was that *we would do nothing to make it necessary for someone else to have to re-invent St Mungo's.*

If one looks into the history of homelessness, from the Black Death until the 1980s, it was a phenomenon associated primarily with *migrant labour*. Certainly in St Mungo's, casual work was prevalent, and we became concerned that the housing that was available for us to resettle people into ('low demand' was the euphemism which preceded 'hard-to-let') was located in unemployment blackspots. In other words, while our resettlement programme might be moving people from insecure to secure housing, it was also moving them from insecure employment to unemployment.

Employment

We began thinking about running an employment programme, but first we wanted to understand the reality faced by our residents. We conducted a survey in 1983 and discovered, somewhat to our surprise, that 86% of our residents were in some form of employment. The scale of the challenge became gradually clearer: the great majority had no qualifications; their employment history was not characterised by long-term unemployment, but by *recurrent* unemployment; and casual work was not just a parallel world of work, it was an active counter-culture to mainstream employment. Training was unattractive, because it equated to a day's cash-in-hand being lost.

It became increasingly clear to us that employment was key to successful resettlement. It conferred an income, and an income conferred choices. We used the Hope Goldthorpe scale (a scheme of occupational classifications) to assess the extent to which homelessness had caused people's occupational options to deteriorate – and discovered that it had had little impact – the majority had always been unskilled workers.

Central government ran services such as the Employment Rehabilitation Centres (closed in the 1990s), but these had more in common with a carousel than a conveyor belt. They were ineffective, and government proved incapable of re-invigorating them. The reason that St Mungo's launched an employment service was due to that archetypical justification of the voluntary sector: we recognised an important need and when it was quite clear that the state had neither the interest nor the ability to run a relevant service, we moved in to fill the vacuum.

We therefore set up our own employment and training programme, funded initially entirely from charitable sources. We gradually learned that the fundamental progression was not provision-led (i.e. from *activity* through *training* to *employment*), but psychological (from *being* through *doing* to *working*). We achieved many successes in terms of occupational, training and employment outcomes – but were also outstripped by an escalating problem. By 2010, 15% of our residents had never worked; 50% had been unemployed for five years or more; and over 50% could not read or write to a functional level. Since the length of time spent unemployed is the most reliable proxy indicator of employability, these figures show that the state had just consigned this population to the scrap-heap.

We knew that labour market re-integration was a long and winding road, with many false starts and dead-ends along the way. The inadequacy of the state's response was shocking: the Department for Work & Pensions was set up in 1948 under the National Assistance Act with the aim of reducing unemployment. In 70 years it does not appear to have understood youth unemployment, women's unemployment, recurrent unemployment or fluctuating unemployment. It had absolutely no understanding of homelessness and unemployment. It is nothing short of scandalous that in the 30 years since our survey of 1983, the employment rate in St Mungo's hostels fell from 86% to 10% in 1997, and to 4% in 2014! This represents a scathing indictment of state inertia, indifference and incompetence, as embodied by the DfEE (Department for Education & Employment – now DWP) and its senior management and ministers[4].

---

4   One later example was the Work Programme set up in 2011, in which St Mungo's agreed to participate only to find that it was completely unworkable and so withdrew accessed 18.12.18 https://www.civilsociety.co.uk/news/st-mungo-s-withdraws-from-work-programme.html A subsequent review of the programme by Parliament's Work & Pensions Select Committee - *Can the Work Programme work for all user groups? 2013* - condemned the Programme for failing vulnerable people, and denounced the widespread practice amongst contractors of 'creaming and parking', i.e. creaming off the easiest to help, and leaving the rest.

Our approach

Over the 1980s we developed a three-pronged approach to tackling single homelessness – to continue to run street-facing hostels for the most indigent and needy; to develop a range of smaller projects, from low-support move-on to specialist high care (e.g. for the frail elderly, or people with mental health conditions – we took advantage of the Registered Homes Act to set up the first care homes for homeless people); and to build on our resettlement expertise, so that people could move on and out of homelessness as quickly as possible. We were also the first homelessness voluntary agency to employ mental health specialists. It is important to recognise just how unusual this tripartite approach was: it was our funders and supporters who recognised this as pioneering, and thus led to us describing ourselves with justification as a *unique organisation*.

Revenue funding came from a variety of sources, but these were the days when central government saw itself as being the guarantor of the prospects of single homeless people. This was welcome since, in central London at least, single homelessness was demonstrably a national issue, rather than a purely local one (which is not to suggest that local single homelessness did not exist). The GLC had a dedicated single homelessness team (because it recognised that provision needed to be pan-London in its scope), which morphed into the London Boroughs Grants Unit (LBGU): this was the main strategic funding body for the homelessness voluntary sector. By today's standards they 'went native', in the sense that our work mattered to them, and they were not afraid to take decisions, which was unusual compared to parts of central government. The progress that we (and others) made in this decade *was due to this sense of a shared vision between funder and provider*. Commissioning was well-informed and characterised by mutual trust, qualities which are very hard to find nowadays.

Most of the people who came to St Mungo's at this time – and they were mainly men – had been living in common lodging houses but had lost their accommodation when the landlords sold up to cash in on rising property prices. Most importantly, they had personal histories: they had had jobs, flats and relationships. Things had gone wrong (we usually found that mental illness preceded homelessness, whereas alcohol problems succeeded it), and they came into the orbit of St Mungo's. Social isolation was a significant issue and too often we heard that their friendships amounted to not much more than the camaraderie of shared circumstance. Twenty years later, many fewer of our clients had these personal histories – indeed, some of them were felt to need re-parenting, something which was far beyond St Mungo's abilities.

The campaigning mantra of the 1980s ('homelessness is a housing problem') was seductive, but homelessness is more complex than simply amounting to an absence of bricks-and-mortar. It has much more to do with inequality and disadvantage, compounded by a total abdication of responsibility by public services. Alongside St Mungo's emphasis on personal fulfilment in terms of progression in housing and work, we also looked much more closely than hitherto into mental illness.

Mental health

St Mungo's had been very tolerant towards problem drinkers, but we knew that alcohol and mental health do not mix well, and our determination to be more accommodating towards the latter changed our organisational strategy. We employed specialist workers; we planned for specialist mental health projects; and opened the first Clubhouse in Britain, based on Fountain House in New York. We tried to exert pressure to improve public services for this very neglected sub-group of the single homeless population, and were largely responsible for the introduction by the government of the Homeless Mentally-Ill Initiative (HMII) in 1991 – a significant example of our lobbying and campaigning role. At the time about 25% of St Mungo's residents were thought to have a mental health condition; over the next 30 years this rose to up to 60%.

One of the criticisms of 'Care in the Community' was that it did not just entail the closing down of the big psychiatric hospitals, but also the closure of psychiatry. This seemed to be confirmed in the 1980s and 1990s by the rise in the incidence of diagnoses of 'personality disorder'. Opinion was divided as to whether this was a real clinical condition or a convenient label to hang on homeless people. Since there was no available treatment, it seemed to justify the withdrawal of psychiatry from those with the disorder.

The 1980s was also the time when the language of dual diagnosis emerged. This referred to people with a mental health and a drugs or alcohol problem, but specifically it meant that someone had two problems of equal magnitude, so that no primary diagnosis was possible – precisely because one condition would impact negatively on the other, which intensified each. This gave way over the years to the less precise term 'complex needs', but what we noticed at St Mungo's was an intensification of need, so that it was not uncommon to find people with up to four co-occurring mental health conditions, let alone (say) a drugs problem. As we engaged more in the 2000s with the health sector, the language of 'tri-morbidity' became more prevalent – but it was essentially describing the same phenomenon.

Over the succeeding 25 years we extended our services and introduced further specialisms (e.g. Life Works, a counselling service), and were a key contributor to the development of the Psychologically Informed Environments approach to homelessness.

St Mungo's always focused on people at the 'severe and enduring' end of the mental illness spectrum, rather than the 'mild to moderate' one. This was almost by definition the segment which had fewest treatment options – which is doubtless why they ended up with St Mungo's in the first place.

It is depressing to recall that the evaluation of the HMII in 1995 which noted, '... the fact remains that homelessness among those with a mental illness is a preventable adverse outcome that ought to be addressed by mainstream services.'[5]

---

5   *The Evaluation of the Homeless Mentally-Ill Initiative: an Evaluation of 4 Clinical Teams* Prof T. Craig, E. Bayliss, O. Klein 1995

The 1980s saw a sea-change in the way that single homelessness was tackled. The typical 'soup-run/night shelter/charity & volunteers/containment' approach evolved into a more professional and effective service, with an emphasis on enablement across the range of an individual's needs. Short-life housing was replaced by fully refurbished properties; dormitories gave way to single rooms; canteens made way for self-catering. *Differentiated provision was created for differentiated needs.* Staff were no longer 'de facto' ex-service users, but people with no lived experience of homelessness who were recruited from outside and were paid (low) pensionable salaries.

But in important ways St Mungo's did not change: *we were unique in running hostels which were open 24 hours a day* (avoiding the humiliating queuing to get in at 6pm – and, more importantly, avoiding throwing people out at 9am regardless of their state of health), *and which had no security screen at the reception desk.* Those hostels run by central and local government (e.g. the DHSS Reception Centres) and some local authorities (e.g. Bruce House in Westminster), as well as by some large charities, had security glass whose cracks testified to the residents' frustration; because we had none, and the residents could therefore punch the staff if they wanted to, they never did. And this was not just because of the absence of strengthened glass: it was also because we knew that *our work was primarily about relationships* – and our emphasis on inter-personal interactions was absolutely fundamental to our credibility with our clients. They trusted us. And we in turn were straightforward with them.

The 1990s

The 1990s was a decade of initiatives. Roger Freeman, a health minister, was sympathetic to the idea that mental illness among homeless people should be tackled. A surprisingly ambitious initiative (perhaps too ambitious for some tastes: Freeman was quickly re-shuffled to Transport by Mrs Thatcher) was launched in four areas of London, in three of which the initiative consisted of small, specialist hostels as access points into the service, linked to permanent flats as move-on. This was re-christened the HMII. Social services received funding to become involved (but unfortunately this local involvement meant that the opportunity to set a national standard was lost in the quagmire of local priorities and accountabilities). St Mungo's ran the housing in two of these three areas: we did not control the referrals in, and the social services teams tended to prioritise admissions from hospital rather than from the streets. This was doubly regrettable, since the Department of the Environment had simultaneously launched the Rough Sleepers' Initiative (RSI). These two initiatives ran in parallel, i.e. they did not intersect and connect with each other.

RSI ran from 1990 to 1999, in three-yearly segments (the first two phases were confined to London, and the initial ministerial boast that RSI would end rough-sleeping in London was watered down by the civil service to just 'central London'). In brief, the first phase focused on shelters, the second on independent housing, much of it shared, and only in the third phase did we see more appreciation of both ends of the spectrum, so to speak. Alongside this, the RSI funded street outreach work, resettlement and also enhancements to hostel staffing levels.

Cold weather

In the late 1980s, St Mungo's had managed to acquire leases to buildings over the winter (and charitable money with which to make them safe and habitable) to run as winter shelters. These were accepted by government as an important component of tackling street homelessness, and became incorporated within RSI as 'cold weather shelters'. For the first couple of years we were in the curious situation of having someone within the DoH monitoring the weather forecasts, so that as soon as the temperature fell below freezing, winter shelters should open, but close again once the temperature rose above freezing: clearly nobody had anticipated that during the winter, the temperature fluctuates, and so we saw shelters opening and closing like jack-in-the-boxes. They had equally obviously given no thought as to how these should be set up and staffed at the drop of a hat). Eventually they were re-imagined as winter shelters, open from December to March.

There was a recognition that temporary shelters could be more dynamic than permanent ones – and of course that it would be easier to get planning consent for short-term use. Accordingly, the concept of 'rolling shelters' was elaborated by the RSU: not only could they bring empty buildings into temporary use, but they could also be located close to 'hot spots' of entrenched rough sleeping. One would additionally ensure move-through by closing the shelter and re-opening it somewhere else. This was also intended to ensure that the staff team was constantly refreshed.

St Mungo's was eventually contracted to manage the whole winter shelter programme on the DoE's behalf: this included selecting organisations to run them. It was quite salutary to discover just how bad at it some well-known voluntary organisations were.

The 1990s also saw the final transfer of the DHSS Reception Centres to the voluntary sector. This process had been going on for some time outside London, on the promised basis of 'transfer and replace', i.e. there was funding for new buildings. This only happened in Camberwell, which was closed and replaced with virtually no direct access element, and a range of other projects based on a rather basic support needs taxonomy of 'low', 'medium' and 'high': otherwise, the buildings were transferred as they were, with a modest refurbishment budget. After a somewhat dubious tendering exercise, most went to Novas-Ouvertures. St Mungo's nevertheless acquired two of the buildings.

In the 1990s there was significant investment from government in both improving the physical environment and amenities of hostels and move-on housing for single homeless people, and in increasing the staffing-levels in those housing projects. Simultaneously, some money was invested in ancillary services (such as specialist workers in drugs/alcohol/mental health) so as to maximise the benefits of utilising core homelessness services. The closure or upgrading of outdated and poor-quality buildings spread beyond these programmes, and covered some local authority-run hostels (Bruce House in Westminster, Carrington House in Lewisham and Tooley Street in Southwark, for example), as well as the Rowton Houses in Camden (Arlington House), Vauxhall and Whitechapel (Tower House).

The DfEE launched an initiative in the late 1990s to tackle long-term unemployment among single homeless people, their most notable contribution being the re-christening of 'pathways' as 'crazy paving'. The initiative only lasted a year (hardly long enough to try anything out, never mind draw any valid conclusions), which was characteristic of a general approach by government: we welcomed initiatives, but would much rather have seen the commitment which a proper policy would have represented.

The 1990s also saw a steep rise in drug use amongst St Mungo's clients. This led to much more volatile behaviours, less interest in resettlement and moving out of homelessness, and ultimately more existential despair.

Drugs and alcohol

In some of our hostels, up to 75% of the residents were drug users – spiking at 95% in one particular example. The nature of drug use changed more than 20 years ago, with users experimenting with combinations of 'Class A' drugs as well as prescription drugs. Most of St Mungo's drug users would take whatever was available, and would have been considered 'problematic' due to poly-substance misuse.

We employed drugs specialists and ran a range of services based on the principles of Harm Minimisation. These included in-hostel substitute prescribing services, needle exchanges, and specialisms, such as a culturally specific service for Portuguese drug users. Some detox and rehab was available, but the big gap was in post-rehab support – Tier 4[6] – but adapted, so that access to treatment was not dependent on motivation and stability (the requirement for which effectively excluded long-term rough sleepers).

---

6   Residential drug misuse treatment

With alcohol, St Mungo's focused on harmful drinking[7]. In the early years, our concerns were twofold – to encourage street drinkers to come off substances such as meths, boot polish etc, and move on to safer, commercially produced alcohol, and to only drink during pub opening hours. From the 1990s onwards, our clients were generally consuming commercial alcohol, such as the strong lagers, but were still binge drinking, and many were dependent. This was illustrated by their reason for going to detox: not to become abstinent, but because they were too ill to continue drinking they needed to dry out so that they could resume drinking.

Alcohol was the most commonly used drug among St Mungo's residents, and the drink of choice was determined by price. This was the reason for the popularity of the white ciders. These are very cheap but potent alcohols: the names of some of the brands ('Polaris'; 'Blackout'; 'Three Hammers') gave a clue; small wonder that, by some, white cider was referred to as 'murder in a can'. Half of white cider drinkers interviewed in a study[8] claimed to drink more than three litres a day, equivalent to more than 10 times the recommended maximum number of units for a male.

Residential treatment options prioritised a fast-track to abstinence. As in other areas, our clients needed a service that would take account of the pace at which they could manage change, including allowing for false starts and relapses; and, as in other areas, they had few options.

The 1990s cemented St Mungo's position as the leading homelessness agency in London (and therefore the country). We were the only organisation to be involved in all four government initiatives to tackle single homelessness (HMII/RSI/DHSS Reception Centres transfer programme/DfEE); and the only one to have run hostels under each phase of RSI[9]. Our central purpose of helping those right at the bottom of the pile was clear and unambiguous. Critically, *we stuck to what we did best – our diversification was into wider services for our core client group, not widening our core client group.*

The 2000s

In the first decade of the 2000s, St Mungo's continued to acquire hostels – a small hostel for drug users in Earl's Court; the YWCA in Euston; and the Girls' Friendly Society hostel in Victoria. In each case the owners lacked either the revenue funding to keep going, or the capital to carry out the much-needed refurbishments. We benefited greatly from their strategy of off-loading valuable sites.

---

7   Defined by NICE (National Institute for Health & Care Excellence) as drinking which *'leads to physical or mental health problems such as alcohol-related injury, inflammation of the liver or pancreas, or depression'*

8   White Cider and Street Drinkers, Alcohol Concern, 2011

9   We continued this area of expertise into the future, where we were the only agency to have run the government's Cold Weather shelter programme, its Rolling Shelter programme, and the Mayor's SWEP (*Severe Weather Emergency Programme*). We were also the only agency to have been involved in two other mayoral programmes – NSNO (*No Second Night Out*) and NLOS (*Nobody Living on the Streets*).

The largest acquisition we made was a bundle of hostels and houses from Novas. This meant that all (bar one) of the DHSS Reception Centres (later rebranded as Resettlement Units) were now run by St Mungo's. We believed strongly that there would always be a need for hostels, because there would always be people facing personal crises and emergencies in their lives; and funders have always preferred generalist to specialist provision (a former CEO of Crisis criticised hostels as being places which created problems for people rather than helping them to overcome them, which is a bit like blaming hospitals for people being ill).

The most valuable aspect of a hostel was usually its planning consent – it was quite clear that if one sold up, then that class of planning consent would be lost for ever. Localism meant it was not transferable, whereas a properly strategic approach to provision in London would have allowed for the portability of planning consent and revenue funding. Of course the profile of homelessness does change over time, and the location of provision must be periodically reviewed – but the hostel estate, which has shrunk by two-thirds[10] since the days when SHiL (*Single Homelessness in London*) monitored it for the LBGU, is a vital resource: only the voluntary sector has the will to maintain the stewardship of such a heritage.

Politically, the decade brought about a significant loss of influence for homelessness agencies. St Mungo's had previously secured revenue funding of more than £1m from four different government departments, at a time when that represented a considerable slice of their expenditure on the voluntary sector. It was therefore possible (at a pinch) to persuade secretaries of state to visit and see at first-hand what else needed to be done. This began to unravel with the bringing together of different funding streams under the Rough Sleepers' Unit (RSU), but at least it had – theoretically – a direct reporting line to the Prime Minister, as well as a committed Housing Minister (Hilary Armstrong). With the demise of the RSU in 2002, the political ring was held by a junior Housing Minister (Barbara Roche), and so the issue lost political visibility.

This was exacerbated by the advent of 'Supporting People' in 2003, which amalgamated disparate funding streams and handed the commissioning of services to local authorities. There is no doubt that this was a very retrograde step. The claim that councils are best placed to commission because they understand the strategic needs of their 'patch' thanks to their close connections with the local population is highly questionable. At best they might have that understanding in relation to the settled population (although the disaster at Grenfell places even that under question), but when it comes to mobile populations or (to use a horrible term) 'unpopular groups', most of

10　In 1985 London's direct-access hostels had a capacity of 4,943. By 2013 the equivalent figure was 1,771, a decline of 64%.

them have little understanding and even less commitment. Those that had actually directly run hostels had a very poor track record. While it is only fair to acknowledge that there were some fine exceptions to this dismal rule, they were in a small minority and the overall standard was very poor.

Initially the funding was ring-fenced, which lasted until 2009[11]. Central government started cutting it back from 2010, even though a report from Cap Gemini found that this investment delivered returns greater than expenditure[12]. We then witnessed a multi-pronged assault on single homelessness/rough sleeper agencies. Funding was cut, sometimes brutally, and in the process years of irreplaceable knowledge about disadvantaged individuals was simply junked; services were dismantled with no regard for the knock-on effects for those which remained; benefits were cut, with no help given to the long-term unemployed to actually find work, despite the honeyed promises of government strategies; and single people were steered away from social housing and into the private sector, where rents were very much higher – and rising.

The homelessness sector's ability to campaign effectively against harmful change was consistently undermined by the inability of most agencies to co-operate and find a collective voice, due partly to ideological differences but mainly by now to the competitive pressures which had been introduced by 'dive-to-the-bottom' competitive tendering.

The RSU had by this time morphed into the Homelessness Directorate, whose stellar achievement was to manage to persuade the Treasury to provide extra capital money to upgrade standards and facilities in hostels in a 2005 programme (called, unimaginatively, the 'Hostels Capital Improvement' programme). This was undoubtedly the most ambitious investment ever undertaken by government, and led to some hostels having, for example, en suite single rooms and facilities to help people find work and tackle their health problems. As with services relying on revenue funding, advances in environment and facilities had to rely on one-off capital initiatives, as opposed to considered policy and strategy.

St Mungo's was the first agency systematically to recognise the importance of health in tackling homelessness: half of our clients had a chronic health condition. Rough sleepers had an exceptionally wide range of illnesses, whose condition was exacerbated by neglect. It is commonplace to focus on their neglect of their own health, but the real issue was the systematic neglect of this population by the NHS, giving the lie to the claim that it is a

---

11 Parliament https://publications.parliament.uk/pa/cm200809/cmselect/cmcomloc/649/64904.htm

12 *Research into the benefits of the Supporting People programme* DCLG, 2009

universal service[13]. We started to use in our public materials the assertion that 'homelessness is a health problem', and launched services such as Palliative Care. We saw homelessness services as needing to address housing, health and work. *In other words, the necessity of a holistic approach in order to effectively support clients with complex, long-standing and inter-connected problems.*

The 2010s

We had toyed for many years with the idea of expanding outside London, an early foray into Basildon having proved unsuccessful when the promised projects never materialised. Eventually, however, we did take the plunge, focusing initially on Bristol and the south west.

This was always going to be a challenge. We were well aware of local sensitivities and wariness of London agencies. We also knew that many of our support systems – IT, HR and finance – would be placed under heavy pressure, especially since we only wanted to expand into areas where there was a real prospect of scale – we did not want 'pepper-pot' expansion i.e. a little here, a little there. We were persuaded, though, by the evident need outside London and the belief, in all humility, that we could offer a very good service, particularly at the 'sharp end' of entrenched rough sleeping.

In this period we also embarked upon two fundamental changes of gear – recovery and client involvement.

The recovery model originated in the mental health field, but St Mungo's adopted the social justice model. (Without being too technical, this meant for example that people did not have to be symptom-free.) The crucial point, though, was that we recognised the personal assets which our clients possessed, and which they brought to their own recovery.

Client involvement turned out to be more radical than we had first anticipated. Terminology had changed – we were being encouraged to see clients as 'customers' (although nobody could explain what difference that made) – and accountabilities had, too. For us to be actually accountable to our clients was a big psychological step-change, but one that made perfect sense. Initially, some of our front-line staff experienced a contradiction between their accountability to people over whom they had some authority. As our approach evolved, we were able to benefit from the

---

13 A GP surgery in Lambeth wanted to de-register the residents of a project we ran for crack-using sex-workers because they were 'too difficult'. We did not think that the NHS was set up just for people who were well; but it was only because we had contacts locally, regionally and nationally that this disgraceful decision was swiftly over-turned.

energy and insights of our clients, which in turn ensured the relevance of our services. We were on the same side, which has actually been a hallmark of St Mungo's since its beginnings.

A summary

My association with St Mungo's ended when I retired in 2014. It was personally a great privilege to have lived through the greatest transformation in services for single homeless people the UK has ever seen. When I started in 1980 we housed around 650 people in a range of projects, all 'short-life', and had a total staffing complement of about 25. When I left we housed around 2,500 people in buildings, which had almost all been refurbished to '30-year life' standards, and employed about 1,100 professional staff, indicating a highly staff-intensive operation[14]. Our turnover has grown from £250k to £55m. We have moved on from warehousing people in dormitories to running differentiated provision focusing on a wide range of needs, from support and resettlement to long-term care in personalised settings. We had basic shelters and well-resourced hostels, including specialist ones (e.g. for street-drinkers), but also intermediate move-on housing – shared housing, group homes and cluster flats – and permanent, independent housing. We had specialist projects for long-term rough sleepers, for arsonists, for Muslim women fleeing domestic violence, and for different age-groups. Our support services spanned the spectrum from street outreach to resettlement follow-up support and we employed specialists in drugs, alcohol and mental health. We had an employment and training service, and ran a Recovery College. Some of our hostels contained recording studios, with professional standard mixing decks. Back in 1980, all of this was simply unimaginable.

Lessons

I am offering only a personal perspective. We were an exceptionally successful organisation, especially given the history of our founder having appeared at the Old Bailey. Our success was not a matter of size (we could have been at least twice as big if we had wanted to be – but that would have taken us away from our core client group, single homeless people/rough sleepers), but of course scale did help us to navigate some difficult times.

I would, though, like to return to the two questions I set out at the beginning of this chapter. First, to what was our success attributable?

---

14 About 65% of our costs were staff salaries. In common with many other agencies, our costs increased by price inflation, whereas our income increased by (at best) wage inflation. This is an idiotic funding model, whose gap can only be – temporarily – plugged by growth.

- **We understood that homelessness is not just about a lack of housing.** The fact that, administratively and politically, it came under the aegis of the Housing Ministry was a limitation that enabled other parts of the state to escape their proper responsibilities – for example the NHS saw homelessness as a diagnosis for which the proper prescription was housing.

- **We were consistently innovative.** From running the first bail hostel in the 1970s to the first asylum seekers project in the 1990s, or launching the first employment service for homeless people, to helping them to obtain bank accounts, St Mungo's has consistently identified gaps and then found ways of filling them. We devised the Outcomes Star (in conjunction with a consultancy) to measure 'soft' outcomes alongside 'hard' ones; we pioneered a 'good neighbours approach'[15], which involved our staff conducting local patrols, our managers being contactable, and our clients helping to improve local amenities, such as clearing up and maintaining local green spaces. But of course the only people with authority to tackle anti-social behaviour were the police. We were the first agency to accept dogs with their owners, and to admit couples into our street-level projects.

- **We had a culture of credibility with our clients.** This was reinforced by usually filling that most difficult of jobs – a hostel manager – from our own front-line staff, and growing our own senior managers. This helped us to retain highly-motivated staff.

- **Our work was always about relationships.** We did not forget that.

- **We tried to be an operations-led organisation.** It is very easy in cash-strapped charities (as most charities are, because of operating in a funding system which is 'unfit for purpose'), for, say, the finance tail to wag the service dog. We made sure that did not happen.

- **We stuck to what we did best** and resisted the lure of branching away from our core client group. Diversification rarely works to their benefit.

- **We had a strong team spirit throughout the organisation.** Our managers' meetings were an example of inclusive leadership from the top, because they were not just top-down briefings but involved collaborative planning. *Where possible, we would follow up on ideas from local managers and staff for improving or introducing new services*, since they were the people best-placed to identify gaps in provision.

- **Thanks to our designation as a housing association, we owned buildings.** This gave us influence (though not decisive) in how they were used. It also made it easier for us to accept the management transfer of services: there was a serendipitous link between our ability to run

---

15 We were conscious of the poor image of homeless people – some will say that our presence caused neighbourhood problems, but we experienced being blamed for every social problem in an area.

services because we owned the buildings, and our ability to acquire buildings because we knew how to run the necessary services. We had specialist development expertise because we knew how to design a hostel or other form of supported housing, something which mainstream housing associations did not properly understand. We also managed the capital finances prudently, including by building up sinking funds.

- **We were successful at raising funds from charitable Trusts and members of the public.** This gave us an important base of ordinary and (sometimes) influential supporters who shared our values, as well as enabling us to launch projects which local or central government would not facilitate.

And what lessons, if any, might that have for the voluntary sector more broadly?

- **The voluntary sector guarded its independence jealously.** At St Mungo's we quite consciously sacrificed slivers of independence in order to be able to run services – we were, after all, set up to provide services, not to be pure and ineffectual (which is the fate of voluntary agencies which made the opposite calculation).

- **We were lucky – and most of that luck we created ourselves,** by constantly reinforcing our reputation for (a) taking on the difficult work, and (b) being able to deliver. We did what we said on the tin, to borrow a phrase.

- **Our governance was very good.** We had a knowledgeable and capable Board, which never interfered in day-to-day decisions or the running of the organisation, and which ensured stability and confidence.

Future challenges

As the number of rough sleepers rises inexorably, and their needs continue to intensify, it may be worth drawing on St Mungo's background to highlight some of the enduring challenges that need to be addressed head-on if the scourge of homelessness is to be arrested and reversed.

- Short-termism is a plague on forward planning, and the parliamentary cycle can put a straitjacket on strategies.

- It was easier to be effective when the funding relationship ran directly from central government to the voluntary sector, without expensive intermediaries. Routing resources via local government, and then removing the ring-fence, has proved an expensive mistake. The risk for an organisation working with people who fall through the gaps between services is that it will itself fall through the gaps in funding

■ We tried – unsuccessfully – to get homelessness considered as a needs category, rather than simply a circumstantial condition. There are many arguments for supporting this: one of the clearest is the example of homeless people who were admitted to hospital in Glasgow with drug problems being seven times more likely to die within five years compared to housed people admitted with the same drug problems. Unfortunately we were subordinate to a regime of Joint Strategic Needs Assessments that was neither 'joint', nor 'strategic', nor 'needs assessments'.

■ There is a sense in which services chuck everybody they find too difficult to work with in a box and label it 'homelessness'. Mainstream public services need to be re-engineered so that they do not just apply 'one-size-fits-all' solutions to problems, but develop bespoke approaches for minority populations. We need segmentation of provision, reflected in funding differentiation.

■ The justification for a determination to end homelessness is not just moral: *it is very expensive to keep people ill, unemployed and homeless.*

■ The All Party Parliamentary Group on Social Mobility found (in 2014) that Britain had almost the worst social mobility in the OECD, with more than 50% of children having their life paths effectively determined by the age of three: 'soul-sapping immobility' they called it. This is relevant to the destiny of homeless people. Once we started to examine the incidence of childhood trauma among our clients, we detected a common trajectory: as children, many had spent their early years in family circles characterised by neglect and sometimes abuse, they had failed to strike up friendships at school and had early exposure to drugs, they had played truant (or been excluded), had left school without qualifications and begun to claim benefits. By the time they turned 18 it was portrayed as their fault that they were homeless, whereas in fact they were unquestionably failed by public services, frequently were failed by their families, and were ignored by the market. It is long overdue that that tape be rewound.

■ Progress will be limited until the inverse care law[16] is overturned.

---

16 This states in effect that those most in need of medical or social care are the least likely to receive it.

Chapter Seven:
Mental health for young people – making an impact with scarce resources

By Sarah Brennan, OBE

Introduction

Mental health is a continuum, not a fixed state. We move up and down this continuum throughout our lives and need others to help us through difficult times. Childhood and adolescence are times when the foundations for our future mental health are laid down. Evidence shows that 75% of long term adult mental illness begins before we are 25 years of age, and half of all mental health problems by the age of 14, yet less than half receive any care[1]. Some children face greater risks to their mental health than others – research has found that adverse childhood experiences can have a lasting negative impact on the life course of our mental health. The severity and quantity of these experiences and how a child is supported through them is critical.

Thus, to effect change among the population's children and young people's mental health, we must understand the risks they face and help prevent them increasing, and address or mitigate them when they exist, while at the same time supporting the development of protective factors.

Services should focus on:

1. Prevention – stop risks to healthy psychological development, and build resilience to cope when they arise.
2. Early intervention – help as soon as problems start to develop, and apply trauma informed services.
3. Giving effective, timely treatment.
4. Offering crisis support.

---

1   Kessler RC et al. (2005) Kessler, R.C., et al. (2005) Lifetime Prevalence and Age-of-Onset Distributions of DSM-IV Disorders in the National Comorbidity Survey Replication. Archives of General Psychiatry, 62, 593-602.

Mental health affects all aspects of life – relationships, academic achievement, employment, physical health. Childhood and youth mental health is particularly important as the only way we will improve the life outcomes and mental health of the population. To do this we need a shared approach that is relevant and appropriate to all disciplines – education, social care, health, justice and mental health. Otherwise we have the fragmented, piecemeal approach we experience today, which too often leaves children and young people with nothing, or even worse, which re-traumatises an already traumatised child or young person.

We talk about building resilience, well-being and psychological health among children and young people. Essentially this is the process of healthy child and youth development. Asking the questions 'What does a child need to develop well?' and 'What disrupts that process?' will help create a basis upon which to respond. Adopting a theory of change, logic model or theoretical framework will explain why the service exists and how it will contribute to healthy child development or the foci above, as well as provide a structure for measuring success or impact. Identifying how the service(s) fits into local or national provision and supports others will also encourage a system-wide approach so that local strategies become strategic and effective.

Some of the main barriers to the increased delivery targets set by government is the challenge of workforce, and how to reach young people who need help (which is why schools have become such a focus).

There is an opportunity for charities to lead nationally:

- We have a trained, committed workforce (837,000 employees in the voluntary sector in 2016 and 40% in social work of some kind).

- Even large charities do not face the long and tortuous path that government and statutory services experience in trying to get things done. Consequently charities move much faster, and can deliver at scale and speed.

- Given the coverage that the large national charities have, and add to that the more niche local or expert organisations and there is astonishing capacity and expertise to be harnessed if the will is there.

- If we are to change the outcomes of the most vulnerable children and young people in our society, and if we are to realise the potential of all children and young people, we need to operate at scale to have an impact. No one charity, and not any single statutory service, can do this alone.

■ Charitable organisations are often the 'agency of choice' for children and young people, because of their values and style of working.

A number of models can be adopted. Many social care charities are delivering some kind of mental health support and have recently been more explicit about that. If we can harness the support that is being delivered using a range of models or methods to ensure common practices which support the same work wherever a child lives or whatever service they receive, it may be possible to significantly increase the positive impact on their lives.

Mental health is an incredible 'turn-around' story regarding stigma, awareness and public interest. In 2008, when I first started work at Young Minds, mental health – and especially children's or young people's mental health – was a taboo subject. Mention what you did at social gatherings and people would politely turn away and speak to someone else; try to get media interest in one of the shocking stories that we heard every day and you'd be turned down repeatedly. Fast forward to today and you can't escape campaigns, new initiatives, discussion and new research being announced every day on all media platforms. Frequently we hear about the 'mental health crisis' among children and young people.

As almost the only area to receive new funding since the government's policy of 'austerity' (£1.4b new government funds agreed from 2015-20, and recent fresh funds promised in the NHS £20b 10-year future plans), the attention given to the mental health of children and young people has escalated particularly. Add to this the Health Minister's and the Prime Minister's declared commitment and the impact of the young royals 'Heads Together' campaign has boosted awareness alongside Young Minds' own tireless campaigning and awareness raising, and suddenly all organisations seem to be redefining their work as 'mental health'. This was a coup in many ways, but how does this help the day-to-day lives of children and young people experiencing distress?

Moreover, for all the attention and new funding, children, young people and their families still face a daily battle to find the right help when a child is in distress. Child and adolescent mental health services are overwhelmed, and parents – the people most often trying to navigate the system on behalf of their child – are at their wits' end trying to find their way through a confusing maze. At the same time, the mental health problems among our youth are increasing. The latest research shows that in 2017 one in eight children and young people aged between five and 19 had a mental disorder. This has increased from one in ten in 2004.

Background and context

In 2014, children and young people's mental health received 0.6% of the NHS total budget. Total mental health NHS expenditure was 11% – so it was almost entirely spent on adult care, of which inpatient and long-term care is the most costly. Today 0.7% of the total NHS budget is spent on children and young people's mental health. In the main this is for treatment delivered through clinical teams called CAMHS (Children and Young People's Mental Health Services)[2]. But there has always been an awareness in CAMHS of the importance of the environment in which the child is living and the need to promote healthy child development and support family interactions.

CAMHS was, and often still is, arranged in a 'tiered' system in an effort to identify and match a person's needs with an appropriate service. It was/is a simple model, which of course never quite reflected reality:

- Tier 1: Universal services (community services available to everyone) (not NHS funded).
- Tier 2: Targeted provision (identified children and young people needing mental health support).
- Tier 3: Specialist provision (clinical services for serious and complex disorders).
- Tier 4: Inpatient care (hospital or crisis care).

So, funding for children and young people's mental health was directed mainly and increasingly at treatment via the NHS, and was restricted through lack of funds. Since 2010, with austerity and local authority cuts, local community services have been reduced, cut, or are struggling. Schools under financial pressure, and teachers under work pressure, reduced after-school activities and clubs and other supports such as breakfast. Youth services and juvenile justice provision in the community were severely cut back.

Add to this the little-understood social changes stimulated by the internet and social media, along with the increased pressure on schools and therefore pupils to 'succeed' with good exam results, and you have the perfect storm for children and young people's mental well-being.

To reflect the growing complexity of children and young people's needs and the interconnectedness between local communities, education and social care services and NHS mental health services, the 'Thrive' conceptual framework for CAMHS was developed in 2014 by a collaboration of authors

---

2   NHS accessed 22.1 19 https://www.nhs.uk/using-the-nhs/nhs-services/mental-health-services/child-and-adolescent-mental-health-services-camhs/

from the Anna Freud National Centre for Children and Families and the Tavistock and Portman NHS Foundation Trust[3]. The Thrive framework aims to be an integrated, person-centred and needs-led approach to delivering mental health services for children, young people and their families. It splits need into five categories, and emphasises prevention and the promotion of mental health and well-being:

1. Thriving.
2. Getting advice: signposting, self-management, one-off contact.
3. Getting help: goals focused, evidence informed and outcomes based intervention.
4. Getting more help: extensive treatment.
5. Getting risk support: risk management and crisis response.

Central to this approach is shared decision making regarding treatment and care, which reflects the growing understanding and recognition of the importance of empowering children, young people and their families by getting them actively involved in decisions about their own care, led by the young people's participation work carried out by Young Minds.

The Thrive framework moves mental health services forward, and recognises the breadth of mental health and well-being needs and provision. It provides a structure within which social care and other children and youth services have a place and are recognised. The approach described by this framework is more familiar for local authorities and social care services who often struggle to provide co-ordinated provision. Thrive provides a framework that services can sit within.

What would further strengthen the psychological well-being of our children and young people would be a shared approach to how we support the development of their emotional well-being and resilience. This needs to be a framework, or theory of development, which social care, education, justice, physical health *and* mental health services can all work to. It may be a high standard framework, but it would enable everyone working with children and young people to have a shared approach and goals in their work.

Why is child development so important?

The changing nature of childhood, alongside wider social changes caused by the advent of the internet, social media, educational pressures and risk-averse parenting, have had an enormous impact on children and

---

3   Thrive accessed 22.1 19 http://www.implementingthrive.org

young people. Because their developing mental health was, historically, not widely understood and largely ignored, the impact of radically reducing local community and school supports and the impact of social change was not foreseen.

Good mental health is defined by the World Health Organisation as:

> '...a state of well-being in which every individual realizes his or her own potential, can cope with the normal stresses of life, can work productively and fruitfully, and is able to make a contribution to her or his community.'[4]

To achieve this, we need to build young people's emotional resilience so they can withstand the knocks that life gives them, provide easily accessible help when it's needed, and specialist or intensive help when treatment is necessary. It takes many different types of service to create a mentally healthy community.

Unfortunately, when the term 'mental health' is used, we most often mean the opposite – mental illness. This has reinforced a negative impression about mental health, directing attention towards medical responses, and slowing any public health approach to supporting genuine mental health – its development and protection, education about it, and the provision of appropriate early help when it is threatened or vulnerable.

Terms are used differently depending on who is using them and what discipline they are trained in. If you are delivering mental health support to children or young people, it is helpful to understand where any intervention 'fits' in the spectrum of provision both locally and nationally, but also, importantly, where it 'fits' with regards to child psychological well-being. In this way interventions can relate to other services and can cross professional boundaries, which is necessary if we are to provide effective, holistic care.

Now that the significance of mental health and mental illness has become more accepted, descriptions of mental health problems can be used too easily and flippantly and can create more problems than solutions by creating unhelpful labels.

The different government departments reflect different cultures in their working and funding practices. The respective lexicons used by each express this most clearly. The same children, demonstrating the same behaviours, will be given different labels.

---

4   WHO accessed 22.1.19; https://www.who.int/features/factfiles/mental_health/en

Table 7.1: Same child, different label

Social services ■ Vulnerable child ■ Child at risk ■ Child in need
Education ■ Child with social, emotional or behavioural difficulties (EBD) ■ Child with special educational needs (SEN)
Health ■ Child with mental illness ■ Child with psychiatric disorders

The language used by different professions demonstrates how they have been taught to think and work, and so has a direct effect on their work. It derives from the theoretical framework and consequently the training those professionals receive, but simultaneously it creates very effective barriers to working together.

The diagnosis of a mental illness is made by identifying defined sets of behaviours which have been codified to indicate types of illness e.g. the WHO International Classification of Diseases[5] and APA Diagnostic and Statistical Manual of Mental Disorders[6]. Diagnosis by a clinician depends on identifying the severity and range of characteristics, but can be problematic for children because it may be affected by their developmental stage and they may not easily fit the diagnostic 'boxes'. Clinicians can be reluctant to diagnose a mental illness or disorder in a child as this can cause them additional problems, for example the child is labelled from then on or unnecessary medication may be prescribed.

Formulation is another way mental health problems can be understood. This involves looking at the child in the context of their life – what has happened to them and their current circumstances – to help understand how problems have arisen and to inform future strategies. Our mental health does not develop in isolation. The accepted biopsychosocial model of mental health (above) helps locate the complex and interrelated nature of mental health. This means our mental health is affected by biology – our genetic predisposition – the nurture we receive, and the impact of life events that are beyond our control, for example the death of a key attachment figure, physical illness, accidents or neglect or abuse etc.

---

5   WHO accessed 24.1.19 https://www.who.int/health-topics/international-classification-of-diseases

6   American Psychiatric Association accessed 24.1.19 https://www.psychiatry.org/psychiatrists/practice/dsm

Historically, research into child and youth mental health has been poorly funded. However, one theory from the 1960s that has informed clinical understanding of child development is Bowlby's theory of attachment. Children who have a secure attachment to their primary caregiver will grow to have higher self-esteem as well as better self-reliance. Additionally, these children tend to be more independent and have lower reported instances of anxiety and depression. These children are also able to form better social relationships.

The development of neuro-science has further increased interest in child psychological development and greatly enhanced our understanding of the interconnectedness of physical and emotional development. It has shown us how the kind of nurture we receive from our first breath affects neural pathway development and therefore emotional and psychological health development, and it has shown how a mother's mental health can also affect their baby's.

Thus, children and young people's mental health is entirely related to healthy child development overall – and therefore their familial, social and educational environment and their physical health development. Services and organisations that support the healthy emotional and psychological development of children and young people are also obviously contributing to their good mental health.

Vulnerabilities and the impact of trauma

Experiencing emotionally challenging situations during childhood is a normal part of growing up. How we are able to manage these and cope is key to our developing mental well-being and later mental health. When these experiences are more extreme, they have a potentially traumatic and long-lasting impact on our development and health.

Children are resilient, but when they do experience ruptures in their care or negative life events, they will have a negative impact on their psychological well-being. Research has found that the greater the number and severity of adverse childhood experiences (ACEs), the more likely it is that there will be a negative impact on a child's developing mental health, and this directly influences mental health outcomes in adulthood. ACEs can include anything from physical or sexual abuse, neglect, bereavement, the effects of racism or disability and many others. Effective and timely care can mitigate against the traumatic impact of these experiences, but the dynamics of how trauma affects children and young people's behaviour and development has to be understood in order to provide effective care.

Certainly, we know that almost half of looked after children have a diagnosable long-term mental health disorder and they are four times more likely to have a mental health condition than those not in care. These are children who have often experienced significant trauma in childhood, and being removed from their family, while safer, is nevertheless traumatic for a child.

However, it can be very dehumanising if children or young people become reduced to a list of disadvantages or traumatic experiences, and are not seen holistically as a young person dealing as best as they can with a complex and challenging life. Each child and young person experiences a unique set of circumstances affecting their well-being – it is by seeing the whole person that we can be the most help to them.

Several years ago, as the co-chair of the Vulnerable Young People's Task Group, as part of the Future in Mind strategy, we were quickly overwhelmed by charities, services and interest groups demanding special attention and funds to address the mental health needs of their specific clients. This might have resulted in dividing children and young people up into 'different vulnerabilities', each competing with the other for resources, and encouraged the already pernicious competition between organisations for a slice of scarce resources.

Even worse, for many young people, vulnerabilities overlap. For instance, being physically disabled plus facing poverty and being unemployed all directly affect a person's mental health. But by looking at each vulnerability separately and not seeing the young person as a whole, we are unlikely to meet their needs effectively. Too often this situation can result in a range of different and uncoordinated services being offered, none of which properly meet the issues the young person is dealing with.

Now, the concept of ACEs and research into the relationship between ACEs and challenging and risky behaviours, and the risk of mental health problems, has helped identify risks and protective factors and can help guide interventions that will mitigate the effects of ACEs the most. Recent research into the impact of ACEs has provided helpful insights into understanding a child or young person's behaviour. Thus, it is understood that challenging or risky behaviours may be a rational response to earlier traumatic experiences; we just need to understand the signs and be able to ask the right questions.

Understanding the impact that life events can have on a child or young person's development, and therefore on their mental health, enables organisations and support staff to consider their behaviour in a new light, and can contribute to understanding them holistically, and thereby make connections between vulnerabilities or disadvantages and mental health issues. ACEs help provide a framework for both theory and practice applying the evidence. As a nationally accepted approach, this is still in its infancy, with considerable debate and discussion about how to uncover previous trauma, precisely what the impact of trauma is on emotional and brain development, and what the most effective responses from both care and clinical services are.

Many organisations, in particular children's charities, are championing a cause to counter the effects of an adverse childhood (or youth) experience. If this work can be put into the context of adverse childhood experiences, and their interventions incorporate a nationally shared trauma-informed support approach, alongside child and youth development AND how we build resilience – THEN we begin to create a system of services that complement and support each other's work, rather than divide and confuse.

What does this mean for services?

Many charities work with specific groups and around particular causes or issues, and they need to start placing their work within a wider context, using a broad evidence framework about the impact of ACEs and how trauma affects childhood and youth development. This means they need to develop a shared understanding of the problems and solutions, better communication between organisations, and approaches that cross disciplines and departments.

A young person's mental health at any point in their development is a blend of risks and protective factors that affect their emotional resilience and ability to cope. It is a dynamic process influenced by their genetics and by their family, friends, and the wider community in which they live. Since the prevention of mental illness is directly linked to a person's ability to cope with adverse life events, there has been an increasing focus on resilience building and understanding a young person's risks and protective factors, so interventions or support can be provided to help them when problems occur. These interventions aim reduce or mitigate risks, and increase their assets and protective factors.

Resilience has been defined in many ways, but Fonagy captures its essence well: 'Normal development under difficult circumstances'[7]. Although many factors can be associated with resilience, there is consensus about the three fundamentals that underpin a resilient child:

---

7   Fonagy, P. et al 1994 The theory and practice of resilience. Journal of Child Psychology and Psychiatry.

1. A secure base and sound attachments with carers providing the child with a sense of belonging and of security.

2. Good self-esteem providing a sense of self-worth and of competence.

3. Self-efficacy or a sense of mastery and control, along with an understanding of personal strengths and limitations.

Daniel and Wassell have developed these three factors into a framework for assessment and planning consisting of the following six domains[8]:

1. Secure base.

2. Education.

3. Friendships.

4. Talents and interests.

5. Positive values.

6. Social competences.

If we are to improve children and young people's mental health outcomes in an environment of scarce resources, organisations should focus on how they support and enhance the assets or protective factors in their client groups and enable those children and young people to understand that they have those assets and how they can make best use of them.

Examples might include:

1. A school counselling service hears how a pupil is having trouble getting on with their parents, but on speaking with the pupil discovers they have very good, supportive relationship with their aunt. The counsellors' response is to help the pupil see and understand this as an asset and encourage them to explore ways of accessing this support more. (Developing their secure base.)

2. A young person is excluded from school because of anger issues affecting behaviour in the classroom. But the local outdoor centre provides rock climbing workshops working in teams and find he is able to succeed in this and his growing self-confidence and achievement reduces his frustration and anger, and builds his self-esteem and confidence. (Developing talents and interests.)

Research on resilience in children suggests three basic strategies for intervention: reduce or mitigate risk; boost assets or reduce barriers to promotive factors for child health and development; and nurture, mobilise or restore as needed the fundamental and powerful adaptive systems that generate capacity for resilience over a lifetime.

---

8   Daniel, Brigid & Wassell, Sally. (2002). Assessing and Promoting Resilience in Vulnerable Children; JKP

Systems thinking: the ecological approach

As much as every child and young person is a part of a complex structure of people and institutions, so too is every service or organisation part of a complex local and national network of organisations, services and people. A child, young person or family is not necessarily aware – nor do they necessarily care – what kind of organisation is helping them. What is of concern is what the help is, whether it is actually helpful, and whether the people helping are trustworthy – do they make the young person feel valued and understood?

Charities, no matter their size, are most effective when they understand their position in the continuum of local and national services (statutory and voluntary), and the needs of the local population. This requires a basic understanding of local demographics and easily available information about other organisations and statutory services operating locally. This will also help the charity determine the need for their services in an area, and they can relocate or change focus if the service they offer is already well taken care of.

Charities and the voluntary sector

Mental health provision in this country has been described as overwhelmed, fragmented and under-resourced given the needs that exist among children and young people. However, responsibility for addressing the mental health challenge to improve children and young people's psychological well-being really should fall on everyone. If all organisations, professions and charities pull in different directions, we will continue to have a piecemeal, short term impact with few long-term gains.

What is needed is a shared approach to underpin our endeavours and to reduce and/or mitigate the risks to a child's mental health, and enhance the protective factors to build their resilience and well-being. We call this the ecological approach.

Charities and voluntary sector organisations come in all shapes and sizes. And because they focus on meeting the needs of their particular client group, they can be extremely effective 'navigators' of the system on behalf of their client, seeing their needs 'in the round', as previously described, and delivering some services themselves. The flexibility afforded by a smaller size and reduced bureaucracy for voluntary sector organisations means that while concentrating on one type of provision, for example social care, they will (and often do) work across other sectors too, such as health, justice or education.

A shared approach can be developed if organisations answer these questions:

- What model of healthy child development have you adopted? What are a child's needs for healthy development and emotional resilience and where does your service/organisation fit in meeting those needs?

- In the local/regional/national system of mental health provision, what does your service/organisation contribute, and how does it complement others?

- Assuming your client group has experienced ACE's, what is your trauma-informed approach and how does your team learn and deliver it?

- How does this all fit together as a framework that complements others?

Providing a mental health care service for specific groups of children or young people by voluntary sector agencies will become compelling if they can demonstrate how their work has a clear place in the 'system' of care, what their contribution is to building healthy child/youth development and thus emotional resilience.

It will be essential to describe the different ways of working in their own language and for their different sectors e.g. how counselling in schools can lead to improved exam outcomes. The role of large national organisations should be one of leadership and joint working e.g. to develop together an appropriate trauma informed approach suitable for informal settings.

Shared approaches would enable scarce resources to have more impact and would mean the scale of the impact will increase significantly, which is what funders want. An example of the impact a shared approach with a strongly evidenced theory of change can have – and impact measurement metrics – is made clear in the anti-stigma campaign 'Time to Change[9] .

Case study

The Royal Foundation 'Heads Together' campaign brought eight mental health charities together to create a shared approach and a shift in the way we view mental health as a nation. The concept of 'starting the conversation' raised awareness of the importance of challenging the stigma around mental health, and while not a 'model' in the way described this chapter, it nevertheless provided a concept that all charities could get behind and work together in ways appropriate for their organisation, but which combined to achieve a national impact. Of course, all of this was helped in no small part by being led by the Duke and Duchess of Cambridge and the Duke and Duchess of Sussex.

https://www.headstogether.org.uk/

---

9   This campaign is a shared partnership between Mind and Rethink and has been credited with significantly shifting the national awareness and attitude to mental health.

Do services reflect the need for a multi-sector, multi-level approach?

There has been a welcome step change in the recognition of the importance of education and mental health services working more closely together. This reflects the recognition that it is often in school where behavioural changes first signal a child or young person's distress. It has been clearly evidenced how important it is to receive help early on when problems do occur. Moreover, there are countless reports of teachers feeling isolated and overwhelmed by the increase in mental health needs among their pupils. However, there is still a long way to go, in particular with welfare and mental health services becoming more 'joined up'. Due to the wide range of issues and vulnerabilities that social care is struggling to address, often the voluntary sector is depended upon to 'fill in' the ever widening gaps.

And there are frustrations on both sides, between CAMHS and local authority services, when children with obvious emotional needs are turned away from CAMHS with the explanation that their issues are social not psychological, or that their social issues need to be addressed if the psychological work is to be successful. As the ecological approach demonstrates, these excuses are both true and not true simultaneously, because all elements are connected into the system around the child. A shared approach to fulfilling the needs of the child or young person could create a more coherent plan of action. Voluntary sector organisations can often intervene successfully due to the fact they are less burdened by protocols and bureaucracy, while their values create an expectation that they will be clearly focused on the needs of their clients.

When areas do jointly plan strategies for local children and young people, often led by Directors of Children's Services, all the local voluntary sector agencies working with children can easily be forgotten or ignored. It is, undeniably, very hard to generate a system-wide approach to ecological resilience. However there have been some effective initiatives, like the Big Lottery funded 'Headstart', which actively promoted and funded joint local resilience building strategies with very encouraging results.

Our better understanding of the need for 'joined up' working provides more opportunities for organisations who give mental health support to schools. This will be the only way to make scarce resources effective. To have an ecological approach, there needs to be a shared, high-level theory of change[10] or logic model across disciplines to aid collaboration between social care, education, health and mental health services, and among the charities and community projects working with them. If a resilience framework, such as Maston's, with a clear approach to trauma-informed care services

---

10 An example of a theory of change is in Chapter Five.

was adopted across disciplines and agencies, this would tip the scales and achieve positive outcomes in the most cost-effective way.

Case study

The Big Lottery has funded the Headstart programme, a five-year, multi-million pound programme aiming to improve the mental health and well-being of young people aged between 10 and 16, and prevent serious mental health issues from developing. The six areas funded have taken different approaches, most led by the local authority, and there have been some useful lessons to learn. For instance, local areas have developed and adopted their system wide theory of change in collaboration with young people, schools and local agencies. The frameworks they have developed provide a structure and shared language for all local services.

Blackpool has taken a direct approach based on Hart et al (2007)[11] with a framework enabling all services to be explicit about their contribution to building young people's emotional well-being and resilience. All services and young people can share the same understanding about what makes up psychological well-being and the public health approach means the whole city is promoting their resilience approach with young people at the centre.

https://www.boingboing.org.uk/resilience-revolution-blackpool-headstart/

Charities have a leadership opportunity in the current environment. Given that even with the very welcome new funding in 2015 to deliver the *Future in Mind* strategy, the NHS nevertheless now only spends 0.8% of its budget on children and young people's mental health[12]. The recent Prevalence Survey evidences that one in eight young people experience mental health problems, and only 25% of these young people receive statutory psychological care. It is therefore easy to see that support delivered by charities and social care is essential and of significant importance.

The route map laid out in the *Future In Mind* strategy is now enshrined in the Five Year Forward View for Mental Health – but starting from such a low resource threshold, with significant workforce challenges, the target for 2020 is just an additional 70,000 children/young people to receive NHS care each year, leaving two thirds with no help at all. And this is still an ambition rather than a detailed plan.

The plans for the newly announced £2bn for mental health have yet to be seen, but this figure indicates how seriously the mental health of the nation is now taken. To turn the dial on the mental health of the nation, charities have the chance to demonstrate how shared approaches can have a sustainable impact in the long term. The resources from charitable and

---

11   Hart, A., Blincow, D., Thomas, H. (2007). Resilient therapy: Working with children and families. Hove, UK: Routledge.

12   NHS accessed 23.1.19 https://assets.publishing.service.gov.uk/government/uploads/system/uploads/attachment_data/file/414024/Childrens_Mental_Health.pdf

voluntary sector agencies spent on children and young people experiencing adversity, while under enormous pressure, is also nevertheless significant. The Charity Commission lists NSPCC and Barnardo's as spending over £422m between them in 2016-17. Millions of children and young people receive care and services each year from these and many other charities.

Funding is insecure, many services come and go, and we have seen a number of high-profile charities close along with a large swathe of local children's and young peoples' services. In truth, social care supports child development without the mental health 'tag'. Striving to achieve healthy child development, which must incorporate building resilience and understanding the impact of trauma, has the potential to bind all services together, whatever department or discipline. It is only by improving children's mental health that we will improve the mental health of the nation over time. As our mental health influences all life outcomes, it is imperative we do this.

Chapter Eight:
The Windrush scandal and Windrush Day

By Dr Patrick Vernon, OBE

Introduction

Although I was not directly affected by the Windrush scandal, I am a child of the Windrush Generation, born in the 1960s following my parents' arrival in Britain in the late 1950s. I grew up in Wolverhampton where my local MP, Enoch Powell, was part of the party that opened my junior school in December 1968, a few months prior to his 'Rivers of Blood' speech. In this speech he branded dependants as immigrant children who should be repatriated back to the countries of their birth. Fifty years later, the same children, now of pensionable age, became the victims of the Windrush scandal when large numbers were wrongly detained and threatened with deportation. Many were actually deported.

A 'hostile environment' is therefore nothing new in Britain, but the Immigration Act (2014), promoted by the then Home Secretary Theresa May, wrote this into law along with the approach by the Home Office to declassify British Citizens of African and Caribbean heritage. According to remarks made by Theresa May in 2012 during an interview with *The Daily Telegraph*, 'The aim is to create, here in Britain, a really hostile environment for illegal immigrants', while setting a high and unrealistic target with regard to numbers.

As the situation deteriorated, more cases came to light, and I became involved in supporting and advising a number of affected individuals and families as a community campaigner and former Councillor in Hackney.

After making my documentary, 'A Charmed Life', about the Caribbean contribution to the Second World War and the legacy of the Windrush Generation, I wrote an article for *The Guardian* newspaper in 2010. Here I argued that we would have failed as a nation if, by 2018, there was still no substantive recognition for the Windrush Generation on the 70th anniversary of their arrival in Britain. I called for a public holiday very similar to Martin Luther King Day in USA to celebrate the Windrush Generation and all post-war migration to Britain. Over the last few years I have been able to convince and work in partnership with a range of individuals and organisations from the trade union movement, faith leaders, politicians and celebrities to support the campaign for a national Windrush Day on 22 June, the anniversary of the arrival of the MV *Empire Windrush* at Tilbury docks in 1948.

The central message of the campaign is that many aspects of British society today would be unrecognisable without the contributions that immigration and integration have made: from the NHS to the monarchy, our language, literature, enterprise, public life, fashion, music, politics, science, culture, food, and even humour. I also developed the concept and idea for a board game called Every Generation Game: Windrush Edition in partnership with Focus Games[1].

Amnesty petition

Between 2010 and 2017, I regularly posted images and messages on social media about the contribution of the Windrush Generation and migration in Britain leading up to Windrush Day with very limited success. Then, in 2018, the whole issue of the Windrush Generation become a major international news story as British citizens of Caribbean heritage, many of whom had spent most of their lives in the UK, lost their rights, their homes, their livelihoods and even their lives as result of the Home Office's 'hostile environment' policy – a policy that saw British citizens treated as illegal immigrants, facing deportation or being refused re-entry into Britain after coming back from holiday. The scandal was further heightened with the discovery that the government had destroyed or misplaced people's Landing Cards – constituting an important and vital part of black history, as well as hampering the exercise of individuals' rights.

In many ways the issue had been brewing for decades, but it was the investigative journalism of Amelia Gentleman of *The Guardian* from November 2017 that elevated this to a national and international news story in April 2018. I was aware of Amelia's articles and the cases, particularly of Paulette Wilson, who was detained twice at Yarlswood Detention Centre, Albert Thompson, who was refused cancer treatment, and Sarah O'Connor, who was on the verge of facing bankruptcy proceedings having not been allowed to work for years. I remember during this period I was tweeting and sharing on social media about these cases. However, for the public, media and politicians, there was no traction, and people still saw these as isolated cases. Many viewed it as the victims' own fault for not sorting out their citizenship years before. Furthermore, the Home Office deflected these concerns by claiming that it was tackling illegal immigration.

---

1   Hackney Gazette Accessed 9.1.19 https://www.hackneygazette.co.uk/news/ heritage/patrick-vernon-s-board-game-every-generation-shows-changes-since- windrush-1-5836727

Alicia Graham, founder of community radio station Reel Rebels Radio, which for the last three years I have been running a monthly show called *Museum of Grooves*, introduced me to Rachelle Romeo and her father, Elwardo, regarding his immigration status. I got to know Elwardo and shared that his young brother was Jazzy B of Soul2Soul fame (we agreed not to disclose this fact to the public as we wanted to focus on his case). Elwardo was subsequently featured in *The Guardian* by Amelia Gentleman, and his situation highlighted that this was a clear breach of justice by the Home Office; they threatened to deport him back to Antigua, a country he had left as a four year old, despite the fact he had already had a British passport and had done jury service. I realised then that this was a class action targeting the Caribbean, and also the African community, in which the state was pursuing the children of the Windrush Generation, who fitted the concept of 'low hanging fruit' and helped the Home Office meet its deportation targets.

Case study: Elwardo Romeo

Elwardo Romeo, 63 years old, received a letter from the Home Office in February 2018 telling him he was in the UK illegally – despite the fact he has been here for 59 years since moving from Antigua at the age of four, with his mother who came to work as a nurse. The letter stated: 'You have NOT been given leave to enter the United Kingdom within the meaning of the Immigration Act 1971' and offered 'help and support on returning home voluntarily'. Romeo did not want help returning to a country he has not visited for almost 60 years. He had worked in London for more than 40 years, has children and grandchildren here, and was dismayed to be told he was here illegally. 'It scares the living daylights out of you – the threatening language on the letters,' he said. The problem may have been caused by an administrative error on his birth certificate in 1955. After publicity about the case, the Home Office said it was 'urgently reviewing' his case. He is still waiting for the problem to be resolved.

In a recent interview in a special Windrush edition of the Big Issue, Elwardo stated, 'Over the last two years my life has been turned upside-down. The mental stress and turmoil caused me ill health and still impacts on my daily life. The government compensation scheme has not been fairly documented, it was constructed behind closed doors, no public input and no one to represent the Windrush victims.'

I believed at the time, after hearing the Elwardo case in late March, there might have been be over 10,000 people affected by the hostile environment. While Amelia Gentleman was exposing this scandal, various organisations such as the Joint Council for Welfare of Immigrants (JCWI), Runnymede Trust, Praxis, Liberty and numerous High Commissioners from the Caribbean, had been lobbying the government regarding their concerns. However there was no acknowledgement or shift in policy.

Based on years of activism and experience as a former councillor, I decided in March 2018 to launch a petition to the government using the Elwardo Romeo case as evidence that the government was unfairly targeting the children of the Windrush Generation and those from other parts of the Commonwealth, who came to Britain as minors between 1948 to 1973 on their parents' passports. It took over two weeks for the petition to be approved on the government website[2], but eventually it went live in early April 2018 calling for an amnesty for the Windrush Generation. While I was waiting for approval, other petitions were launched. Councillor Cleo Lake, a Bristol-based Green councillor and activist, launched her campaign on change.org[3], while 38 Degrees had a similar petition[4]. When my petition went live, I worked closely with Cleo to promote both our petitions, until mine got more media attention and she supported my campaign.

Graphic image

Alongside the petition, I wanted to have graphic images reflecting the nature of the campaign in order engage the public and the media. I approached Pen Mendonca, a graphic facilitator[5] who worked with me in promoting Windrush Day by developing a series of images highlighting the key demands of the campaign and encouraging people to sign the petition.

Figure 8.1: Windrush graphic, Pen Mendonca[6]

---

2   Petitions Parliament Accessed 10.1.19 https://petition.parliament.uk/petitions/216539

3   Change.Org Accessed 10.1.19 https://www.change.org/p/home-office-we-demand-an-immigration-amnesty-for-commonwealth-citizens/u/22611880

4   38 Degrees Accessed 10.1.19 https://you.38degrees.org.uk/petitions/allow-commonwealth-citizens-who-arrived-here-as-children-automatic-right-to-remain-in-the-uk

5   Pen Mendonca; accessed 5.1.19; http://www.penmendonca.com/portfolio/windrush-day-campaigning

6   Ibid

When the petition reached over 10,000 signatures after four days, a large number of people started to get involved, such as MPs such as David Lammy, who, through his role as Chair of the All Party Committee on Race, was already getting letters signed by Parliamentarians about the scandal during April. In addition, a number of celebrities came on board such as Lenny Henry, David Harewood, Beverley Knight and June Sappong, encouraging people to sign the petition. An open letter was written by four Bishops condemning the government and encouraging the public to sign the petition. Trevor Phillips, the former Chair of the Equalities and Human Rights Commission, signed the petition and also wrote a series of articles in April 2018 in the *Daily Mail*, which then led to a rush of newspapers such as *The Sun*, *Daily Express* and *The Telegraph* attacking the government over the treatment of the Windrush Generation and criticising Theresa May for her actions during her time as the Home Secretary.

The speech made by David Lammy on the first day of the opening of Parliament after Easter, when the petition had already hit 100,000 and a date was fixed for the formal debate in the second chamber on the 30th of April, went 'viral' around the world and further raised the profile of the campaign and awareness of the scandal.

My petition played an important function as the glue that held the national campaign together, which reinforced the stories in the media and engaged 'Middle England' with the scandal, and soon the petition had been signed by over 180,000 people showing their anger and disgust at the government. In addition, the petition led to a fantastic social media campaign where celebrities, faith leaders, Caribbean diplomats, MPs from all political parties, activists and concerned members of the public all stepped up to show support of the Windrush Generation and their children. Between April and June the terms 'Windrush Scandal,' 'Windrush Generation' and 'Hostile Immigration Environment' were trending regularly on Twitter, becoming a major cause célèbre. The voices and stories of the victims were featured on television and social media regularly throughout this period, along with the Pathé News reel of the calypso rendition of Lord Kitchener's 'London is the Place for Me' on board the *Empire Windrush*.

Ironically, the public have learned more about Empire Windrush and the Windrush Generation during April 2018 than in the previous 50 years, which further exposes the invisibility of the BME community's lived experiences and contribution to Britain.

This pressure from the social media campaign highlighted the impact of the hostile environment of the Windrush Generation and was one of the factors that led to a major U-turn in government policy and the resignation of Amber

Rudd, the Home Secretary[7]. The petition was also used as part of the lobbying by the 13 Caribbean High Commissioners ahead of the Commonwealth Summit taking place in April. The High Commissioners were supported by JCWI and the Runnymede Trust in making the legal and policy case to the government on the impact of the hostile environment on the Caribbean community in the UK. The migrant sector, through case work and lobbying organisations like Praxis, IMAX and Migrant Organise, Migrants Rights Network and Amnesty, had been lobbying over the last four years on the hostile environment and the racist 'Go Home' vans.

Between April and May, the Windrush Scandal was debated on a regular basis in Parliament. A special debate on the 30th of April was organised in Parliament, which was triggered as result of my petition reaching 100,000, which I attended with Rachelle Romeo. Caroline Nokes MP, the Immigration Minster, accepted the key points from my petition demands and further apologised for the government's failure in dealing with the Windrush Scandal.

Windrush Justice Fund

With the increased media attention and public response, this created the environment for people experiencing the impact of the scandal and other victims of the hostile environment to seek urgent assistance. However, this became a major issue for under-resourced and under-funded migrant advice centres, law centres, CAB, grass roots organisations, faith and other agencies as they became overwhelmed with enquiries for help, especially as people do not trust the Home Office. Thus, on the 16th of April, I launched the Windrush Justice Fund to support children of the Windrush Generation to access free legal advice from a range of third sector organisations specialising in immigration, migrant centres and community organisations. The fund was instigated on the GoFundMe platform, with JCWI holding the money as an independent organisation[8].

Over £18,000 has been raised on the site plus private donations. I am in discussion with Sadiq Khan and his advisers on obtaining additional funding to match that raised by the Justice Fund from the GLA. A number of publishers and organisations are using proceeds from Windrush-related products and merchandise to support the campaign, particularly the #WeAreAllWindrush campaign, whose clothing was sold as part of the 70th anniversary commemoration – a mother and daughter have raised £3,000 in the last six months[9].

---

7   A subsequent Government report appears to blame senior civil servants not the Home Secretary.

8   Go Fund Me Windrush Campaign Accessed 10.1.19 https://www.gofundme.com/windrush-justice-fund

9   The Voice Accessed 9.1.19; https://www.voice-online.co.uk/article/fundraiser-t-shirts-launched-support-windrush-generation

The focus of the fund is to provide a small grant scheme for migrant grass roots, third sector and faith groups who are supporting victims of the Windrush Scandal to cover the following key activities:

■ provide free legal advice sessions for the Windrush Generation and other Commonwealth citizens affected by the hostile environment.

■ to support migrant and third sector organisations to extend their services to meet the increased caseload as victims apply to the Home Office Windrush fast track scheme and forthcoming compensation programme.

Ideally, the Home Office would provide additional resources and support to the sector and for the Windrush Justice Fund to ensure people receive independent advice, that promotional materials are developed, and to support community events when the compensation scheme is launched in 2019.

Hardship/interim payments

With the government refusing to make any emergency and hardship funds to the victims or the families of the scandal, I have launched two separate appeals to cover the funeral costs for Dexter Bristol and Sarah O'Connor.

Dexter Bristol

I was approached by the family solicitor of the late Dexter Bristol[10], Jacqui McKenzie, who over the last several years has supported clients affected by the scandal and has played a key role in establishing Windrush Action, a network of over 400 victims to lobby the government. I helped to raise about £2,000 towards his funeral costs working with GoFundMe[11].

Case study: Dexter Bristol

Dexter Bristol, who was 57 when he died, moved from Grenada to the UK in 1968, when he was eight, to join his mother who was working as an NHS nurse. He spent the rest of his life in the UK. He was sacked from his cleaning job the year before he died because he had no passport and was denied benefits because officials did not believe he was in the country legally.

He spent the last year of life trying to untangle his immigration situation, repeatedly attempting and failing to get the Home Office to acknowledge that he was not an illegal immigrant. Until he was sacked, he had no idea there was any problem with his immigration status. He was born a British subject in Grenada but had never been able to get a British passport, and he had struggled to gather

---

10 Camden New Journal Accessed 10.1.19 http://camdennewjournal.com/article/windrush-scandal-victim-died-under-enormous-stress

11 Go Fund Me Dexter Bristol Justice Fund Accessed 10.1.19 https://www.gofundme.com/dexter-bristol-justice-fund

the extensive documentation required by officials to prove that he was not an overstayer. On 31 March he collapsed in the street outside his home and died.

On August 28, 2018, an inquest at St Pancras Coroner's Court concluded that Bristol had died of natural causes, namely 'acute cardiac arrhythmia', though the coroner acknowledged that stress had been a factor in his death. Bristol's family walked out of the inquest following the coroner's refusal to allow that the UK Home Office should be named as an 'interested party' to the inquest[12]. The family had sought to have the Home Office's role in his death examined by the coroner's inquest. Bristol had not accessed NHS healthcare since August 2016, believing himself to be ineligible because of his immigration status.

The Guardian[13]

Case study: Sarah O'Connor

Sarah O'Connor died of hypertension on Sunday 16th of September, 2018, at the age of 57 years old. She was a victim of the Windrush Scandal and campaigner for the rights of the Windrush Generation who was on the verge of bankruptcy. I met Sarah on a number of occasions and I approached the family to raise money for the funeral costs. I raised £5,550 towards the cost under the GoFundMe platform[14]. What is clear is that an interim or hardship fund payment was something that could have saved Sarah's life, but it had been refused, which then increased the amount of stress she was under and ultimately led to her death.

In a recent interview in the *Big Issue* in June 2019, the daughter of Sarah O'Connor, Stephanie, stated:

'The Windrush scandal impacted on my mum Sarah, both on her health and emotionally. Before the scandal was exposed, she felt on her own and like she had done something wrong, despite contributing to the country for many years. For my mum the compensation scheme has come too late and I'm so disappointed that it is still taking this long for people to get compensated fairly for everything they have been through. This scandal has ruined people's lives, and in today's world it is terrible that we have allowed that to happen to this extent.'[15]

Over the last few months there had been constant lobbying of government by Diane Abbott MP, the Shadow Home Secretary, third sector organisations and victims of the scandal for interim and emergency payments. The Home Office reluctantly agreed to this on the 17th of December, with new guidance issued 24 hours before Channel 4 were due to cover the story of two survivors of the scandal[16]. These two are members of Windrush Action[17], a newly formed network of over 400 individuals who have been affected the scandal, which is chaired by Elwardo Romeo and which I support as an adviser.

---

12 Ibid

13 Guardian accessed 10.1.19 https://www.theguardian.com/uk-news/2018/jul/20/windrush-mother-wants-home-office-role-in-sons-death-looked-at

14 Go Fund Me Sarah O'Connor Funeral accessed 10.1.19 https://www.gofundme.com/djc2w4-sarah-o039connor-funeral-fund

15 The Big Issue (2019) Patrick Vernon: 'The government was in denial over Windrush injustice' [online]. Available at: https://www.bigissue.com/latest/politics/patrick-vernon-the-government-was-in-denial-over-windrush-injustice/ (accessed August 2019).

16 UK Government accessed 10.1.19 https://www.gov.uk/government/publications/windrush-scheme-support-in-urgent-and-exceptional-circumstances

17 Facebook Windrush accessed 5.1.19: https://www.facebook.com/Windrush-Action-274736539802353/

Compensation cap

At the heart of my original petition was for the government to have a compensation scheme which covered the emotional and financial loss as result of the scandal. I felt that a fair compensation scheme for the Windrush Generation had to be in line with compensation awarded by the courts in civil cases. The government needed to consider immediate payments for hardship alongside the full payment of compensation, within the development of a comprehensive compensation scheme.

Thus, there should be no artificial cap that will inadequately compensate those who have suffered emotionally, financially and who may have lost their homes and citizenship. However, when the Home Office announced in July the launch of a consultation process in the design of a compensation scheme, they announced that they would consider a cap on payments.

The Windrush Generation, plus others from the Commonwealth, have paid their taxes and contributed to the wealth, prosperity and cultural identity of the UK since the Second World War and this should be the starting point of a scheme; it should not devalue human suffering caused as a result of structural racism. After meeting Martin Forde QC in August in London, who was appointed by the government to advise on a Windrush Compensation scheme, I felt that the government, despite all the apologies, would short change the Windrush Generation and create a 'pound shop' compensation scheme. This was especially so after I read a complex and onerous 63 page consultation document that was launched in July with a closing date for responses on the 11th of October[18]. In fact one person described the process of filling it out as an 'unpleasant 'psychedelic experience'.

Thus, I launched a new petition in September 2018 with a focus around questions 15A and 15B in the consultation, which would place a potential cap on all compensation claims that the Home Office would impose. I started another social media campaign that was picked by the public and various stakeholders such as trade unions and local government. Although it did not get the same numbers as to my petition in April, over 4,000 people have signed it protesting the idea of a cap or limit on compensation claims. This is a bigger response to the Home Office consultation when the deadline was extended in November[19]. Martin Forde QC, who is designing the scheme, stated at various public meetings between September and November 2018 and in the media, that Windrushers should receive a compensation that covers all their losses and that no cap or limit should be imposed[20].

---

18   UK Government accessed 10.1.19 https://www.gov.uk/government/consultations/windrush-compensation-scheme

19   Petitions Parliament accessed 10.1.19 https://petition.parliament.uk/petitions/227821

20   Daily Mirror accessed 10.1.19 https://www.mirror.co.uk/news/politics/windrush-victims-could-receive-hundreds-13450577

Deportation flights

One of the big issues over the 12 months was the use of deportation flights as a form of repatriation back to Africa or the Caribbean. Although flights were suspended for 10 months, the Home Office in February 2019 controversially resumed them again even though many people deported had spent their adult life in the UK with strong family ties. The campaign group Movement for Justice, and BME Lawyers for Justice, played an important role in forcing the Home Office to reduce the numbers that eventually got deported. I was in Jamaica in March and I had the opportunity to speak to five people who were deported in February. They all shared the following concerns:

■ They all have no money and are dependent on family and friends.

■ All had served their sentences and were moving forward with their lives before deportation.

■ Most of them have caring responsibilities as fathers and/or supporting elderly parents with health problems such as dementia.

■ Some of their children are not aware that they had been deported and may not see them again.

■ The impact of deportation is imposing tremendous pressures on their partners and family members in the UK.

■ All are experiencing anxiety and depression regarding leaving UK, with high levels of anger about being deported by the British government.

■ All of them stay indoors most of the time. One person described life as like being back in prison.

■ Several of them have physical health problems. One person was given six months of medication for their kidney problems, but he is not sure what will happen when supplies run out.

■ They all feel they have no real future in Jamaica.

To make matters worse, not only were people deported to Jamaica without any plans for support or rehabilitation, the charity supporting deportees in Kingston, National Organisation for Deported Migrants, had all their funding cut by the Home Office. This was brought to my attention by Oswald Dawkins from the charity when I was in Kingston. I shared my concerns with the UK High Commissioner in Jamaica, Asif Ahmed, and Pernell Charles Jr, the Jamaican Foreign Minister. Back in the UK, I shared this news with several media outlets and *BuzzFeed* took on the story about the Home Office in May and successfully helped to reverse the funding cuts to the charity.

The role of local government

Since 2014, local government have implemented aspects of the hostile environment policy from the Home Office around workforce, social care and housing. With the Windrush Scandal breaking in April, local politicians and councils could not respond as 'purdah' was imposed in the period leading up to the council elections in May 2018. Once the election was over I was in contact with a number of councils to develop full council motions on the Windrush Scandal and the hostile environment. On 18th July, Hackney Council was the first local authority in the country to have a debate with elected representatives. The debate was led by Councillor Carol Williams, Cabinet Member for Equalities, and Deputy Mayor Councillor Antoinette Bramble[21]. The following key points in the motion were passed by the full council:

■ *'Continue actively campaigning for an end to all "hostile environment" policy measures and to continue to call on the Government to enable the Windrush generation to acquire British citizenship at no cost and with proactive assistance throughout the process.*

■ *Lead the way, by celebrating an annual Windrush Day in Hackney and for Hackney to welcome the Government's announcement to make 22 June each year an annual celebration of recognise(ing) and honour(ing) the enormous contribution of those who arrived between 1948 and 1971.*

■ *Press the Prime Minister to call for an independent public enquiry into the Windrush scandal.*

■ *Demand the Government fully supports advice agencies in their work to achieve justice (and compensation for all losses, injury and damages to date where necessary) for all Hackney residents of the Windrush generation.*

■ *Review our own policies and procedures to ensure we support those affected.*

■ *Support the call for fees for naturalisation to be waived for all those who have been affected.*

■ *Oppose the criminalisation of Windrush families.'*

As a result of Hackney Council being the first local authority to pass a full motion, the following local authorities adopted similar motions: Lambeth, Southwark, Croydon, Cardiff City, Luton, Newham, Barking and Dagenham, Lewisham and Brent. It is certain that more local councils will adopt and take forward Windrush motions throughout 2019.

---

21 Hackney Council accessed 10.1.19 http://mginternet.hackney.gov.uk/ieListDocuments. aspx?CId=112&MId=4348 Hackney Council accessed 10.1.19 http://mginternet. hackney.gov.uk/ieListDocuments.aspx?CId=112&MId=4348

Lessons for government

Although the compensation scheme is focused on individuals, the government should also make recommendations on wider issues on community development and education. This should include recognising racism and discrimination over the last 70 years and promoting the heritage of the African and Caribbean community. This would fit in to the wider work around the government's own Race Disparity Audit[22] and the Wendy Williams Lessons Learned Review around any strategic recommendations, which will require dialogue and conversation with key stakeholders in the community[23].

One of the key lessons that the government needs to learn is that in 2018, as part of the 70th anniversary, we as a nation have failed in creating substantive recognition the contribution of the Windrush Generation and other migrant communities. It is critical that the Windrush Compensation Scheme does 'right the wrongs' inflicted by this scandal, as promised by the Home Secretary.

Windrush Day and promoting tolerance

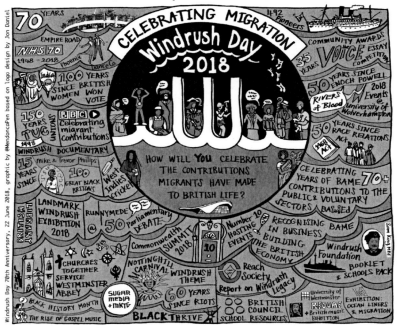

Figure 8.2: Windrush Day poster by Pen Mendonca (copyright permission)[24]

---

22 UK Government accessed 10.1.19 https://assets.publishing.service.gov.uk/government/uploads/system/uploads/attachment_data/file/686071/Revised_RDA_report_March_2018.pdf

23 UK Government accessed 10.1.19 https://www.gov.uk/government/publications/windrush-lessons-learned-review

24 Pen Mendonca accessed 5.1.19; http://www.penmendonca.com/portfolio/windrush-day-campaigning

Conclusion

Over the last 15 months there has been some progress, including a taskforce trying to fast track citizenship claims, a Lessons Learned Review, two consultations on a Windrush compensation scheme, numerous apologies and admissions from the Prime Minster and other government ministers, and the adoption of a National Windrush Day, with funding and a proposal for a national Windrush memorial at Waterloo Station. However the National Audit Office report into the Home Office's handling of the scandal, which criticised the government for failing in its duty of care by not responding to or taking on board the assertion that the hostile environment was unjustly targeting British citizens of African and Caribbean heritage[25].

In the spring of 2019, the Public Accounts Committee, a Parliamentary select committee, published a damning report on the Windrush Scandal[26] and the Home Office. Wendy Williams, the appointed Independent Adviser for the Windrush Review, will also publish a report on the scandal in the autumn of 2019. However, the draft recommendations were leaked to Channel 4 News in June providing further evidence of system failure and civil servants' lack of understanding about the history of the British Empire and the Commonwealth in dealing with the Windrush Generation. David Olusaga's BBC documentary 'The Unwanted: The Secret Windrush Files', found evidence of 70 years of surveillance, monitoring and racism against the Windrush Generation, which further demonstrated the deep-seated structural racism which is at the heart of government.

Nevertheless, without the petition and support of many stakeholders that created a coalition for action, and we can reflect on the following lessons around the impact of the campaign:

- The launch of a petition on the government's website, which contributed to raising awareness of the scandal with the public and led to debates in Parliament between April and June 2018.

- The role of the media helped to create a positive perspective in the debate on immigration and migration as a result of the Windrush Scandal.

- The Home Office failed to provide any emergency support or assistance to the victims of the scandal, especially those who died as a result of the hostile environment, but, with additional campaigning and pressure, they were forced to introduce an emergency fund in December 2018.

---

25 London Live Accessed 9.1.19 https://www.londonlive.co.uk/news/2018-12-06/the-national-audit-office-report-on-the-windrush-scandal

26 Public Accounts Committee Accessed 9.1.19 https://www.parliament.uk/business/committees/committees-a-z/commons-select/public-accounts-committee/inquiries/parliament-2017/inquiry19/

■ The role of third sector, race equality and migrant organisations has been important to support victims, but they require additional funding to provide independent advice and to liaise with the Home Office Task Force.

■ An independent mobilisation and social media campaign are now required to encourage those affected by the hostile environment to come forward to regularise their status prior to Brexit, especially as there is a lack of trust with Home Office.

■ Further work is required to assess the impact of how local government, the NHS and other bodies implemented the hostile environment policy, and what is required to mitigate the impact of victims of the scandal who have been denied local services.

■ The Windrush Compensation Scheme needs to cover all financial and emotional loss, with no artificial cap imposed.

■ A national strategy around mental health and wellbeing needs to be developed to support Windrush Generation families between the Department of Health and Social Care, NHS England and the Home Office[27].

■ The government has acknowledged and will fund a Windrush Day from June 2019 to promote the history and contribution of the Windrush Generation, but this should be extended to other migrant communities.

■ Proper consultation with community stakeholders on the proposed Windrush memorial at Waterloo Station.

■ The hostile environment is part of a long history of structural racism and discrimination, and it raises issues about how the Public Sector Equality Duty is implemented by the Home Office, the rest of the Civil Service, and by private sector contractors.

In addition to the above lessons and with the appointment of Boris Johnson as the new Prime Minister in July we need to have a 10 point plan to resolve the scandal and to create a permanent legacy around the contribution of the Windrush Generation and mainstreaming the migration history as part of the national narrative[28].

Achievements

One of the key achievements of the Windrush Scandal campaign has been the response of the public in signing the various petitions. I launched

---

27 Mental Health Today Accessed 28.7.19 https://www.mentalhealthtoday.co.uk/blog/
   inequality/will-boris-johnsons-new-government-support-the-mental-health-of-the-
   windrush-generation

28 Class Accesses 27.7.17 http://classonline.org.uk/blog/item/a-plan-to-right-the-wrongs-of-
   the-windrush-scandal

several petitions including an Amnesty, 70th Anniversary Stamp for Royal Mail, Windrush Day and No Cap to Windrush Compensation scheme. In total just under 200,000 have signed these petitions. If we add Councillor Cleo Lake and 38 Degrees' petition numbers then just over 350,000 people have supported our respective campaigns for the rights of the Windrush Generation, plus the millions who were captivated by the news story of their suffering and by the contribution they have made to the UK.

In addition, the public, fundraisers, and the Mayor of London have contributed to over £50,000 to the Windrush Justice Fund, the funeral costs of Dexter Bristol, Sarah O'Connor, and recently a holiday break for Mrs Delsie Gayle, a member of the Windrush Generation who was racially abused on a Ryanair flight[29]. The crowdfunding campaigns have had great support from Dina Rickman and the team from GoFundMe have made a practical difference. In addition, *The Guardian* and *The Observer* newspapers launched Windrush Christmas Appeals which raised about £1 million for five charities that support victims of the scandal[30].

The Windrush Scandal, in the context of Brexit and the national debate on immigration, has brought the country together, and media and politicians from across political parties came together in a rare moment to inflict one of the worst public humiliations of a Prime Minster in a generation, and forcing the government to make one of the biggest concessions in immigration and social policy in the last 30 years. This will be lasting a legacy of Theresa May as she transferred reins of power to Boris Johnson.

---

29 Huffington Post accessed 10.1.19 https://www.huffingtonpost.co.uk/ entry/virgin-atlantic-to-fly-ryanair-racism-victim-out-for-luxury-holiday_ uk_5bd1ddf1e4b0a8f17ef55879

30 The Guardian accessed 10.1.19 https://www.theguardian.com/society/2019/jan/01/ guardian-and-observer-charity-appeal-passes-750000?utm_source=gdnwb&utm_ medium=onplatform&utm_campaign=ca18_site&utm_content=key_tag

Chapter Nine: 'Survive or die – critical management challenges in non-profit organisations'

By Don Macdonald

Overview

Non-profit organisations are under enormous pressure at the moment with regard to funding, and face many other issues such as staff conduct, reputation and governance. Society is facing rapid and enormous change, so all organisations must keep evolving continuously or face stagnation, decline or even closure. Leaders and managers have to make crucial decisions that could make or break the future of their organisations. In this chapter I examine cases of non-profit organisations that have closed down (Kids Company, Novas Scarman) and compare them to non-profit organisations that have changed and survived over 20 years, staying true to their mission (Ashford Place, Jericho Foundation etc), drawing out lessons about relevant management skills.

Survival or collapse?

Big household names in the UK, such as Oxfam, Save the Children and the National Trust, with annual incomes above £10m, make up less than 1% of UK charities, though they account for almost 50% of the total income (and inevitably, one could argue, most of the bad publicity, though their size must be one reason for this). They generate this income though large fundraising teams and can rely on legacy income, commercial sponsorship and investments, as well as contracts, of course. Smaller organisations, defined as those whose annual income falls between £10,000 and £1 million, are under much greater financial pressure, with 84% of local government funding going to larger charities and with a quarter of smaller charities having no reserves.[1]

As managers, staff or volunteers in non-profit organisations, we will have received rejection letters or emails from funding agencies or trusts, which left us without the funding we needed or threatened the future of our

---

1   NCVO (2015) *What do we know about charities' reserves?* [online]. Available at: https:// blogs.ncvo.org.uk/2015/08/07/what-do-we-know-about-charities-reserves (accessed August 2019).

organisations. The first duty of a community organisation is to survive, according to management guru Peter Drucker[2], and effective management is obviously crucial in leading the organisation through difficult times. When non-profit organisations collapse, the clients, staff and the community all suffer.

In fact, non-profit organisations are expected to do much more than private companies, who just have to meet the bottom line of profitability, which is why management in this sector is so complex; our organisations have to achieve social objectives and meet the hopes and aspirations of stakeholders and service users.

With austerity introduced by the coalition government in 2008, times have become much harder indeed for charities and other non-profit organisations; grants from councils and central government are being reduced by around 29%; if statutory funding still exists, it has mostly been transformed into contracts with high targets to meet. Many of these contracts are put out to competitive tendering in which price is an absolutely critical factor. Some charities are even subsidising these contracts with their own funds[3], and there is also much more competition for grants from trusts.

Austerity and cuts have therefore brought about the demise of some non-profit organisations, but there are other causes too, which this chapter will explore along with case studies of successful smaller non-profit organisations.

Why do charities collapse?

The reasons why non-profit organisations collapse or close down are multifarious:

- The need which they were set up to overcome never really existed in the first place, so projected income does not reach targets or cover actual costs. Age Concern set up Heyday, for example, a social enterprise, in 2006 that offered services and benefits to members, hoping to attract three million members by 2011. However, the services it offered were similar to those already offered by the NHS, so membership only reached 40,000, despite the £22m the charity spent on the project. So Heyday was wound up in 2009, senior staff left and Age Concern soon merged with Help the Aged.

- The need exists but the funding is cut, because government, either central or local, does not see it as a priority. Many women's refuges,

2   Drucker P (1990) *Managing the Non-Profit Organization: Practices and principles*. New York: Harper Collins.

3   Civil Service World (2017) *Charities using own funds to subsidise public sector contracts, research finds* [online]. Available at: https://www.civilserviceworld.com/articles/news/charities-using-own-funds-subsidise-public-sector-contracts-research-finds (accessed August 2019).

for example, have been closed over the last few years in Exeter, South Gloucestershire, Bury St Edmunds, Welling-borough and more towns, due to government funding cuts.

■ The need exists but procurement procedures have been changed to favour wealthy non-profits or companies. Several training and employment organisations closed after changes and cuts to programmes under the Conservative governments from 2010-18, which penalised small organisations supporting harder-to-reach clients. Consequently Tomorrows People, Red Kite, Westward Pathfinder, Eco Actif, Create Motorvations and others have all closed.

■ Poor financial management, including 'poor contracting and poor controls', led to the collapse of Lifeline, a £60m drug and alcohol charity in 2017[4]. Relying on a single contract also poses problems. Secure Healthcare had a £5 million contract to provide health services in prison but it was a fixed-price contract, and, with costs rising and a £1 million debt, Secure had to be wound up in 2009.

■ Mismanagement. One of the most destructive causes is a charismatic CEO directing an organisation down the wrong path, without their ideas being properly researched or examined by an informed group of trustees or senor staff. One example of this was the well-documented case of Kids Company. Another example was Novas Scar-man, founded in 1998 as a care and homeless charity, which crashed from a 2008 turnover of £21 million to closure in 2012, with redundancy for 300 staff (see case study below).

Case study: The demise of Novas Scarman

The initial genesis of the UK Novas Group in 1998 seemed both innovative and rational, merging three small charities that provided care and housing for homeless people in London, Northern Ireland and Liverpool at a time when homeless charities were too small, creating a much more effective organisation. Novas then expanded its provision into other towns increasing housing units to 2,000 across the UK, which stretched management capacity further.

In 2006 it was planning a £50 million redevelopment of its hostels and housing provision, but a Housing Corporation report of June 2006 warned that its proposed redevelopment could prove too ambitious as it lacked proper development capacity at this scale. However, by 2008 turnover had increased to £21 million per annum.

In 2004 Novas merged with Scarman Trust, a regeneration charity, and, as part of the hostel redevelopment, it then embarked on a highly ambitious arts centre development. Arts funding in the UK provided much lower incomes when compared with running hostels, where 40% of the income was derived from government subsidies and then topped up with another 40% in government

---

4   Civil Society accessed 05.10.18 https://www.civilsociety.co.uk/news/lifeline-project-collapsed-owing-over-4m.html

grants. In addition, the steady increase in property prices in the UK, particularly in London, increased the asset base of hostel non-profits, which owned their hostels, like the Novas Scarman Group (NSG).

In addition, the difficulties were compounded by developing two arts centres in two different cities, with the one in Liverpool costing £17 million, albeit with £6.5m regeneration grants. Furthermore, the founding CEO, who also sat on the board, embarked on an expensive spree buying antique fittings, Malaysian art and other fripperies, which were exposed in a government agency investigation, publicised in the *Daily Telegraph* and he was forced out. The report raised concerns over 'alleged cronyism, nepotism bullying, and mismanagement' and 'collective failure by NSG's board and executive team'.

A new board was appointed in 2009 after the investigation. NSG had to sell a large number of properties to its competitors (who purchased them with part government funding), but still failed to sort out its finances and eventually had to sell its flagship, Arlington House, where George Orwell stayed in the 1930s. The organisation was holed under the waterline by the time an experienced new senior management team was brought in, with a new chair and CEO appointed. The organisation was relaunched as People Can in 2010. However the pension commitments of £17m incurred since its set up proved too great, its steady income from housing benefit had been reduced by the disposal of most of its hostels, some commissioners were wary about renewing contracts, and the financial situation became irretrievable. It was wound up in 2012 and almost 300 staff lost their jobs, though a few services and staff were transferred to other charities.

One could argue that some government grants were being so heavily cut back that it was wise for NSG to try to reduce dependency on these and switch to more trading activity. However, the lessons are that organisations should not be led into a new risky business area - arts funding - if they have insufficient knowledge or experience to embark on this and they have not fully researched the operational context. It is difficult enough for those arts projects that already have experience. It is made worse if new ventures are not thoroughly assessed, along with the risks of damaging an existing and stable organisation.

The move by NSG seems an example of 'mission creep', venturing into the unknown without any clear evidence that this would benefit either the clients or the organisation set up to serve them. The regulator stated there were failures in management and clearly there was over-reliance on and lack of supervision of the charismatic founder. The new chair said the real lesson for organisations was that risk management and the ability to look at real case scenarios were critically important.

But closure and change can also happen to long-established organisations. The English YWCA, set up in 1855, has now virtually disappeared apart from a single branch in Yorkshire, yet the YW used to be a well-established charity with a very strong identity, pioneering really interesting youth work, including outreach work with young women and men in the East End of London in the 1960/70s. The YW also provided 4,000 beds for young women, centrally managed in 1996. Sometime after this, the YW was hit with a huge demand to install essential fire precautions in its hostels for which it had not saved sufficient funds. They therefore sold all their hostels, invested the proceeds and just carried on with youth work, rebranding as Platform 51 in 2010. Two years later, as Civil Society reported, 'Platform 51's spending ... (had) outstripped its income by more than £1m each year since 2008[5]. So in 2014 it transferred its remaining youth and community work to the Cyrenians and initially became a research and lobbying organisation, called the Young Women's Trust. Since then, however, it has restarted, providing services for young women on a substantially smaller scale, including a coaching service.

If an organisation takes the right action at the right time, however, it is possible to rescue itself from severe deficits. The UK Outward Bound Trust had a deficit of £3 million on a turnover of £8/9 million in the 1990s and was 'close to insolvency' according to its director. The organisation was turned round by an interim CEO with experience of running a similar charity, the Duke of Edinburgh Awards. He implemented a swift and thorough restructure, which provided different and shorter courses, while revamping fundraising.

Mergers

Mergers can often be a way for non-profits to survive in some form or other as the example of Rainer Foundation below shows. A recent report by NPC, a philanthropy think tank, suggested that more mergers should take place and that too many charities were reluctant to take this step, prioritising organisational survival over mission.

However, this situation may be changing; several branches of national charities, which are local to each other in London, such as those of Mind and Age Concern, have merged recently and so can share overheads across more services. A consultancy has even drawn up a list of charities that it believes it would be beneficial if they merged[6].

The Rainer Foundation has survived over the years through a variety of mergers. It was started in 1848, running the London Police Court Mission, the forerunner of the probation service. When the probation service was setup in 1907, Rainer carried on running residential homes for children, an outdoor activities centre and approved schools; the most famous of which was the Cotswold Community, which eventually became independent before finally closing in 2011. Rainer closed its homes and residential centres in the 1970s and became one of the pioneers of supporting young offenders in the community, including setting up supported housing schemes. However it failed in its attempt to become a registered housing association

---

5   Civil Society accessed 05.10.18 https://www.civilsociety.co.uk/news/platform-51-transfers-services-to-changing-lives.html

6   Firetail accessed 17.1.19 https://static1.squarespace.com/static/59f0ea5051a584d3bb9881a8/t/5b080c98aa4a99be08b7f8f2/1527254168820/Merger+Survey+2018+-+key+findings.pdf

and it ran into financial problems in the 1990s. It then merged with the Royal Philanthropic Society, a charity founded in 1788, which sold a large residential centre in the Home Counties but retained the Rainer name. In 2008 it then merged with Crime Concern, a crime prevention charity, and rebranded as Catch 22; it has now taken over a small charity, Only Connect, under its wing. It has moved into new areas of work, setting up an academy schools trust that focuses on learners who might benefit from small, supportive alternative and its income is now around £50m each year. The mergers have meant that the charity has survived because it becomes more cost-effective, with overheads spread across more services. The downside is that very large organisations may lose touch with their staff. The recent report on Oxfam highlights this danger, but as Charles Fraser explains in his chapter on St Mungos (Chapter 6) it is possible to create structures to consult staff and service users.

When charities lose a large contract they may be able to still transfer staff and services across to the winning contractor and make sensible downsizing cost adjustments, such as reducing office space. The Refugee Council lost a large national contract but survived by downsizing its building and transferring staff to other charities.

Digital technology

There are also lessons to be learned from the private sector. Recent research by the ERC has shown that there is enormous potential for growth in UK micro businesses (those with less than 10 staff) if they adopt five key digital technologies. Since around 80% of UK charities have incomes below £100,000, these lessons are mostly applicable to them. The technologies include cloud-based services, customer relationship management software, web-based accounting software, computer-aided design and online sales, the latter being probably the least applicable to most charities.

Success stories

If one looks at charities and social enterprises that have succeeded in surviving or prospering during austerity, there are a number of common factors in their success. This applies particularly to small local organisations, without the resources of large national organisations. I have interviewed the managers of and researched four small charities or social enterprises, namely Bounceback, Sidings Community Centre, Ashford Place and the Jericho Foundation, which have all survived austerity successfully and still thrive.

They are all located in inner city areas, the first three in London and Jericho in Birmingham. Each provides different services: Bounceback provides training and support for ex-offenders, both in prison and in the community[7]. Sidings is a general community centre, catering for children, young people and older members of its local community in Camden, London[8]. Ashford Place provides accommodation and services for homeless people, alongside community support for local older people, particularly the Irish community, and others with needs such as dementia in Cricklewood, London[9]. Jericho is a social enterprise providing a range of building and recycling services in the community, providing jobs and training for the long-term unemployed and other excluded groups[10].

They all, however, share certain qualities. They all have managers who are skilled and experienced, who have been in post managing their projects for between eight and 20 years, so that they understand both their specialist service area and their 'political' environment, and so carry weight both with funders and other supporters. This experience may have been gained in the private sector, as with the Bounceback and Jericho CEOs, who both had gained substantial experience previously at a senior level in the private sector. Professional development is seen as critical, with one completing an MBA and others focusing on mentoring and leadership development.

All four managers are held in justifiably high regard: all projects have won competitive tenders. Two were the founding CEOs and they have all built up stable workforces with trusted staff in key posts providing continuity. One CEO pointed out that it is vital to have experienced and trusted staff in key positions because they bring 'organisational learning' about what is effective and what is ineffective[11], rather than having to start from scratch and reinvent the wheel, and to prevent making avoidable mistakes.

The managers had to be creative, to explore new ways of working or new forms of funding. But they have not pursued new projects regardless of consequences, and they are prepared to change or cut back a service if it does not work or the finances do not add up.

Austerity has hit hard, as the director of Jericho stated:

'[Our] Biggest difficulty remains finding the relatively small amounts of grant income that we still need to cover the support costs of the disadvantaged clients who work in our businesses. Almost all of our government money is gone. It's now grant making trusts and corporates, a continual battle to find in an increasingly crowded market.'[12]

7   Bounceback accessed 05.10.18 http://bouncebackproject.com/
8   Sidings Community Centre accessed 05.10.18 http://sidings.org.uk/
9   For more information, visit www.ashfordplace.org.uk
10 Jericho Foundation accessed 05.10.18 https://jericho.org.uk/
11 Interview with Ashford Place Director 02.04.18
12 Email to author from Jericho CEO 17.11.2015

Creativity is important. At Sidings, when Sure Start funding was cut for children's services by central government, the manager had to rethink its children's service and its funding completely; the government was offering financial support for a different 30-hour service which the centre took up and they 'had to run it as a business, but still maintain the caring element'[13].

But creativity must be tempered with realism, as shown by another example at Ashford Place, who tried to take on a social enterprise approach using a Meals on Wheels contract, making use of their existing kitchen facility. However the payments for the contract had been drastically cut back from previous levels by the commissioners, namely the local council. Ashford Place felt duty bound to spend extra funds providing additional services to keep quality at the right level. This was expensive, costing the charity £100,000 per annum more than the £200,000 the contract paid and in the end the charity decided that this was too great a drain on resources.

A great deal of funding from trusts is now project-based, which makes it hard to acquire essential core costs, however carefully you try to allocate these to individual projects. Three of the four have significant contributions to their core costs in different ways, which then ensures stable management; Sidings still has (so far) a grant from Camden Council, while Ashford Place receives a grant from the Irish government for its work with Irish migrants.

Diversification is also important. Sidings runs sports services for local schools with its trained sports leaders and gets paid for this. Jericho spreads its income, with enterprise income from ten different enterprises set up as different companies and topped up by trust grants for its support for excluded groups such as ex-offenders, former homeless people, long-term unemployed, and slavery and abuse survivors.

In spite of good management, there are always risks and some services have had to be changed, cut back or eliminated. Ashford Place had to cut back its youth and employment project because the council cut its grant (see the following case study). At the same time other services at this centre have been expanded with NHS funds, for example services for older people and people with dementia and similar conditions. Jericho lost a lot of money in 2012 when a big customer went bust and their biggest ever construction project got delayed by three months at the last minute.

---

13 Interview with Sidings Director 05.06.18

Case study: Ashford Place

Ashford Place was set up in 1983 by volunteers from the local Catholic Church in North West London as Cricklewood Homeless Concern (CHC). Its mission was to care for local homeless men, mainly from the Irish community. The church rented it a building, which had originally been a camera plate factory and latterly a young peoples' community centre. Initially the volunteers, with funding from Brent Council and support from local churches, provided basic services such as food, winter shelter and advocacy for those who needed it. As requests for help increased, however, the decision was taken to employ specialist staff.

The current director, Danny Maher, joined in 1996 and CHC expanded its work with homeless people by setting up a range of services including a day centre, training services and employment programmes, drug and alcohol services and medical services. CHC also took on the management of a couple of local houses to accommodate homeless people. These services were funded by the local council, a grant from the Irish government and from charitable donations.

CHC became a non-profit company in 2002 and then a registered charity in 2003, and the building was bought at market price from the Catholic Church in 2004 with a large donation from a successful Irish construction businessman and others. Over this period more support was given to local over 50s, particularly older Irish people and people suffering from dementia, and the centre is now a resource for the whole local adult community. The name was changed to Ashford Place in 2013 to demonstrate this change of function.

In 2008 the building was converted into a modern, fully DDA-compliant building with a kitchen and dining room, laundry facilities, offices, medical consulting room, staff offices and training/meeting/activity rooms spread over five floors. One floor is set aside for emergency accommodation for up to 25 homeless people, with separate facilities and entrance.

New services for young people, such as sports, specialist enterprise and employment support, were started in 2008 and 2009. However these had to be cut back in 2015 when the council ceased its funding and four staff were made redundant. (The good news is that most of this staff group has since set up a viable youth social enterprise, Youth Engagement Solutions https://yes-ltd.org.uk.) As mentioned above, Ashford Place also tried a social enterprise approach, through a Meals on Wheels contract, using their kitchen facility, but sadly this failed, as outlined above.

The building itself now generates income with 16 desks rented out to other charities, providing 12% of current income. The housing project generates 35% of the income from housing benefit. Volunteers are still essential, while new forms of work such as peer-to-peer support has been developed in several fields, including supporting local residents to create a local place that everyone can be proud of. Community capacity building has also been part of the new work.

Adequate reserves, which had been built up over the good years, were essential to tide the charity over when cuts hit. Expenditure has been reduced; in 2016-17, expenditure (£847k) exceeded income (£786k). Income and expenditure peaked in 2014-15 at £1026k with expenditure at £1082k.

Council funding has been reduced from around 75% of the budget 20 years ago to around 4% currently. Irish government support is around 25% and is still very important. Projects from the lottery and other trusts bring in around 10%.

For projects to survive, high quality networking is essential, taking up 95% of the director's time, including good links with other community groups. Flexibility is important and Ashford Place runs a range of programmes on other sites in the borough. A holistic approach is followed on health, mental health and social inclusion, encouraging self-help and using preventive strategies such as exercise. An NHS contract took two years to negotiate and is still not enormous, at £130,00 for three projects together. This contract is still yearly renewable, providing around 15% of the income.

Strategies to avoid closure

There are numerous reasons why non-profit organisations collapse or close. These include the following:

- Non-profit Senior Management needs to commission thorough research in their field of operations the viability of new projects before starting them (agencies with research available in different specialisms, such as Barnados, are listed in the Evaluation Chapter).

- Government, both local and central, does not fund vital services, even when there is a demonstrable need or when cutting funds for provision leads to an increase in other problems, such as abuse and homelessness, or in other costs such as benefits.

- Senior managers fail to manage their organisation's finances carefully, plan ahead and diversify their income streams.

- CEOs are not challenged in a constructive way by a strong and informed group of trustees or senior staff. This is particularly true if the CEO is also the founder, as was the case with both Kids Company and Novas Scarman.

There are numerous reasons why non-profit organisations survive, with most linked to the quality of management:

- **Strong stable leadership** is essential at all levels. The demise of Kids Company and Novas Scarman taught us the valuable lesson that a charismatic CEO needs to be challenged by a strong and informed group of trustees. Good leadership requires difficult decision-making, while being resilient and avoiding panic. It is important to set a positive example, keeping staff informed without letting any potentially difficult situations become exaggerated. Developing resilience in your team is also important.

- **Change and grow in a rational and logical way**. In the case study above, Cricklewood Homeless Concern evolved into Ashford Place, a project serving a wider community. Remploy, meanwhile, closed 32 factories making thousands of disabled workers redundant after the government removed most of its funding in 2012. One factory re-invented itself as Ability Tec, a social enterprise, and has carried on successfully providing work for local disabled people[14].

■ Successful non-profit organisations are **realistic**; one homeless charity lost a contract to manage a hostel that it owned, but then realised that they made fewer losses renting out the hostel to another homeless charity than they did managing the contract themselves.

■ **Keep evolving and developing your organisation and its services**, so you do not get stale or complacent.

■ With regard to contracts and funding, it is critical that organisations **do not put all their funding eggs in one basket** – so attempt to diversify rationally so that if one fund ends or a contract winds up, you have other options.

■ **Do not change a winning formula too radically**. If they do, organisations may lose service users' buy-in or staff may not be able to cope with too much change. It is important not to diversify too fast and too far from your organisation's original strategy and expertise base in case they start to get out of their depth.

■ Before starting a new service, **it is essential to research very thoroughly to see if there is sufficient demand**. Investigate other services and visit other projects to acquire ideas on what really works and what is just good PR in their annual report. Running a pilot first is also a crucial first step.

■ **Recruit and retain experienced staff in key posts**. If consulted regularly, staff can also feedback their experiences from the 'front line' so that both policy and practice are kept properly informed.

■ **Be realistic about the capacity of your organisation's' team, and be cautious about ambitious new ventures to ensure that you have the capacity to deliver**. One social enterprise took on a project that trained ex-offenders, but the director, who had substantial experience in this field, then discovered that one of his training staff, who was excellent with almost all other client groups, found this group daunting and could not engage with them. He left the project shortly afterwards.

■ **Manage your finances effectively and build up reserves**. Finding funds for core costs is essential, as is allocating realistic proportions to all projects. It is crucial that the manager remains fully in control of the organisation's finances. Another strategy is to create a sinking fund for building repairs or other irregular outgoings and to build up reserves for emergencies.

---

14 Ability Tec accessed 05.10.18 http://www.abilitytec.co.uk/ http://www.bbc.co.uk/news/business-20970906

■ **Avoid short termism and think long-term**. Networking and staying well-informed is essential to be able to predict trends in policy accurately, in both local and central government, as well as understanding comparable services being provided by other non-profit organisations.

■ **It is critical to produce a practical work or business plan**. Help and advice is available from support agencies. The plan should look ahead for at least three years; this is also a requirement for grants from trusts. As part of the plan, a risk analysis should be included, while the whole plan should be updated and changed regularly as appropriate.

■ If your organisation is so small that you do not employ a specialist fundraiser or consultant, **it is important for managers to seek support or get training in fundraising** (from organisations like NCVO[15] or FSI), or get small grants from trusts to explore and sharpen your strategy and identify new funding opportunities.

■ Successful non-profit **organisations are level-headed and do not rush into taking on unsuitable contracts**.

Conclusion

Perhaps it is something of a cliché, but good managers see opportunities where others just see problems, and small organisations are more nimble and flexible than large ones. In the 1980s, research suggested that most innovations in community care originated from local centre managers. The reason is that managers of small and medium organisations are invariably more in touch with what is going in their service user group and community than national organisations, in which new proposals have to go through various layers of the hierarchy and can end up unconsidered in a pending tray.

It can be relatively easy to ride a wave of success with a fashionable new charity. One prime example of that danger was Kids Company, with its 'charismatic founder… high profile trustees' and its highly publicised services and support from government, which proved to be an unsound basis for survival. On the other hand, long-standing organisations can build a reputation for good work and sustainability that attracts other funders if they take the right steps and recruit and train good staff and trustees.

Networking and research are essential to keep in touch with changing policies, practice and needs, as is being aware of the potential outlook for your project. It is essential not to jeopardise the long term future of your project by focusing on short term gains. However, as we argue in Chapter 4, which deals with procurement, it also requires government to amend

---

15 NCVO Knowhow accessed 05.10.18 https://knowhownonprofit.org/funding/fundraising

the Social Value Act and for local councils to make contracts smaller and therefore more manageable for smaller organisations. Smaller non-profit organisations can survive and prosper over time if they adopt appropriate strategies that they have properly researched and follow the right processes. There are no magic answers to survival, but perhaps Edison came close when he described genius – 99% perspiration and 1% inspiration.

Chapter Ten:
Youth activism

By Kathryn Engelhardt-Cronk

Introduction

In 1903, Mary 'Mother Jones' Harris marched with 400 child labourers
on strike demanding an improvement to working conditions in the textile
mills – one of the earliest modern youth community-based actions intended
to change people's lives for the better. Fast forward to 6 April 2008, when
young activists in Egypt planned the first of the mass strikes that marked
the beginning of the end of Hosni Mubarak's government. The power,
idealism, strength and courage of youth community organisers have left
their imprint on social change movements of all types, but never more so
than today. Whether bringing attention to the plight of women without
access to feminine hygiene products, to lack of educational opportunities
for those in occupied or war-torn countries, to racism, to bias against the
LGBTQ community, to school shootings or to lax gun control rules, to name
but a few social issues, young people are making their voices heard and
initiating profound societal awareness and change. This chapter explores
these movements and their different aspects.

Background

Community youth activism has always played a fundamental part in
driving social change in societies around the world. Young people's natural
questioning of accepted norms asks society to re-examine itself, raises
awareness of social issues and often leads to societal transformation. The
ongoing challenging of social norms by adolescents and young adults shows
no sign of abating. It is a recurring theme: a youthful segment of society
seeks a fundamental change to a system of beliefs or practices in their
countries, in their communities or across the world. They work to reduce
inequality, to fight injustice, to curb violence, to increase opportunities and
to carve a path forward for themselves and others, towards a better future.

These powerful movements to effect change can sometimes be violent
or chaotic, are rarely constrained to local geographies and are almost
universally met with resistance by that society's controlling forces seeking
to maintain the status quo. Yet the idea that, as a group, young people can
make a difference continues with each generation.

Young people often seem to be motivated to organise for social change because it is their nature to challenge what previous generations have done or what they have held to be true. As Robert Kennedy said, 'This world demands the qualities of youth: not a time of life but a state of mind, a temper of the will, a quality of imagination, a predominance of courage over timidity, of the appetite for adventure over the love of ease.'

As adults, with mortgages, taxes to pay, children to raise and jobs to hold down, many settle for the status quo and accept uncomfortable limits. The young, however, are by and large less unencumbered by notions of their own limitations, and this allows them to proceed despite unfavourable odds and intrepidly pursue right over might. It is our collective understanding that these are the traits that define youth and that lay the path for social change.

Youth-driven activism in the 20th and 21st centuries

Since the industrial revolution, and long before the term 'teenager' was coined, young people have been an integral part of protests driving changes in child labour laws, access to housing and other social problems that were a direct result of population movements from the countryside to cities, and the consequent labour movement from agriculture to industry. Beginning in the early 20th century, Jane Addams, known as the 'mother of social work', established recreation programmes for children designed to foster democratic co-operation and collective action and to educate young people in using the power of the group to create social change.

From that time up to the present, social change through youth community activism has grown to become a force that influences public policy and legislation around the world. In the late 1930s, for example, community organiser Saul Alinsky started the Industrial Areas Foundation in Chicago, Illinois, with the goal of uniting ordinary citizens of all ages to demand better, safer neighbourhoods and living conditions. Many consider Alinsky's approach to be the blueprint for community organising movements, an approach that embraces youth inclusion.

In Europe in the 1960s, students were at the forefront of a range of protest movements. Probably the most significant of these took place in France in 1968 and, arguably, led to the downfall of President de Gaulle.

During the tumultuous period of the 1960s in the United States, young black people were at the forefront of the civil rights movement. Starting with the lunch counter sit-ins in Greensboro, Northern Carolina, which eventually turned into the Student Nonviolent Coordinating Committee (SNCC), young people were the key actors in protesting racial discrimination and related violence. Other campaigns, such as the Little Rock Nine and the Birmingham Children's Crusade in 1963, also played an important part in raising awareness of the social injustices of segregationist laws and policies propping up institutionalised racism in the US.

Student-led protests of the 1960s and 1970s against US involvement in the Vietnam War brought youth-driven activism to America's more white and suburban populations. A seminal moment during that era – the deaths of four students marching at Kent State University in Ohio – eventually triggered national political change and was a factor in the eventual end to the presence of US armed forces in Southeast Asia.

Community youth organising is a global phenomenon. The Tiananmen Square protests in China in 1989 were instigated by Chinese students demanding an end to institutionalised corruption, as well as better economic conditions and employment opportunities. The Tiananmen protests resulted in many violent deaths. A full accounting of the Chinese government's actions and a final death toll have never been established or made publicly available.

Young people were also at the forefront of the Hong Kong pro-democracy movement Umbrella and its demonstrations, which started in 2003.[1] China has its own social media companies, which are heavily restricted but still used by organisers. Tear gas was used to break up demonstrations, elected members were disqualified and organisers sentenced to prison. In 2019 anti-extradition bill protests started, again led by young people, which have been larger and more successful than 2003, but they have been as heavily attacked by the authorities and by Triad gangs.

The threat to Turkish civil society after the constitutional referendum of 16 April 2018 spurred groups of young activists to demand change. At great personal risk, people rallied in the streets, about ten per cent employing digital platforms as an organising tool. While their perilous actions had no immediate benefit, mainstream media reported their courage, and some may be inspired in the future to take their own stand against tyranny.

On 14 February 2018, in Parkland, Florida, a gunman opened fire on his classmates at Marjory Stoneman Douglas High School. It was the most recent in a long string of gun-violence incidents in the US after decades of inaction by adults to address a societal problem which seems to have no conceivable end. The students of the school formed the 'March for Our Lives' organisation[2]. A global protest was held on 24 March 2018 in 800 cities

---

1   Parker, Emily New Yorker accessed 24.1.19 https://www.newyorker.com/tech/annals-of-technology/social-media-hong-kong-protests

2   March for our Lives accessed 24.1.19 https://marchforourlives.com

around the world, attended by 1.2 million people. Well organised, articulate and determined, the young people who spurred this movement have sparked a movement towards safer communities and schools.

Adults: adversaries and allies

Adults play an important dual role in youth organising and youth activism: as sceptics and as supporters. Too easily adults will belittle young people's protests against injustice, dismissing them as a matter of inexperience or a lack of knowledge or understanding of the world. Youth organisers and community activists often find themselves dismissed by adults, particularly adults in positions of authority or control. Yet time after time today's youth have exhibited persistence, consistency of message and a compelling argument. Young people have established themselves as a legitimate force to be reckoned with and have gained the respect of many community leaders.

Municipal policymakers and community political influencers repeatedly put up barriers to young people's and grassroots efforts. Confronting this establishment resistance to change can seem a daunting task for young people, who have fewer individual rights and less economic capital.

Consider One Mind Youth Movement (OMYM), which describes itself as 'a group of youth leaders organising out of the Cheyenne River Sioux Tribe in South Dakota'[3] protesting the construction of a massive oil pipeline – a project slated to move half a million barrels of oil a day under the nearby Missouri River, which the tribe claims threatens its main water supply and desecrates sacred ancestral lands. After joining activist adults to confront the guns of the National Guard and sometimes violent physical assault by corporate security guards, the OMYM found the resistance of pipeline stakeholders hard to break. Nonetheless, the youth members of OMYM feel the fight was worth the hardships suffered and they stand ready to try again. As Tokata Iron Eyes, one of the activists, said, 'Our communities have such a hard time. But we don't want to be victims anymore … Now, with this generation of youth, we're just trying to pick ourselves up and start over and live in a good way'.[4] The Federal Court ruled the pipeline illegal in 2017 so the protesters won that step, but the Army Corps simply came back and carried on.[5] The fight will continue,[6] and neither side appears likely to back down.[7]

3   OMYM accessed 24.1.19 https://www.omym.org/
4   You Tube accessed 24.1.19 https://www.youtube.com/watch?v=S2uubENv6MU
5   Earth Justice accessed 24.1.19 https://earthjustice.org/features/faq-standing-rock-litigation
6   The Star Tribune accessed 24.1.19 http://www.startribune.com/standing-rock-sioux-pledges-support-for-pipeline-protests/494524401/
7   The Guardian accessed 24.1.19 https://www.theguardian.com/environment/2018/sep/20/keystone-pipeline-protest-activism-crackdown-standing-rock

Adults can mitigate hesitation and uncertainty by welcoming youth organisations, helping to make connections between youth and other community groups and paving the way for youth to participate in the community.[8] Austin Voices for Education and Youth, a community-based organisation that works to create opportunities for students and families, maintains a public resource centre, the efforts of which include coaching parents to support youth organising. 'When young people interact with adults who value their voice as they participate in community, they begin to use their voice in powerful ways. When young people feel valued and needed and are treated with respect, they are drawn into the community.'[9]

Engaged and involved youth make for healthy, strong communities

In what ways do communities benefit from youth organising? In 'Enhancing Local Capacity and Youth Involvement in the Community Development Process', researchers say 'community involvement provides young individuals with empowerment, skills, and a direct connection to society'.[10]

If youth organising and engagement lead to strong communities, what then is the initial impetus for youth to participate in action? How can young people, in general, be encouraged to become more engaged? Surveyed students were asked what motivated them to become more engaged within their communities. Their answers included social injustice, institutionalised inequality and lack of opportunities in education and employment.

Results also showed that forming a strong and meaningful personal connection to a social cause was a key element. Respondents described this personal connection as occurring through developing knowledge, skills, values and future goals, and in their perception of the value of achieving social goals.

Increased engagement can also be attributed to peers' acknowledgment of their contributions. Peer connection can lead many youths to feel a greater sense of purpose, 'including moral, civic, and social change goals'[11]. 'Perhaps

---

8   M.A. Brennan et al 'Enhancing Local Capacity and Youth Involvement in the Community Development Process', Community Development, 38:4, (2007) 13-27, DOI: 10.1080/15575330709489816

9   Evans, Scot. D., 'Youth Sense of Community', Journal of Community Psychology, Vol. 35, No. 6, (2007): 693–709.

10   M.A. Brennan et al 'Enhancing Local Capacity & Youth Involvement in the Community Development Process', Community Development, 38:4, (2007) 13-27, DOI: 10.1080/15575330709489816

11   Dawes, Nickki Pearce, Reed Larson. 'How Youth Get Engaged: Grounded-Theory Research on Motivational Development in Organized Youth Programs.' Developmental Psychology 47, no. 1 (2011): 259-269.

more than with adults, the community represents the entire context and backdrop for youth life. As a result, they may be actively interested in efforts to develop community and to take leading roles.'[12]

How technology has changed the ways youth organise

Technology is playing a critical role in communication and inspiration in an overwhelming number of current youth activist engagements. Since the advent of text messaging in 1992, the ability to instantly reach millions has changed the global social movement organising landscape. It is claimed that Twitter's advent in 2008 went on to aid political protests in Egypt in 2011 and in other countries, and it has even been blamed for the London riots in 2011.[13]

The scale of use and anonymity that comes with modern communication technologies can support those who act or organise for a cause, along with those who seek to infiltrate and disrupt the activist process. In the past decade, many countries' governments, from Turkey to Thailand, have shut down social media during times of unrest. While both tech tools and user creativity continue to keep a step ahead of attempts to thwart such communications, political crackdowns on internet and social media platforms will continue to be a challenge.

Technology and social media platforms played an interesting new role during the Arab Spring in 2010. Like the students of the Tiananmen protests, young people in Middle Eastern countries such as Egypt,[14] Tunisia and Algeria were protesting corruption and lack of opportunity. They took to the streets and to the internet in protest. Some organisers of the protests communicated via Twitter and Facebook, spreading their messages and information in ways that were not yet restricted by government controls. Nonetheless, these technologies were not enough to tip the scales and successfully bring about revolution.

Twitter has been banned in Iran, even though its effect on protests in 2010 was probably exaggerated. According to Professor Annabelle Sreberny,

---

12 M.A. Brennan et al 'Enhancing Local Capacity and Youth Involvement in the Community Development Process', Community Development, 38:4, (2007) 13-27, DOI: 10.1080/15575330709489816

13 Buettner, Ricardo & Buettner, Katharina (2016). A Systematic Literature Review of Twitter Research from a Socio-Political Revolution Perspective. 49th Annual Hawaii International Conference on System Sciences. Kauai, Hawaii: IEEE. doi:10.13140/ RG.2.1.4239.9442.

14 'Seeds of Change: Revisiting Egypt's April 6 activists,' April 6, 2018, accessed 24.1.19 https://www.aljazeera.com/programmes/rewind/2018/04/cloneofseeds-change-revisiting-egypt-april-6-act-180406164917804.html

'Twitter was massively overrated. But spaces like YouTube and Facebook have been very important for sharing information ... the protests were best organised using SMS.' The importance of social media is perhaps best illustrated by the Iranian government's response, with web sites including YouTube and Facebook being blocked and internet speed deliberately slowed.

More recently, youth activist groups have effectively leveraged technology to get their messages out: the Parkland student groups discussed previously and Black Lives Matter (BLM), which protests police brutality,[15] have effectively utilised social media channels to organise and refine their messaging and effectiveness.

Black Lives Matter is an activist movement which was initiated by three black women to campaign regarding violence and racism towards the black community. It was started in 2013 after George Zimmerman's acquittal after shooting Trayvon Martin dead in Florida. BLM then organised protests over further deaths in New York and Ferguson and has carried on protests over other killings. It has a decentralised structure with local chapters and no formal hierarchy. BLM signifies a new approach: Professor Frederick Harris argues that this 'group-centered model of leadership' is distinct from the older charismatic leadership model of older civil rights organisations. Harris states that 'Black Lives Matter has done more to put issues of institutional racism and criminal justice reform front and centre than a two-term black Democrat in the White House, the 40-plus members of the Congressional Black Caucus, and traditional civil rights leaders and organisations, combined ... Black Lives Matter activists have already won by pushing an issue that was dormant in American politics.'[16]

The growing use of digital media presents another avenue through which social movement organisations (SMOs) can recruit youth participation. While social media platforms, for instance, have been used to communicate, collaborate and recruit in youth-led SMOs, the jury is out on how much of a security risk they may bring for individuals and groups. There are also ongoing questions about such platforms' effectiveness in terms of long-term community action engagement.

Digital technology options are always expanding and are likely here to stay. Nonetheless, digital methods and tools via which youth activism is fuelled and managed are in flux and may be so for some time to come. The best and most effective uses of digital technologies in different types and stages of social activism are still being explored by all generations, but particularly by youth.

---

15 Black Lives Matter accessed 24.1.19 https://www.newyorker.com/magazine/2016/03/14/where-is-black-lives-matter-headed

16 Harris, Prof Fredrick accessed 24.1.19 https://news.columbia.edu/content/5-Questions-Fredrick-Harris-on-Race-in-2016-Election

Where once texting was considered a private and revolution-friendly platform, people around the world today are using Facebook Live and Twitter to share videos in real time, while apps like Signal allow protestors to communicate behind the wall of encryption. So how might new technologies such as social media affect uprisings and activism in the near future? Dr Ramesh Srinivasan of UCLA says: 'I believe that increased access to technology all over the world is fait accompli. That's going to happen. That does not mean that democracy will spread, or that there will necessarily be more effective protests, but it does mean social media is going to be central to how people communicate and network around these issues.'[17]

Much of the research on the use of social media as a tool to propel social change shows mixed results. The assumption that movements for social change always benefit from digital connection is still being debated. 'Studies suggest that the spread of social media among young people and the broader public has had salutary effects on political engagement, but at the same time suggest that the relationship between social media use and engagement may be limited to individuals who would likely be relatively engaged without social media.'[18] It is generally accepted that, while youth are early adopters of the newest technologies, those same technologies may not play a predictable role in organising and social change.

Clay Shirky, author and professor of journalism at NYU, says that much of the narrative on the role of technology and social media has been driven toward the disruptive societal elements, but suggests that 'the potential of social media lies mainly in their support of civil society and the public sphere'.[19] Shirky also observes that 'the adoption of [social media] tools as a way to coordinate and document real-world action is so ubiquitous that it will probably be part of all future political movements.'

Many politicians support policies to reduce climate pollution, such as renewable energy tax credits and fuel economy standards. However, many young activists feel much more is needed – in other words, that Intergovernmental Panel on Climate Change (IPCC) policies are required. The Sunrise Movement is one of the movements for young people fighting climate change in the political sphere.[20] A plan has been proposed, the Green New Deal (GND). While there have been occasional splits in the movement,[21] in general

17 Srinivasan, Dr Ramesh accessed 24.1.19 https://www.inverse.com/article/21806-how-social-media-could-influence-uprisings-2026

18 Xenos, Michale, Ariadne Vromen, Brian D. Loader 'The great equalizer? Patterns of social media use and youth political engagement in three advanced democracies.' *Information, Communication & Society*, 17, no. 2 (2014): 151–167. DOI:10.1080/1369118X.2013.871318

19 Shirky, Prof Clay 'The Political Power of Social Media Technology, the Public Sphere & Political Change', *Foreign Affairs*, Jan/Feb 2011.

20 Sunrise accessed 22.1.19 https://www.sunrisemovement.org/

21 The Atlantic accessed 21.1.19 https://www.theatlantic.com/science/archive/2019/01/first-fight-about-democrats-climate-green-new-deal/580543

the movement has become incredibly successful: a story in Vox analysed the effect of the campaign with regard to social media, such as Google searches over 2017 to 2018, and the results can be seen in Figure 10.1.[22]

Figure 10.1: Google in Vox

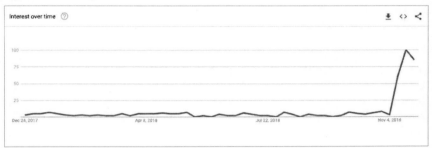

Google

Political activists working on the GND 'expressed surprise at the speed and intensity with which both media attention and activist energy have centered on it. There is a sense among those involved that they have caught a tiger by the tail' and have 'thrust climate change into the national conversation … and created an intense and escalating bandwagon effect … everyone involved in green politics is talking about the GND.' This is shown clearly by the exponential growth in Google searches and Tweets about the Green New Deal.[23]

The school strike movement has developed together with other environmental movements, such as Sunrise, across the world. Greta Thunberg, a Swedish 16-year-old, started the first school strike in August 2018 to protest failures by government to take action on the environment. Since then, the movement has expanded exponentially, into an international climate movement with around 1.6 million students worldwide organising and joining demonstrations to demand stronger action and policies to address climate change.

Undeniably, social media has played an indispensable role in publicising recent political movements. It could be argued that the Arab Spring, for instance, would not have had a worldwide impact without technology – but then it could also be argued that the Arab Spring has ultimately failed, with the exception of Tunisia.

Today it is agreed that social media will be a component to enhance, not replace, traditional youth organising elements such as protests, letter writing campaigns, working with community adults and leaders or canvassing.

22 Vox accessed 21.1.19 https://www.vox.com/energy-and-environment/2018/12/21/18144138/green-new-deal-alexandria-ocasio-cortez

23 Ibid.

What's on the horizon for youth organising?

'The generation underneath the millennials is larger than the generation of millennials. It is also the generation that is starting to vote in 2018 ... and 2020 ... Voting is how we can shape the country going forward and this is our future.' Haley Zink, co-organiser, St Louis 'March for Our Lives' rally

The majority of people in the world are under the age of 30 and more than a quarter of the world's population is under 15. The maths tells us that all baby boomers will soon be outvoted by the youngest of our adult population. While it is appropriate to welcome these new voters and social activists, most experts in social movement organising agree that the youth of today are not waiting for a welcome; they are forging ahead with a new social agenda.

'There's a renaissance of political activism going on, and it exists on every major campus', says Harold Levy, a former chancellor of New York City's public schools who now oversees the Jack Kent Cooke Foundation.[24] Levy attributes this resurgence in part to the growing inequality in educational opportunities in the US. This inequality has contributed to great tensions between institutions and the public they are supposed to serve.

There is some discussion about how youth unemployment is accurately reported. Even though it is particularly high in certain countries (Greece, Spain, Portugal, Italy) for the so-called millennials or Generation Y, some argue that 'American youth is today idler and worse affected by the crisis than their EU and UK counterparts'.[25] A specific feature of Generation Y is that 'their demands are significantly higher than those of their predecessors. These are demands for a better quality of life, a good education, a developed society, a stable labor market, but also demands for themselves. Why do they want more? Simply because they dare to work for more. They are the most educated generation in history but are also trapped in the "Eurocrisis". Disappointed in the authorities, Generation Y finds its own ways to handle the problems it faces.'[26]

Adults, watching from the sidelines, see youth activists attempting to secure justice while determining their own destinies. They admire young aspirations but hope that idealism is not crushed by reality. Some adults suspect that youth activism stands as a tacit criticism of their own past

24 The Atlantic accessed 24.1.19 https://www.theatlantic.com/education/archive/2015/05/the-renaissance-of-student-activism/393749/

25 CEPR accessed 24.1.19 https://voxeu.org/article/youth-unemployment-europe-it-s-actually-worse-us

26 One Europe accessed 24.1.19 http://one-europe.net/debates/youth-activism-in-europe

social and political action (or inaction), as traditional theory suggests that youth comes to the fore of activism in times of structural strain or the collapse of social order.

It may be more likely that today's youth community organisers have their own vision of the future, as have most generations of the 20th and 21st centuries. Already questioning the status quo and willing to take personal risks, while increasingly empowered by media and digital communication platforms, youth are acting with imagination and determination to better the world through youth-led community activism.

Further reading

Astor, Maggie, '7 Times in History When Students Turned to Activism', *New York Times*, 5 March 2018.

Christens, B. D., B. Kirshner (2011). *'Taking stock of youth organizing: An interdisciplinary perspective'*. In C. A. Flanagan & B. D. Christens (Eds.), Youth Civic Development: Work at the Cutting Edge. New Directions for Child and Adolescent Development, 134, 27–41.

Dawes, NP, Reed Larson. 'How Youth Get Engaged: Grounded-Theory Research on Motivational Development in Organized Youth Programs.' *Developmental Psychology* 47, no. 1 (2011): 259–269.

Dunfey, Theo Spanos. 'What Is Social Change and Why Should We Care?,' *Southern New Hampshire University,* 7 November 2017. https://www.snhu.edu/about-us/news-and-events/2017/11/what-is-social-change

Ginwright, Shawn, Tai James. 'From Assets to Agents of Change: Social Justice, Organizing, and Youth Development', *New Directions for Youth Development*, 96 (2002): 27–46.

Green, Matthew. 'The Youth Activists Behind the Standing Rock Resistance (with Lesson Plan),' KQED Learn, May 23, 2017. https://www.kqed.org/lowdown/27023/the-youth-of-standing-rock

Flanagan, Constance, Peter Levine. 'Civic Engagement and the Transition to Adulthood', *The Future of Children*. ERIC Accessed September 3, 2018. https://files.eric.ed.gov/fulltext/EJ883084.pdf

Howard, Philip N., Aiden Duffy, Deen Freelon, Muzammil Hussain, Will Mari, Marwa Mazaid. 'Opening Closed Regimes: What Was the Role of Social Media During the Arab Spring?' *PITPI Working Paper* (2011).

Knefel, John, 'Encrypted App Signal, the Preferred Tool of Cleveland GOP Protesters,' *INVERSE*, 19 July 2016, https://www.inverse.com/article/18505-encrypted-app-signal-the-preferred-tool-of-cleveland-gop-protesters

Mott, Nathaniel. 'Facebook Live Is Becoming the Future of News Before Our Eyes,' *INVERSE*, 8 July 2016, https://www.inverse.com/article/18035-facebook-live-becoming-future-news-before-our-eyes

Chapter Eleven:
All women count:
organising an action
with refugee women

By Marchu Girma

Women for Refugee Women

Women for Refugee Women (WRW) is a small, dynamic charity founded in 2006 to support refugee women and challenge the injustices they experience. WRW works in three connected ways: to empower refugee women to tell their own stories; to influence target audiences by sharing these stories through the media, events and arts; and to create change in the asylum process. To achieve the latter, we publish research and support refugee women to speak directly to politicians and policy makers, so enabling them to understand the impact of current policies and encouraging them to take steps to build a world in which all refugee women in the UK can live with safety, dignity and liberty. By working in these interconnected ways, WRW can enable individual refugee women to become advocates, and work on a wider scale to tackle systems that deny them their rights.

Refugee women's groups in the UK

Women have an incredible gift for coming together to build communities throughout the world. As such, refugee and asylum-seeking women in the UK are coming together throughout different cities in the UK and building communities for themselves. These grassroots groups are founded on the value of helping one another to overcome the incredible pressure and struggles of going through the asylum process.

Some of these groups of women are as small as ten, others as large as 250–300. They come together to support each other, to tell their stories to each other and to share a meal. Some have organised classes and advice workers. Many are run by volunteers in churches and small halls throughout the country. These grassroots groups are the small buds of an alternative society, with alternative ways of doing and being in the world. They are full of diversity, co-operation and creativity that inspires change.

The work of WRW is part of the wider movement of women coming together to make change. WRW has built an effective model of grassroots organising, which centres on our supportive space for refugee and asylum-seeking women in London. Every week more than 100 women come to our centre for English classes, advice, yoga and a warm lunch. However, we don't see our work as just service delivery. Women are encouraged and enabled to find pathways to build their confidence as advocates and to join and lead our work at every level.

We have been working with different groups throughout the country to harness and channel this energy for change. Below is a case study of a Parliamentary lobby we organised called All Women Count. It is an example of how communities can come together and organise for change from the grassroots up. It highlights some of our success and learning.

Case study: All Women Count

Introduction

On International Women's Day 2018, we organised the #AllWomenCount lobby, led by migrant and refugee women to ask Members of Parliament to listen to and support our demands for safety, liberty and dignity. More than 200 refugee and migrant women came together in a room in the House of Commons, a few short doors away from MPs debating women's issues on the day.

An introduction to the issue

Community actions have to be built on the foundations of a firm understanding of the context in which they operate. We can never know all the information about the issue at hand, but it's important to understand the political, social, cultural and economic contexts that will impact or shape our actions. It's important to understand the challenges and injustices experienced by the community, as well as to develop understanding about the wider context that enables such injustice to take place.

The defining issues of the past three years have been the refugee crisis and the rising tide of feminism. Thousands of people have marched under the banners of #RefugeesWelcome[1], started in response to the death of a refugee boy, Alan Kurdi, and #MeToo,[2] started by Tarana Burke. There seems to be real hunger for change. The work of WRW saddles both issues: we are

---

1   The Guardian accessed 19.1.19 https://www.theguardian.com/uk-news/2015/sep/12/london-rally-solidarity-with-refugees

2   New York Times accessed 19.1.19 https://www.nytimes.com/2017/12/07/us/the-metoo-moment-no-longer-complicit.html

committed to supporting refugee women; therefore our work crosses both the refugee and migration sector and the women's sector.

For refugee women, our gender and immigration status are intersecting issues and the scars of their consequences are woven into our everyday experiences. The systemic oppression of being a woman is magnified by not being a citizen, not belonging and not having official papers. Many refugee women find themselves destitute in the UK, with no accommodation, support or access to education and health care.

The root cause of this sense of being unheard, forgotten and ignored is our broken asylum system, which is not gender sensitive.[3] Women have historically found it more difficult to qualify for refugee status than men. The 1951 Refugee Convention states that to qualify for recognition as a refugee, claimants must demonstrate that they have a 'well-founded fear of persecution' which prevents them from returning home, and that their feared persecution is 'for reasons of race, religion, nationality, membership of a particular social group or political opinion'. The wording of the Refugee Convention does not include 'sex' or 'gender', and it has only been in the past two decades that widespread forms of persecution against women, such as rape, honour violence and female genital mutilation (FGM), have been recognised.[4]

Refugee women are not only fleeing persecution by state actors, but sometimes are escaping persecution by non-state actors, such as rape, domestic violence and FGM. One refugee woman told me: *'We may not have come fleeing a war-torn country, but we have come escaping war on us [women].'*

Female migrants and refugees are at greater risk of exploitation and abuse, including trafficking, on their route to safety. Helen (name changed), from Eritrea, had to flee her country and make a horrendous journey to the UK. She told me: *'We crossed the Sahara Desert in a lorry, travelling day and night for 15 days. It was so sandy and hot. Sometimes the men were forced to get off and lie on their backs in the desert. A bright light was shone into their eyes so they couldn't see, and then we women were taken to the back and raped. All of us. They didn't use any protection, nothing.'*

When Helen made her asylum claim in the UK she was refused because the Home Office authorities did not believe her. There is a culture of disbelief in the asylum system and wrong decisions are made at the onset, which then

3   WRW accessed 19.1.19 https://www.refugeewomen.co.uk/wp-content/uploads/2019/01/women-for-refugee-women-reports-refused.pdf
4   WRW accessed 19.1.19 https://www.refugeewomen.co.uk/wp-content/uploads/2019/01/women-for-refugee-women-the-denial-of-asylum-to-women-fleeing-gender-related-persecution.pdf

leads many asylum-seeking people, including women, to a life of destitution and detention.[5] Another woman who was detained in the UK told me: '*It is not what happened to me in my country that broke me, but what happened to me here.*'

Generating ideas from the grassroots

The idea for the All Women County parliamentary lobby came about at the National Refugee Women's Conference held in Manchester in November 2017. This conference was put together in partnership between Women for Refugee Women and Women Asylum Seekers Together (WAST), Manchester. At this conference refugee women from cities across the nation came together to discuss the two pressing issues that are affecting them: detention and destitution.

At the conference, refugee women's community groups from Halifax, Bury, Coventry, Liverpool, Birmingham, London, Swansea and Manchester came together with many supporting organisations from the refugee sector to discuss and hear from each other about the issues of detention and destitution. Here we can see the importance of bringing people face-to-face to generate ideas as well as to inspire people into action.

After listening to many stories from refugee women, many felt that the way forward was to discuss these issues directly with MPs, as the women felt that 'if MPs knew of our ordeal in the asylum process, they would change the policies'.

During the final panel, a decision was made that we needed to raise awareness and connect with MPs about the issues affecting refugee women and we decided on an action to make International Women's Day, 8 March 2018, International Refugee Women's Day. Having a clear date and goal in mind enabled us to focus our energies and develop an appropriate strategy for action.

'Strategy is turning the resources you have into the power you need, to win the change you want', said campaigner and organiser Marshall Ganz.[6] In this case our resources were the many refugee women who attended the conference from different parts of the country, and the networks of people who support us and whom we could galvanise into action on International Women's Day. The spread of refugee women across the country made it possible to target a wide range of MPs over their local constituencies.

---

5   The Independent accessed 19.1.19 https://www.independent.co.uk/news/uk/home-news/number-of-people-granted-asylum-in-uk-down-26-in-a-year-a8504206.html

6   Marshall Ganz accessed 19.1.19 https://marshallganz.com/

At the close of the conference we all had a clear strategy in terms of what we wanted to do and who we wanted to target. The next step was to scope the wider movement to discover what else was happening for International Women's Day and how our idea of making it International Refugee Women's Day would fit. To make this action a success, we needed to secure the participation of the wider refugee and migration sector as well as the women's sector.

Adapting our ideas

Following from the conference, we researched what other plans existed for International Women's Day 2018, and discovered that many women's sector organisations were coming together to mark the centenary of some women gaining the vote in the UK in 1918. 2018 was set to be a year of women's activism around the issue of gender inequality that still exists in society, even though some women have been able to vote for 100 years.

This new information meant that we had to go back to the drawing board to think about how we could merge the ideas of dedicating International Women's Day to refugee women and the centenary celebration of women's vote.

We were willing to adapt our initial idea to flow with the general consensus in the movement. We saw the opportunity to bring these two ideas together, as the struggles of asylum-seeking women today are comparable to women's struggles for the vote a hundred years ago in the UK. We went on to develop the idea further and came up with the All Women Count Parliamentary Lobby on International Women's Day.

Key moments

Collaboration is an important aspect of community action. Women for Refugee Women is a small charity with mainly part-time staff members. Many of our actions are taken with others, to draw together our resources and amplify our voices to make an impact.

Once we had developed the idea of the All Women Count Parliamentary Lobby from the grassroots at the conference in Manchester and from scoping in the wider movement, we invited potential partners to attend a roundtable discussion to consult on the demands for the lobby. More than 15 organisations attended from the women's sector, the migration and refugee sector and grassroots refugee women's organisations.

Choosing a wide message and pledge

It is important to be inclusive to enable as many organisations as possible to join the action you set out to do. Although WRW campaigns specifically on refugee and asylum-seeking women's issues, we widened the demand to also include migrant women, to enable more organisations to join the action.

We also set up a separate, unbranded website to ensure that organisations felt this was a truly joint action, not just a project of WRW. We asked different organisations to contribute to the creation of the website by submitting a blog about their specific campaign asks, under an umbrella pledge to which everyone could sign up.

Together, we decided to ask MPs to take the pledge: '*I pledge to listen to refugee and migrant women and support their rights to safety, dignity and liberty.*' This was a broad pledge that many organisations could coalesce behind and support. Its aim was to inspire people to take action by tapping into their values and beliefs. It galvanised many organisations and grassroots groups as it aligned with the campaigns and actions they were working on already.

At the same time, the pledge was a symbolic stance that MPs could take to show their support for refugee and migrant women, no matter what their political allegiance.

When organising the All Women Count lobby, it was important for us to develop actions that a large number of people could take to create a broad base of support and involvement. Among the plethora of actions were: writing letters to MPs; promoting the #AllWomenCount pledge on social media; meeting MPs to discuss the issues raised by refugee and migrant women; attending the lobby event in Parliament; and asking MPs to take a picture with the pledge and posting the picture on social media.

Having different options for participation allowed supporters to engage at different levels, and to take on as much, or as little, as they could to be part of the All Women Count action.

Galvanising the grassroots into action

Training and knowledge building is a key part of any community action. In organising the All Women Count lobby, we delivered targeted training which gave refugee women an understanding of our strategy, story and structure and the tools they needed to be involved in the action.

The refugee women already had a lot of knowledge about the issues that were affecting them, but we needed to increase knowledge on what Parliamentary lobbying means and about the Suffragette movement.

We devised workshops to build on the knowledge women have already about the political system that exist in the UK. Refugee women come from different backgrounds and educational levels. We wanted as many women as possible to understand the Parliamentary process as well as the significance of the timing of the event, therefore the workshop content was rich in imagery, discussion and performance.

Over a period of few months we delivered workshops for refugee women in London, Birmingham, Coventry and Manchester. Political education was key to ensuring women's participation at the grassroots level. It was important to increase their knowledge of political processes, who their local MPs were and how change happens in the UK context. This enabled them to see why it was important to have a Parliamentary lobby.

Education about the Suffragette movement was important to understand why this moment, International Women's Day, 8 March 2018, was a key moment in the movement. These workshops were filled with 'A-ha!' moments, when we demonstrated the similarities between the issues that British women campaigned on a hundred years ago and refugee women's struggle in the UK today. This helped refugee women to realise that they can consider themselves as modern-day Suffragettes, struggling and fighting very similar issues as British women did a hundred years ago. We made these connections by looking at some of the posters and campaign slogans that were used by the Suffragette movement.

Refugee women come to the UK in the hope of rebuilding their lives and making a new start. They want to belong here and contribute meaningfully. This is made extremely difficult by punitive Home Office policies. Emmeline Pankhurst's words 'we are here, not because we are law-breakers; we are here in our efforts to become law-makers'[7] chimed with the refugee women we work alongside: refugee women are here in the UK not to break laws, but to be law-abiding citizens.

One woman who is currently seeking asylum told us that learning about the Suffragettes has helped her to see her struggle as part of a long line of women's struggles. She does not feel isolated any more, as she has realised she is part of a continuum of women in this country fighting for their rights.

---

7   Thought Co accessed 19.1.19 https://www.thoughtco.com/emmeline-pankhurst-quotes-3530007

This connection between British history and refugee women helped refugee women to feel empowered and draw inspiration from the activism of the past. They recognised that, through participating in the All Women Count lobby of Parliament, they were challenging the government to look at how the most vulnerable in our society are being treated. There has been enormous change for women over the past century because of the struggles of the Suffragettes. Looking at this success helped refugee women to see that their current efforts to challenge the government have consequences for the future, and that they can affect change that can build a better society for everyone.

Everyone can take action

Part of community action is to enable groups to act together as well as alone. As part of the workshops to increase knowledge about the Parliamentary process and the significance of the timing of the event, we encouraged every refugee woman to find out who her MP was and what support she could expect of them. This opened up a new avenue for some to explore ways of getting support for their asylum claim. An MP has a duty of care to everyone who lives in their constituency regardless of their immigration status. We had a high level of participation from refugee women because they felt they could gain something out of this action individually as well as collectively.

We also designed template letters to invite MPs to attend the lobby and meet their constituents. These letters gave an opportunity for individuals to add the specific issues they were concerned about. Some used this opportunity to write about the desperate housing conditions in which they were living, while others wrote about the wrong decisions made by the Home Office on their cases and pleaded for their MP to intervene. More than 50 refugee and asylum-seeking women wrote letters to their MPs.

The template letters were also available on the website, and we encouraged our supporters and the wider network through social media to use it to invite MPs to the lobby. Having a template letter enabled everyone who wanted to take action in a small way to do so, as well as making everyone feel that they were important in making change as part of a collective.

Speakers at the lobby

Our work at WRW is now part of a growing movement to enable those with lived experience of campaign issues to join and lead those campaigns. Early on during the planning stages, we made a decision that the All Women Count lobby was to be led by refugee and migrant women and to ensure that, at the event itself, all the speakers would be migrant and refugee women, except for the MPs.

Over the years WRW have developed different ways of supporting refugee women and providing pathways for them to become advocates for the issues they care about. Harnessing the power of individual and collective stories of the experiences of refugee women in the UK plays a huge role in influencing public opinion. In the lead-up to the lobby we worked with individual women to enable them to shape their speeches and to align their story with the bigger message of the All Women Count pledge.

It takes a great deal of courage for an individual woman to stand up and tell her story of trauma in public, and many women in our network find it very challenging. In view of this we worked with groups of women to develop poetry and performances to tell those stories of trauma, without leaving one person vulnerable in front of an audience.

One of the ways we enabled sensitive stories to be told was through the creation of a group poem. For example, over several weeks leading to the lobby we worked with the grassroots group in Coventry to help the refugee women develop a short poem about destitution. This poem included individual women's struggles with homelessness and sexual abuse, but it was constructed so that the audience did not know which individual woman's story was shared.

Performing using songs and poetry enables the audience to connect to people's stories and the emotion and pain. At the same time, it can be used to uplift and energise the room, leaving the audience inspired by refugee women's journeys.

Resource, resource, resource!

Both the migration and refugee sector and the women's sector are underfunded. Research suggests that while the field of organisations supporting refugees and migrants in the UK is broad, it is also shallow. There are currently around 930 charities working with these groups, but less than one per cent have a turnover of more than £1m, and less than 20% have a turnover above £100,000.[8] Many organisations operate only at local level and are focused purely on service delivery. There have been huge funding cuts to women's sector organisations, and austerity policies have significantly reduced the capacity of the women's voluntary and community sector. At WRW, we have seen how the underfunding of the refugee and migration sector and the cuts to women's sector has had an impact on refugee women's lives.

Organising at the grassroots and working with the most vulnerable in society is resource intensive. At WRW we run a weekly drop-in, which more

---

8   New Philanthropy Capital (2016)

than 100 women attend. We provide transport expenses and lunch for every woman who attends. It is through the consistency of meeting face-to-face on a weekly basis, that we are able to build an action together. The weekly drop-ins are not just a service we provide; they are the stepping stones that provide pathways for greater participation.

Many women who attend our weekly drop-ins took part in the All Women Count lobby, by participating in the training, writing letters to their MPs and attending the event. A group of the women who attend our drama classes performed poems and sang, and one woman who we worked with was empowered to give a speech that included her story.

Organising the All Women County lobby was resource intensive, as WRW provided transport expenses for nearly 200 refugee women who participated. Participants from places such as Manchester and Birmingham came alongside the many women from London. For effective grassroots participation, resource provision is key, as this can be a barrier to participation.

Unexpected moment

While planning a community action, it's important to be flexible and respond to other actions, and to think strategically about how these other events can amplify the action you are planning.

A couple of weeks before the All Women Count lobby, more than a hundred women detained at Yarl's Wood detention centre started a hunger strike. There was lots of media coverage about their resistance. WRW had spent five years working on a campaign to end detention, called Set Her Free,[9] so we were well placed to bring the demands of the hunger strikers to the lobby.

We drew on the point that the hunger strike in Yarl's Wood was reminiscent of the Suffragettes using hunger strikes to protest their innocence when they were locked up for campaigning for their rights. Among the historical photographs of the Suffragette movement, there is an unnamed woman with a banner that reads: 'To ask freedom for women is not a crime, suffrage prisoners should not be treated as criminals'. This criminalisation of women is a sentiment strongly felt by refugee women. If you change the above quote to reflect the experiences of refugee women it would read: 'To ask asylum is not a crime; asylum-seeking women should not be treated as criminals'.

---

9   WRW accessed 25.10.18 https://www.refugeewomen.co.uk/campaign/

We asked the women on the hunger strike to send a message to be read out on the day of the lobby. On International Women's Day they sent a statement saying: 'It is true that women have made much progress in the past century since the Suffragettes won the right for some women to vote, but a hundred years does not negate an entire history of women being treated at best as inferior and at worst as property. We have a long way to go.'

Ensuring the voices of the women detained in Yarl's Wood were heard in Parliament on the day of the All Women Count lobby amplified their voices. Their statement was also published in full by the *New Statesman* magazine and quoted in other media coverage.

It is important while planning a community action, therefore, to be flexible and react to other events coming up from elsewhere. We could not have planned the hunger strike, nor did we know that it was going to take place. However, we were able to support an unexpected action, to amplify both the voices of the hunger strikers and the women involved in the All Women Count lobby.

Media coverage

The media is a key aspect of amplifying the actions we take as a community and ensuring others know about it. Framing the issue in the right way and having a 'hook' is essential in getting media coverage.

The All Women Count lobby enabled us to frame the issue of migrant and refugee women's rights in terms of women's rights. We linked the story of the past, the history of the heroism of the Suffragettes, to the story of the now – the lack of rights of refugee and migrant women. We also had a hook: the lobby was being held on International Women's Day.

Before the event we prepared a press release to distribute to mainstream media outlets. On the day of the event, we created a photo opportunity outside the Palace of Westminster. We invited everyone who was attending the event to bring their banners and placards. We also designed a huge All Women Count banner that was held at the front. We invited journalists to come to the photo opportunity to get the best pictures of the day. We also had our own photographer, who took pictures and uploaded them to our social media and the lobby website.

As a result we were able to secure media coverage across a range of TV, print and digital channels, ensuring that the messages of the lobby reached beyond the walls of Parliament.

Volunteers

Volunteers are a key aspect of community action. As a small organisation we rely on volunteers to run our drop-ins, and to provide support when we have events. We invest a lot of time in recruiting the right people for the roles, as well as ensuring that the right policies are in place to support their growth and work in the organisation. A clearly defined role and expectations are important at the onset of a volunteer's journey to enable them to carry out their volunteer role properly. Volunteers provide a huge pool of resources that can uplift community actions.

At the All Women Count Lobby, there were ten volunteers who had different roles and supported the day in diverse ways, including meeting different groups, meeting speakers, greeting guests, taking photographs and handling social media. We invited experienced volunteers from our organisation who already knew the way we work, and who had an understanding of why the action we were taking was important. We held one-to-one meetings with them before the lobby so that they knew their role clearly and were familiar with who to contact in the case of unexpected events.

After the action

After a one-off action such as the All Women Count lobby, it is important to reflect on the success of the action as well as any learning. Decisions need to be made about how the energy from such an action can be carried forward into continuing the campaign.

The All Women Count lobby was a success in the following ways. It enabled us to reach new MPs as well as strengthen existing relationships. It helped to bring together many of the refugee and migration grassroots groups as well as the women's sector, forming a coalition of 40 organisations. There was media coverage, including in the BBC's *Victoria Derbyshire* show, the *Daily Mirror*, *Stylist* magazine and various online platforms. Most importantly, it inspired the many refugee and migrant women who attended and empowered them to continue acting together to create more change.

As 2018 was the centenary celebration of the women's vote, we were presented with other opportunities to continue the energy of the All Women Count pledge. For example, on 10 June 2018, thousands of women processed in London, Edinburgh, Cardiff and Belfast to mark the centenary of some women gaining the vote. WRW joined the London procession with our hand-stitched All Women Count banner, calling for safety, dignity and liberty for all women. This event has enabled us to continue to raise awareness about the particular challenges faced by refugee women. The banner will now be part of an exhibition, placed alongside other banners from the event. This has enabled us to continue to reach new audiences with our messages.

Conclusion

There are many aspects to a community action. Some of the key points are highlighted above in using the example of the All Women Count Parliamentary Lobby, including the importance of knowing the context, bringing people and ideas from the grassroots, setting a clear goal and being able to adapt the ideas generated to complement the wider movement. We found that it is important to be inclusive and open to collaboration, as well as being ready to act on opportunities that arise. Training, resources and having a wide range of actions are necessary for wider participation especially in making sure people with lived experience can fully take part. The All Women Count Parliamentary Lobby has strengthened the national network of refugee women's organisations and formed the foundations for a bigger grassroots movement for change.

Chapter Twelve: How austerity has damaged the foundations of UK civil society

By Andy Shields FRSA

Introduction

In 2008 the global financial crisis caused a worldwide recession and a marked shrinking of the UK economy. According to analysis by the Institute of Fiscal Studies (IFS), there was a significant reduction in GDP per capita and the recovery that followed produced weaker growth than had been projected before the financial crisis. By Q3 2017 this had resulted in a gap of 15% between GDP per capita achieved and the pre-crash estimates[1].

By the 2010 general election, the financial crisis had already had a significant impact upon the tax take of the government, and public sector borrowing had increased significantly to fill the gap. The new government decided that the increased public borrowing was unsustainable and introduced a programme of austerity. This chapter seeks to offer an analysis of the impact of the cuts that have been made. These cuts have resulted in the closure or decommissioning of services, while for many of the services that remain there has been a reduction in the input that service users can receive; one example is that the numbers of health visitors are being cut, so that some health visitors now have 829 children under the age of five on their caseload, instead of the recommended 250[2].

Austerity has affected both the members of the public who receive the government funded services and the providers that deliver them (both third sector and for-profit providers). Some of the changes brought about by austerity could have resulted in increased efficiency and better value for the tax payer. Some services were perhaps not necessary and their closure has had little impact. However, there is without question a measurable negative impact of austerity on areas that affect people's quality of life, and we give examples

---

1   IFS Autumn 2017 Budget: options for easing the squeeze, Nov. 2017 accessed 1.1.19
    https://www.ifs.org.uk/publications/10010

2   The Guardian accessed 1.1.19 https://www.theguardian.com/society/2018/sep/23/health-visitors-struggle-with-dangerously-high-caseloads

later. We are also seeing the creation of problems that will cost more to fix than they would have cost to prevent: one example is the escalating effect of homelessness, which we explore later.

Austerity

The programme of austerity has not been applied evenly across government departments with spending on health and education being protected and a number of departments experiencing deep cuts. Perhaps the most notable reductions in budgets that have a direct impact upon local communities include the following:

- Grants from central government to councils have been reduced by 49.1% in real terms over the period 2010–11 to 2017–18,[3] although councils have been allowed by government to raise council tax by a relatively small amount to fund additional social care.

- At the same time there have been controls on local government's ability to increase council tax and we have seen a real terms reduction in councils spending power of 28.6%.

- Ministry of Justice – analysis by the IFS indicates a 40% real terms reduction in the Departmental Expenditure Limit between 2010–11 and 2019–20[4].

- Department of Work and Pensions – Analysis by the Institute for Government indicated a 37% real terms reduction in the Departmental Expenditure Limit between 2010–11 and 2016–17[5].

Impact

Cuts of the magnitude described cannot be absorbed without a very significant impact upon services and the impact can be seen in every community. Some headlines that show the types of impact experienced by the austerity agenda are:

- According to the Nursing and Midwifery Council, the number of registered mental health practitioners dropped from 92,027 in 2010 to 89,065 in 2016. Yet mental health services are universally recognised as being chronically underfunded.

---

3   National Audit Office (NAO) Financial sustainability of local authorities 2018 accessed 1.1.19 https://www.nao.org.uk/report/financial-sustainability-of-local-authorities-2018/

4   IFS Autumn 2017 Budget: options for easing the squeeze Nov 2017 accessed 1.1.19 https://www.ifs.org.uk/publications/10010

5   Institute for Government accessed 1.1.19 https://www.instituteforgovernment.org.uk/explainers/departmental-budgets

■ The number of young people arriving in A&E with psychiatric problems has doubled since 2009.

■ There has been a sharp increase in the number of care home providers becoming bankrupt: in 2010, 32 failed; in 2015, the number was 74, and in 2016 the number was 75. Care homes have been hit not only by cuts to local authority funding, but also by the increased costs of providing the higher national minimum wage.[6]

■ Many local authorities are at 'breaking point' and some, such as Northampton[7] may have had to declare insolvency; others are near that point[8]. Their spending on public services was 22% lower in 2017 than in 2010[9]. The County Council Network, a Conservative-dominated organisation, is predicting £900 million of further cuts from 2019[10].

■ According to one piece of research, by 2020 authorities will have faced real-terms cuts of up to £30 billion over the preceding decade.

■ Since 2011 there has been a reduction of 20% in the amount spent on policing by the Home Office. The number of police officers dropped from 143,769 in 2009 to 124,066 in the year ending March 2016.[11] There is clearly a link with increased crime.

■ Post-2015 welfare reforms will take almost £13bn a year from claimants by 2020–1. This brings the cumulative cuts since 2010 to £27bn a year – equivalent to £690 a year for every adult of working age.[12]

More specifically, there are a number of types of services that are funded from public sources (often provided by charities) that have suffered a significant impact as a result of austerity. The case studies below outline and quantify the impact of these cuts.

6   The Guardian accessed 1.1.19 https://www.theguardian.com/society/2017/may/05/social-care-crisis-record-number-of-uk-homes-declared-insolvent

7   The Economist accessed 1.1.19 https://www.economist.com/britain/2017/01/28/britains-local-councils-face-financial-crisis

8   Daily Telegraph accessed 1.1.19 https://www.telegraph.co.uk/politics/2018/08/09/crisis-hit-council-expected-cut-vital-services-effectively-declared

9   The Guardian accessed 1.1.19 https://www.theguardian.com/society/2018/may/18/tory-council-at-risk-of-bankruptcy-slams-broken-funding-system

10 County Councils Network accessed 1.1.19 https://www.countycouncilsnetwork.org.uk/englands-largest-councils-set-to-outline-another-raft-of-savings-this-winter-with-1bn-in-new-reductions-needed-to-balance-budgets

11 House of Commons Library: Social Indicator 2615 accessed 1.1.19 http://researchbriefings.files.parliament.uk/documents/SN02615/SN02615.pdf

12 Sheffield Hallam University accessed 11.10.18 https://www4.shu.ac.uk/research/cresr/sites/shu.ac.uk/files/welfare-reform-2016_1.pdf

Rough sleeping

Rough sleeping was an issue that was largely under control before austerity, but the wholesale closure of supported housing schemes and mental health services and cuts to substance use programmes has had a direct impact. People with multiple problems, who, when there were appropriate services, managed to remain housed, have ended up on the streets, and the increase in every city centre is obvious. The Ministry for Housing, Communities and Local Governments street count figures indicate that, for the whole of England, there were on any given night in 2010 an average of 1,768 rough sleepers. By 2017 this had risen to an average of 4,751 (nearly a threefold increase). For every rough sleeper counted there will be many individuals who are precariously housed, and it is reasonable to assume that the number of these people has also increased in a similar way[13].

Supported housing

Social housing has reduced sharply in number since 2012 and is predicted to fall by 230,000 units by 2020[14]. In addition, supported housing has been under significant pressure since 2010, with cuts to budgets year on year. This initially resulted in providers trimming staffing, but over time the levels of savings that councils needed to make meant that schemes were decommissioned. Supporting People as a funding stream was simply rolled into local authority funds; the ring fence was removed; and, as the amount of grant paid to local government was reduced by central government, the local authority focus was inevitably to discharge their statutory duties first, which resulted in a significant reduction in the funds available for supported housing.

A report produced by the National Housing Federation and Sitra[15] concluded that demand for supported housing for people of working age was 125,196 lettings during 2015/16. Sitra estimated that there were 109,556 available places in supported housing for those of working age in 2015/16, amounting to a shortfall of 15,640. If current trends continue, the annual shortfall will grow to 29,053 by 2019/20.

Adult social care

The pressure that the adult social care system is under has rarely been out of the news since the financial crisis in 2008. The estimated number of people aged 65 and over increased by 14.3% between 2010–11 and 2016–17,

13 UK Government accessed 1.1.19 https://www.gov.uk/government/statistics/rough-sleeping-in-england-autumn-2017

14 Channel 4 accessed 1.1.19 https://www.channel4.com/news/factcheck/factcheck-jeremy-corbyns-housing-claims

15 National Housing Federation and Sitra 2015 accessed 1.1.19 https://www.housing.org.uk/resource-library/browse/supported_housing_understanding_need_and_supply/

yet day-to-day spending on adult social care fell by nearly ten per cent in real terms between 2009/10 and 2014/15. However, since then it has begun to grow; the IFS estimated that in 2016/17 spending was around five per cent below 2009/10 levels. The IFS estimated that adult social care made up 35.6% of 2016/17 council-controlled budgets (compared with 30% in 2010/11) and that it would rise again to 36.9% in 2017/18[16].

With regard to social care spending, increased demand and reduced available funding has caused a number of issues that are a real challenge for the sector. These include:

- The reduction in the rates paid to providers against a background of rising costs, especially staffing costs relating to the recent increases in the minimum wage. As a result, some private and charitable care providers are closing homes[17].

- Some local authorities are unable to let domiciliary care contracts because no one can afford to deliver the service for the funding available. In March 2017 *The Guardian* reported that 95 councils had contracts cancelled by care providers that could not afford to deliver services at the available rates[18].

- The amount of care available to many users of domiciliary care contracts is inadequate. According to Age Concern in April 2018, more than 1.2 million older people did not receive the help they needed with essential activities. This means nearly 1 in 8 older people now live with some level of unmet need with vital everyday tasks[19].

- The largest funding cuts to services supporting poor families have occurred in the most economically deprived areas of England, potentially trapping them in a 'downward spiral' of poverty, according to new research by the Lloyds Foundation[20].

Youth services

Youth services are funded from a variety of sources, but local government is perhaps the most important. Given that local authorities have seen their real-terms spending power diminish by nearly 30% in the past eight

---

16 Ibid

17 Daily Telegraph accessed 1.1.19 https://www.telegraph.co.uk/news/2018/01/13/nhs-crisis-fuelled-closure-1000-care-homes-housing-30000-pensioners/

18 The Guardian accessed 1.1.19 https://www.theguardian.com/society/2017/mar/20/care-contracts-cancelled-at-95-uk-councils-in-funding-squeeze

19 Age Concern 'Why call it care when nobody cares?' April 2018 accessed 1.1.19 http://www.edf.org.uk/age-uk-campaign-report-why-call-it-care-when-nobody-cares/

20 www.lloydsbankfoundation.org.uk/

years, they have had to decommission numerous services and focus on the provision of services that directly address their statutory duties. This has meant that many preventative services have closed, including many youth services. Between 2012 and 2016, 603 youth centres were closed; between 2011 and 2014, 35,000 hours of outreach youth work were cut, according to a Unison survey[21] (and presumably more since 2014). For the first time since the 1970s there is no specialist youth employment project, even though the number of young people not in employment, education or training has risen. In addition, cuts in mental health services have put young people at risk.

Mental health

There has been extensive media coverage about mental health services being underfunded and much talk about the length of time it can take for an individual to be diagnosed and accepted as a patient by services, and the increased distance that patients have to travel for treatment[22]. Even though the NHS has overall has seen a small real-terms increase in funding since 2010, this funding has primarily been used to pay for services associated with the aging population. According to the Royal College of Psychiatrists in 2018, the total income available to Mental Health Trusts in 2016–17 was £105m lower than in 2011–12 at today's prices.[23]

Substance misuse

Substance misuse treatment is also under pressure, according to an article published by the Independent in August 2017[24]. Freedom of Information figures show that the 118 councils that replied are spending a total of £452m on alcohol and drug misuse strategies from public health grants in 2016/17, compared with £535m in 2013/14 – a cut of 15.5%. This must in turn have a knock-on effect on problems such as crime and mental health.

Offender services

The problems within the prison system have been widely reported, with a cut of more than 25% in the number of prison officers causing all sorts of difficulties in running any regime that is rehabilitative. In 2018 an initiative to recruit and train 2,000 new prison officers was undertaken, which is

---

21 Unison accessed 1.1.19 https://www.unison.org.uk/content/uploads/2016/08/23996.pdf

22 The Guardian accessed 1.1.19 https://www.theguardian.com/society/2018/aug/29/children-forced-to-travel-hundreds-of-miles-for-nhs-mental-health-treatment

23 Royal College of Psychiatrists accessed 1.1.19 https://www.rcpsych.ac.uk/mediacentre/pressreleases2018/mentalhealthtrustincome.aspx

24 The Independent accessed 1.1.19 https://www.independent.co.uk/news/uk/home-news/spending-on-drug-and-alcohol-treatment-slashed-by-105m-in-four-years-a7912531.html

expected to help. At the same time that we have seen a significantly falling head count of prison officers, we have seen a large increase in assaults on staff in prisons (more than doubled since 2013), prisoner-on-prisoner assaults (up more than 50% since 2013) and self-harm (up more than 60% since 2014). We have also seen a decrease in the provision of education within prisons and a consequent fall in the number of prisoners achieving Level 1 and 2 qualifications in English and Maths[25]. There must also be a link between these cuts and prison riots and deaths in custody.

It is also the case that the services provided to offenders and ex-offenders in the community have been both reformed and cut considerably. The reform of the Probation Service through Transforming Rehabilitation (TR) has brought positive changes, including the supervision of those sentenced to 12 months or less. However, TR also involved a cut of 25% of the funding for probation services and this has had a considerable impact upon the amount of support individuals can expect to receive. The performance of the Probation Service has been criticised by the Justice Committee, chaired by the Conservative MP Robert Neill.[26]

Recidivism rates in Britain are very high – 44% of adults are reconvicted within one year of release. For those serving sentences of less than 12 months this increases to 59%. This is even higher for young people, with nearly 69% reoffending within 12 months of being released from custody. Yet Youth Offending Teams (YOTs) have been cut from £145 million in 2010/11 to just £72 million in 2017/18, although they had achieved huge success in supporting young people to prevent their involvement in crime, with an 85% drop in first time entrants to the youth justice system.[27]

The race to the bottom

The cuts in funding that commissioners face mean that they want more for less and are often caught between having a legal duty to provide an intervention and yet not having enough money to pay for a service.

Efficiency measures were taken long ago and now commissioners are often left with a choice of further trimming services to the point where they are no longer effective, or even cutting entire services.

25 Institute for Government accessed 1.1.19 https://www.instituteforgovernment.org.uk/publication/performance-tracker-autumn-2017/law-and-order/prisons
26 UK Parliament accessed 1.1.19 https://www.parliament.uk/business/committees/committees-a-z/commons-select/justice-committee/news-parliament-2017/transforming-rehabilitation-report-published-17-19
27 Prison Reform Trust accessed 10.6.18 http://www.prisonreformtrust.org.uk/portals/0/documents/bromley%20briefings/s ummer%202017%20factfile.pdf

The consequences of this have been decommissioning of services, some providers withdrawing from markets and some bankruptcies. This is not just something that affects third sector providers; austerity has also caused difficulties for some very large multinational companies, such as Carillion, who have been bankrupted, and others that have issued profit warnings. While there is still a market and plenty of tendering activity, the margins that providers can make are so low that the long-term viability of many services is questionable and the quality of provision has inevitably suffered.

If, for example, we look at the adult social care sector, we have had local authorities seeking to commission services at an hourly rate that makes it hard for providers to comply with the law and pay carers the minimum wage; at the same time, the care managers at the council are reducing the amount of input each individual can get, which means that carers are often left with only enough time to meet very basic needs. This in turn means that many professional carers have chosen to leave the profession, both because they cannot provide services in a way that they are comfortable with and because they can earn more in other jobs. The social care sector has been on the verge of collapse for years. With an aging population the situation will continue to get worse and the lack of proper spending on social care is without question putting pressure on the NHS, with people in hospital who could be cared for in the community if suitable services were available. This is evidenced by recent winter pressures which have been well publicised, and recognition that that the NHS and social care need new real-terms investment to prevent complete collapse.

The Prime Minister announced new funding for the NHS in June 2018[28]. This new funding, which represents an average real-terms increase in funding of 3.4% a year over the next five years, is aimed at enabling the NHS to cope with changing population demographics and get out of its current difficulties. The NHS is one of the services that has been protected from the cuts that have been applied to other public services; nevertheless, it still in very real difficulty. This extra funding is still seen as inadequate by many, including the National Audit Office[29].

False economies

The cuts that are the result of austerity have saved public money in the short term but they have also created problems that will cost money to put right. Austerity is unsustainable and eventually will need to be reversed, either because public opinion demands it or because the problems created start to cost more to resolve than they cost to prevent.

28 UK Government accessed 1.1.19 https://www.gov.uk/government/news/prime-minister-sets-out-5-year-nhs-funding-plan
29 The Guardian accessed 1.1.19 https://www.theguardian.com/society/2018/jul/01/mays-extra-cash-for-nhs-is-not-enough-says-spending-watchdog

For example, the increase in the number of rough sleepers can be reasonably assumed to be caused at least in part by the decommissioning of the supported housing schemes that have traditionally been used to get people off the streets. Street homelessness is known to be stressful and that can result in an increase in both the prevalence of mental health conditions and substance misuse. Rough sleeping also can result in the development of physical health problems which need treatment. Finally, many rough sleepers get into trouble with the law, often because they feel they have little to lose. A single problem can often create a set of circumstances where an individual develops multiple problems, and all of these problems can cost the taxpayer money. As well as the personal suffering that that austerity causes for the individual who can no longer access services, there is a long-term cost for the taxpayer of resolving a set of issues that have become entrenched.

An individual who is street homeless but goes on to have deteriorating mental health, a substance misuse problem, physical health issues and a history of offending no longer just needs help with housing and finding a job, but will additionally cost:

■ the NHS additional funds for treatments that would not have been necessary if they had not become an entrenched rough sleeper

■ local authority finance to pay for substance misuse services

■ the police time and money to investigate any crimes they are involved in

■ the Ministry of Justice resources to take the individual through the court system and put them in prison.

By this time the individual has most likely become unemployable and is likely to spend the rest of their life on benefits and in relative poverty. This is not only a human tragedy, it is also an enormous waste of public resources.

Impact funding

A case can be made for austerity and the importance of cutting our cloth according to our means, but more thought needs to be given to the scenario where a cut will ultimately cost more than the saving made.

Perhaps an answer is to seek to commission services that demonstrate an impact with a greater financial value than the cost of the service (i.e. the cost of a supported housing service can be offset against a demonstrated reduction in crime and hospital admissions).

The Treasury is deeply suspicious of cost–benefit arguments, as they have often been used during comprehensive spending reviews but the promised savings never actually materialise (e.g. prisons don't close, hospital wards don't close).

However, this does not mean that there is no merit in such an argument. If there is not an immediate way to relax austerity and provide a little more money for community services, then perhaps the available funds can be better targeted to pay for services that can demonstrate the most impact.

Importantly, the service that can demonstrate the most impact is not necessarily the cheapest service. It is clearly better to spend £2 achieving an outcome that results in savings of £5 elsewhere in the system than to spend £1 creating an outcome that ultimately saves the taxpayer just £2. Too often because of siloed thinking we see commissioners seeking the cheapest way to achieve the specific outcome in which they are interested, rather than considering the bigger picture and the additional impact that provision can and should be expected to deliver.

An example of how impact funding might work would be a service that provides mentoring and other support to 100 young offenders who have been released from Youth Offender Institutions (YOI) and costs £200k a year to deliver. We know that seven in 10 children (69%) sent to prison are reconvicted within a year of release and that this rises to 78% for those serving sentences of less than six months[30]. We also know that a place in a YOI costs £75k a year[31]. If the provider of the service was paid based on the reoffending rate of the cohort of young people that it worked with, then to be cost neutral it needs to demonstrate a reduction in reoffending that might result in the young people not serving a further two years and eight months between them at a YOI. The metric of what the breakeven point is would be quite easy to demonstrate and such approaches have been trialled through Social Impact Bond projects. Of course, there would also be further benefits to society, such as that young people are more likely to finish their education and become more employable if they are not reconvicted (a similar scheme, the Peterborough Social Impact Bond project for young adult offenders, seemed to be working well but was cut short by the Probation Service reorganisation)[32].

This type of approach does result in some challenges for organisations in terms of cash flow, with potentially long periods of time between work being undertaken and payment for the ultimate outcome being made, but if adopted a scale could make real and sustainable savings.

---

30 Crisis accessed 1.1.19 https://www.crisis.org.uk/ending-homelessness/homelessness-knowledge-hub/cost-of-homelessness/

31 Answer to a written Parliamentary question to Andrew Slaughter 19/01/16 accessed 1.1.19 https://www.parliament.uk/business/publications/written-questions-answers-statements/written-question/Commons/2016-01-19/23107/

32 Barrow Cadbury Trust accessed 1.1.19 https://www.barrowcadbury.org.uk/news/peterborough-sib-worlds-1st-social-impact-bond-shown-cut-reoffending-make-impact-investors-return

Many of the issues that services seek to address are issues that can endure and cause disadvantage to individuals throughout their lives, and in some cases the problems can become intergenerational. Intervening and breaking the cycle with these issues is not easy, but can result in very large savings.

Conclusion

It is of course for the government of the day to decide on taxation, the levels of borrowing and the allocation of available resources. However, the approach chosen needs to be kept under review to ensure that the consequences of austerity do not cost more to put right than the money saved through the cuts in the first place. A false economy must be avoided, both for economic reasons and due to the human suffering that cuts can cause.

The recent announcement of increased real-terms funding to the NHS has come in response to very real problems in the delivery of effective health services and is perhaps a partial reversal of the austerity agenda. There is a real issue of how to find the increased funding, with further borrowing not being acceptable to the government and the expectation of growth or a 'Brexit dividend' paying for the increased funding not being credible in the short term. The government has concluded that the only way to meet this new cost is to increase taxation. Increasing taxation is unpopular and unlikely to be used as a way to reverse austerity across public services.

Growing the economy, and as a result increasing tax revenue, is a much more sustainable way to increase the funds available for public spending. To do this, we need investment both in public infrastructure and in developing new enterprise. There are a number of think tanks suggesting that we need to borrow more to invest in R&D and infrastructure to stimulate growth and as a result enable the economy to grow[33]. This growth will enable tax revenues to increase, which in turn can be invested in further services and investment that will stimulate further growth. This is the type of virtuous circle that the German economy benefits from and there is no reason why such an approach cannot be successful in the UK.

Publicly funded services do need to be accountable, and to demonstrate the impact they have both on individuals and in savings that can be taken down the line. A shift in focus to 'impact funding' is one way that this could be achieved.

Public services and many of the charitable organisations that help deliver these services have been badly damaged by austerity. It is also the case

---

33   Bath University accessed 1.1.19 http://www.bath.ac.uk/publications/alternatives-to-austerity/attachments/alternatives-to-austerity.pdf

that austerity and welfare reform has had the greatest impact upon the poorest in society. At the same time, we see record numbers in work; this should mean more prosperity and growth, but we are not seeing that. The evidence points to the economic burden of the global financial crisis of 2008/9 being disproportionately borne by those that can afford it least. The current approach is not equitable and is demonstrably not working; an injection of investment into services and infrastructure will both stimulate the economy and produce growth, as well as addressing some of the problems faced by society. Over time, austerity may reduce future borrowing, but if the economy is smaller then the national debt measured as a percentage of GDP still increases.

(Note: As I am writing this in October 2018, the Prime Minister has just announced at the Conservative Party Conference 'an end to austerity'; whether this will actually materialise and feed through as improved public services is disputed both by the IFS[34] and by the Resolution Foundation[35]).

Case study
Austerity has destroyed the community projects that equip young offenders and truants with new skills and a sense of purpose
By Don Macdonald

I have been involved in youth services for more than 50 years, starting as a volunteer for a Bermondsey youth club, when the docks were still open, running summer camps for boys and girls. I believe that if the government really wants to reduce knife crime, they need to give us back our youth services, our youth training projects and hostels for young people.

In 1969 I became a teacher. I soon found that some children, bored at school, were completely different in the adventure playground that I ran at weekends. One lad, Mickey, got into trouble; his school report was appalling, but in court I spoke about how positive he was in the playground, making structures and being helpful, and eventually he started on building work with his father. **(Note to Education Secretary: adventure playgrounds are best for children when there are staff to encourage and guide them.)**

I trained as a youth worker and in 1972 got a job with a charity working with young offenders and truants. We set up a small education project and decorated a shop and basement ourselves. We did schoolwork in the mornings, cooked lunch and then did an activity. Some days I would pick up three brothers from a dysfunctional family, who had each slept in a different house, none of them their own. For two brothers the project was too late; one continued to offend, never learned to read and received a lengthy custodial sentence for armed robbery; another did learn to read, but 30 years later died in a drug deal gone wrong. However, most of the children did well and turned their lives around. Some years later I bumped

---

34 Independent accessed 1.1.19 https://www.independent.co.uk/news/uk/politics/end-austerity-theresa-may-promise-20bn-public-cuts-institute-for-fiscal-studies-a8568071.html

35 Resolution Foundation accessed 1.1.19 https://www.resolutionfoundation.org/media/blog/the-end-of-austerity-not-so-much

into one of them. He had been a chronic truant and petty criminal but had learned enough maths and English to become a mechanic and had settled down. **(Note to Home Secretary: community alternatives are much more effective than prison, and cheaper.)**

By the 1980s youth unemployment had started to bite, so for another charity in a different part of London, I set up a youth centre as an alternative to custody, including an employment project with training in computers, electronics, construction and basic skills. This practical project helped Derek, a young lad who had been caught up in street robbery, who used the project's support to settle down and get a job, as most young men do in the fullness of time if they can be kept out of custody. **(Note to Employment Minister: apprenticeships have declined in number and this government does not fund any specialist youth employment projects.)**

By the 1990s another problem surfaced as youth homelessness increased. I was asked to set up a national network of hostels to support young people with no home and no job. An enormous effort by local community groups, including the YMCA and housing associations, helped build a network that now numbers more than 100 hostels. As well as providing housing, projects educate and mentor more than 5,000 young people with issues such as offending – young people like Kelvin, who was, in his own words, angry, aggressive and immature after spells in prison, but who feels he has grown up since living in a Foyer hostel. In addition, these projects generated local investment and employment in those towns left behind by the UK's economic inequality. But funding cuts have reduced staffing and services in these projects and several have had to close, including work in Ipswich, Chichester and Newham. **(Note to Housing Minister: how is the government going to solve homelessness if hostels close as funds are withdrawn?)**

I now chair a small youth integration charity, London Football Journeys, which uses football, video-making and group work to enable young people from deprived areas to learn new skills, introduce new experiences and run exchanges between youth groups in different areas. We work with some young people, who are at risk of being excluded because they are unlikely to contribute to their schools' exam target**s (Note to Education Minister: allowing schools to exclude pupils on this basis only builds up trouble in the future).** However, cuts to our partner youth projects and schools mean there is now less staff involvement and follow-up work to support them.

Young people have been hit hardest by austerity, while my generation retains free bus travel, index-linked pensions and other benefits. Yet there is one youth programme that I would cut: the heavily criticised National Citizen Service, David Cameron's pet project, which wastes money, according to MPs. These funds should be diverted to something worthwhile.

If the government is serious about tackling youth crime, it should dump austerity and support proper preventive services in the community.

(A version of this case study was first published on *The Guardian* web site and permission has been given to reprint): https://www.theguardian.com/public-leaders-network/2018/apr/14/worked-young-people-50-years-advice-amber-rudd-knife

Opinions: Getting back to being connected: how housing associations should change

By Charles Fraser

Introduction

For 35 years after the war, the responsibility for building new homes on any scale rested with the private sector and local councils. The high point of council house building was reached in 1953, when 220,000 homes were built. 1978 was the last year when the total number of new homes built (private sector, council and housing association) reached 250,000.

While new public house-building was seen as the job of councils, housing associations had a different purpose. Social reformers and philanthropists had played a pioneering role in the 19th century in developing high-quality housing for the working poor. This provision was not that extensive, with the result that by the 1960s many households had no option but private sector landlords, some of whom were notoriously exploitative. A new grassroots social activism emerged in response to this, where locally credible groups competed with these landlords in order to provide housing free from harassment and overcrowding. They formed housing associations, and surfed the wave of determination to tackle the cruel human consequences of housing shortage which had been so vividly exposed in *Cathy Come Home*. They were close to the communities they served, as could be seen in their names (Notting Hill Housing Trust, Brent People's HA, Paddington Churches HA etc). The cornerstones of their professional and emotional appeal were good quality housing, community engagement, hands-on management and human-scale accountability.

Thatcher government

A step-change took place in 1980 with the election of Mrs Thatcher and the introduction of Right to Buy: between 1980 and 2013, 1.6 million council homes were sold. More than that, they were not replaced – councils stopped building. By 2016, just under 8% of us were living in council housing (compared to 42%

in 1979). By the 1990s housing associations were being encouraged by government to assume the responsibility for building public housing, and, under political pressure to cut public spending, government also expected housing associations to compensate for reduced grant levels by borrowing private money – a precursor to the rather idiotic and lazy slogan of 'more for less', one consequence of which was to significantly curtail risk-taking.

Backing the housing association sector became ideological, but not just along party political lines: the Blair/Brown governments of 1997–2010 only built 7,870 council homes. Housing associations did a reasonable job of delivering new housing, within the limits of available finance, but their supply was inevitably not adequate to meet the demand. For decades Britain has produced insufficient housing to accommodate not just population growth but also the changing demographics of household composition. Politicians have been slow to understand the imperative of new housing supply, and ideology has held sway over action. It is widely accepted that about 250,000 new homes need to be built each year in England: since the turn of the century the average has fallen about 75,000 short each year.

Housing associations

It is now quite common to hear complaints about housing associations being remote, empire-building megaliths, interested much more in development than in management. But if housing associations are so unloved, why is this? There are, of course, a variety of reasons – a belief that size has not generated efficiency of scale but remoteness and an uninterested arrogance; instances of poor quality workmanship in new-builds and then, critically, an unwillingness to take complaints seriously, take responsibility and put things right; an insensitive bureaucracy; and that old perennial – poor maintenance. Perhaps underlying all of these is a disappointment that they so willingly forfeited any sense of independence, and acted largely as sub-contractors to the local state, which swallowed up all the nomination rights to new lettings.

Some of the charges do justifiably stick. With their stupid 're-branded' names and vacuous assertions about tenants/services/communities 'being at the heart of all we do', one is right to be unimpressed, even suspicious. But at the same time one needs to beware of a simplistic approach which equates 'small' with 'good' and 'large' with 'bad'. It is not the fault of large housing associations that government abandoned its role of funding council housing. That withdrawal left a vacuum which housing associations have partially filled. It was government which collapsed the grant rate, forcing associations to borrow privately. Avoiding a default became the absolute priority of the regulator so as to ensure that all the wheels didn't come off the sector's credibility with private lenders. Big associations do use their financial muscle to build new homes, and a good thing too – but isn't that the least that they should be doing with financial muscle?

The problem perhaps lies in the fact that the sector (and the regulator) has allowed power and influence to flow from spreadsheets – the number of units; the asset base; and strong cash flows – rather than from successfully identifying what makes associations different from other housing providers, and then strengthening that. Tenants risk simply being viewed as rent-paying units. At the same time there is far too little protest about the relentless cuts in government funding – down (for example) from £11.4bn in 2009 to £5.3bn in 2015 (a reduction of 47%!) – as well as cuts to 'adjacent' services (e.g. health and employment) which are so critical to the prospects and well-being of their tenants. The sector has lost any radical edge it had, and is felt by some to be too cosy with governments which do not put housing, or people, first.

Then Boris Johnson lobbed a pebble into the pond: when he campaigned to become Mayor of London, he struck a chord when he complained that the label of 'affordable housing' was applied too narrowly to housing for people on low incomes or state benefits alone and that, given the high cost of housing in London, it should be extended to (for example) young couples with a joint income of up to £60,000. As the 'cake' was shared out more widely to address this hitherto unheralded example of housing need, it was inevitable that some resources would be diverted from building for social rent. The sweetener for associations – but not tenants – was that 'affordable rent' was defined as a rental level up to 80% of market rent.

Funding models

I do not pretend to have an insider's understanding of the funding models of large housing associations. Many of them seem to have raised money using very complex financial instruments: the business model is paramount. But there is an issue of mission drift: in 2015/16, out of almost 190,000 new homes built in England, only 6,500 (3.6%) were for social rent, i.e. low-cost housing for people on low incomes. A year later the comparable figure was below 5,400, or 2.5% of all completions. It looks as if the profits from developments for sale on the open market are going to 'affordable rent' programmes rather than to social rent, and that people who need social rent housing are being left to the tender mercies of the private sector.

It is not completely fair to criticise all large housing associations for being in some ways unresponsive. Some have been genuinely innovative, and have sought new approaches to the rapidly evolving needs of their tenants. And yet, and yet … there is a problem. It lurks within the very terminology 'housing association'. The term covers too many disparate types of organisation. It is very hard to see what it is that links together a large association, a medium-sized one and a small specialist one – beyond a commonality of constitution and a common (but 'one-size-fits-all' and unimaginative) regulator. 'Association' is defined as 'a connection or cooperative link between people or organisations', or 'uniting in a common purpose'. It is increasingly unclear how that concept applies to housing associations – should there be a commonality of purpose between landlord and tenant? That seems to be increasingly rare. Customer care programmes and call centres may well have cut costs, but they are extremely impersonal, and entirely unaccountable. They only partly answer human-scale needs.

We seem to have forgotten that housing is not just about bricks and mortar, it is about people. In the early 1980s, some London local authorities still had housing welfare officers, whose job it was to help new tenants deal with practical issues so as to aid their settling in. That seems like a very distant dream today. Housing associations with their roots in the 1960s were not set up in order to build an asset base – they were a front-line, humane response to the abominations of landlords like Rachman, offering security of tenure and dependable housing management. One of the great lies of recent times was the fatuous assertion by the DoE (as it then was) that it was 'the department of place' – all government departments are departments of people, and it behoves them to remember that fact.

Are housing associations private or public?

An interesting question is whether housing associations are private or public organisations. The answer varies, and will depend on the size and focus of each association. The reality, though, is that nowadays most housing associations are indistinguishable. They have lost local connectedness, which does not mean connectedness with an area on Google Maps, but with real people living in a locality. While it is true that the big associations re-invest their profits – sorry, 'surpluses' – into providing more units of housing, they behave in many ways like private housing companies. Nothing wrong with that, perhaps, but it then becomes questionable whether they can justify their charitable status, especially since most of them pay their board members. It looks more and more as if 'charitable' describes their privileges, not their obligations.

The supported housing sector ('supported housing' refers to the integrated provision of housing with support, which can sometimes be so intensive as to border on care) has been struggling badly due to unsympathetic government and generally uninterested (and sometimes downright hostile) local government, but there is precious little show of solidarity between the different 'wings' of what likes to portray itself as a single sector. Indifference does, though, seem to have been sanctioned – the regulator has failed to promote the well-being of small and medium-sized associations, and especially specialist supported housing providers. But then this is the same regulator which has consistently refused to countenance any nuance of designation, which in turn has led to the endless idiocy of small supported associations being exploited by their larger, property-owning 'peers', and of being assessed by the regulator against criteria which are patently irrelevant.

Perhaps this is not all the regulator's fault – after all, it was central government which abdicated its responsibilities in 2003 by handing control of funding streams for vulnerable people to local councils, despite pretty clear evidence that they had a negligible track record in assisting the client groups which are covered by that rather unforgiving label. What started off as a ringfenced fund of £1.8bn had by 2014 become an unringfenced fund of £1.6bn.

Funding cuts

Many councils took proactive steps to cut the funding further. Nottinghamshire was one of the most celebrated and brutal councils: an SP budget of £27m in 2004 was cut by 65% in 2012; a further 35% cut was planned for 2014, leaving an overall budget of £8m in 2017. Derbyshire cut its budget by 81% over three years. These were by no means the only councils which, when faced with the need to save money, visited savage cuts disproportionately on those least able to fend for themselves. Local government claims to be the natural strategic housing body, a claim which is tested by the fact that homelessness has risen by 169% since 2010. The great difficulty for the providers caught in these crosshairs, of course, is that organisations which seek to support people who fall between the gaps in services are themselves likely to fall between the gaps in funding. It is a cruel irony that supported housing should be cut when it saves money: the problem is that it saves money to the public purse, rather than only (or mainly) to its funder. Thanks to the embers of localism, the local tail wags the national dog.

These cuts matter for two reasons. First, supported housing providers work with and on behalf of those whom mainstream housing associations choose to ignore; second, they maintain a close relationship with their clients, thereby ensuring the sort of connectedness and advocacy which the best housing associations once promoted more routinely. By working with marginalised groups, however, these providers risk themselves becoming marginalised. We are frequently reminded of the benefits of communities, without seeing their drawbacks. I recall a colleague from a homelessness agency who sought planning consent for a development of six flats in central London, for which the council received 840 written objections! Apart from the obvious disappointment in realising that 840 people had such strong feelings against homeless people that they were moved to put pen to paper, this does raise compelling questions about the validity of a planning system which is so immune to social progress. Is there a case for taking social housing developments outside the remit of the planning framework? But of course communities rarely define themselves by what they are, and much more frequently by what they oppose. They are intrinsically excluding: and it is at least arguable that social innovation takes place despite communities, not thanks to them.

Connected organisations

This is why it is important to have organisations which 'smell the cordite', that is, which are able and willing to stand up to powerful interests on behalf of their client groups, and which are able to harness the talents and experiences of their client groups in themselves helping to shape the services they receive.

I am not trying to argue that 'small is beautiful'. Just because an organisation is small does not mean that its connections to its client base are exemplary: on the contrary, small organisations are just as capable as large ones of being manipulative, ineffectual and self-important. The important factor is the quality of their relationships with their clients, and then whether those relationships assist their clients towards Maslow's notion of self-actualisation. At its best, that is the strength of the voluntary sector.

It is beyond doubt that there are sub-sections of the population who have been left behind. The cliché declares that 'a rising tide floats all boats' – not if they are holed below the waterline it doesn't. These sub-sections have been failed: they have been failed by public services; they have been failed by the market; tragically, they may also have been failed by their own families. The voluntary sector, in the form of specialist supported housing providers, may well represent their best (and last) chance of having a future.

And it is here that the large housing associations can have a valuable role to play. They should stick to what they do best – but they could and should offer more practical assistance and financial support to their more precarious colleagues in the supported housing world who are trying to maintain that connectedness with their clients in housing need (and 'financial support' does not mean clever wheezes to make a quick buck out of them!).

What matters is almost always that which cannot be counted. When George Peabody established the Peabody Donation Fund he declared that the aim of the organisation would be to 'ameliorate the condition of the poor and needy of this great metropolis, and to promote their comfort and happiness'. Promoting happiness would be a noble goal for today's housing associations – but are any of them up to the challenge?

Final thoughts

by Don Macdonald

Introduction

Writing these final thoughts in July 2019 is rather difficult, to say the least, given the current situation in the UK with both main political parties split, the threat of worldwide economic slowdown and the uncertain political landscape in the UK and other countries such as the US and Italy. As one economic commentator stated, the effects of recovering from the 2008 crash include 'distorted prices, hidden inflation, constrained wages and conflated debt with equity'[1]; *The Guardian's* economics editor wrote: 'sooner or later there will be a serious downturn ... because there has not been a recovery from the "big one" a decade ago'. There is also the Brexit effect, currently unknown, let alone the effects of a 'No Deal' Brexit, while tariff wars and economic uncertainty have heightened the risks of world-wide recession.

Then there is the prospect of an unpredictable Prime Minister Boris Johnson, bringing with him 'a powerful sense of trepidation', according to one conservative newspaper's business editor. The new Prime Minister also has an aversion to the so-called 'nanny state' and measures like the sugar tax, and has 'no natural affinity for the voluntary sector'[2].

We argue elsewhere for an end to austerity, but this Prime Minister's economic approach has been described by a City editor as, 'a path of fiscal incontinence the likes of which the UK has never seen'. The Prime Minister also supports 'deregulation in areas as diverse as medical research and the environment, free ports (…free enterprise zones) reforms to stamp duty and infrastructure'. Since then the list of 'incoherent spending' has increased to include hospitals, HS2, 20,000 police (are there enough police stations for them?), fibre broadband, additional school spending, funds for forgotten towns and shipyards, social care for the elderly and other pledges. The total bill goes up all the time, and yet substantial tax cuts have been promised – there will be an October budget and it is unclear how this will all be funded. The aforementioned editor concludes, 'It's even less credible than Jeremy Corbyn's election manifesto last year'.

---

1 Bill Blain City AM accessed 1.1.19 http://www.cityam.com/270222/we-have-paved-way-next-financial-crisis

2 Third Sector accessed 23.7.19 https://www.thirdsector.co.uk/boris-johnson-win-mean-voluntary-sector/policy-and-politics/article/1591240

These final thoughts are about how civil society could be regenerated and the role of the non-profit sector in this process. Regeneration must also encompass economic regeneration, and so I will try to look at that. I believe that economic regeneration is too important to be left to the politicians or economists. These are very uncertain times. In July 2019, whatever we write, we will undoubtedly get something wrong.

Failure of the system

Civil society is confronted by many issues. First, it must overcome the enormous divisions within UK society. Poverty and inequality have recently increased, with young people being the most pessimistic about their future here. As John Harris wrote in *The Guardian*:

'*Social mobility stalled. Deindustrialisation carried on apace. Insecurity skyrocketed. The complexity of modern society burst into public debate. And our sources of information eventually fragmented, with two key effects. Malign forces found new openings. More generally, we are now close to losing any coherent sense of who "we" are.*'

Sir Paul Collier, one of the UK's most distinguished economists, states that 'capitalism is not working' across most of Britain, particularly in our 'forgotten communities'. This is especially true in English and Welsh regions. He adds that 'George Osborne talked of a "Northern Powerhouse" but we remain as far as ever from a capitalism that works for many British towns'. This led to 'a mutiny against injustice' in the Brexit vote. Collier criticises the government for allowing London to suck in so many resources and for its laissez-faire approach, such as allowing 'outright managerial looting such as at BHS'. Others point out that London has the highest poverty rates[3]. Collier is also critical of the Labour Party's current policy, stating that 'it is easier to imagine it wrecking those parts of the economy that still function than rescuing those that don't'.

Austerity

The failure of the economy has been compounded by the May government's continued imposition of unprecedented levels of austerity, as Chapter 12 demonstrates. The cuts have been spread across every area, including social care, public health, policing and education, but not pensions and health, though many experts think the proposed increase in spending on the NHS is still insufficient. The imposition of cuts via Universal Credit (UC) has met almost universal criticism from many agencies, including the Audit Commission and the Resolution Foundation (chaired by a

3   Institute for Fiscal Studies accessed 23.7.19 https://www.ifs.org.uk/publications/14193

former Conservative minister). The government is now responding with a few changes to UC, though it still maintains a freeze on benefits except pensions. A hostile environment on benefits and tax credits seems to have come into force among benefits staff, with long delays and cuts, while numerous appeals are being won by claimants.

The results of this austerity, at levels that seem unprecedented since the 1920s/30s, are that it appears that people's health has declined, prospective life spans have deteriorated, poverty and debt levels have grown and crime has increased, along with problems such as homelessness. The Brexit vote showed the dismay and disillusion of vast numbers of people whose economic situation has either deteriorated or not improved since the 2008 crash. This also means that non-profit organisations are facing greater demands, while at the same time smaller organisations are finding it harder to acquire funding.

The May government's claim that it was ditching austerity would appear rather insubstantial, according to most commentators[4]. Apparently many of the cuts are still to come through. The government has now met its spending target and surely should increase spending, if only to forestall the impending slump predicted by the Bank of England, OECD, the IMF and many others. It is short-sighted in the extreme, as any first year economics student knows, to reduce investment – low productivity and poor growth have resulted, whatever other damage the worldwide downturn and Brexit are also doing.

Community stress

Another example of the stress on civil society is that community cohesion has been hit by the closure of numerous post offices, libraries, pubs and working men's clubs, while public transport has been allowed to decline outside London and conventional church attendance has reduced severely. Longstanding working-class solidarity has been hit, with trade union membership declining; traditional employment has been attacked, with service jobs exchanged for manufacturing jobs and full-time employment exchanged for limited or zero hours contracts. Social media has exacerbated divisions and, possibly as a direct result, racism seems to be on the increase and reports show that discrimination against BAME people is still pervasive in many different spheres, including employment[5] and juvenile justice.

The government has also enforced a 'hostile environment' on Windrush residents, as Chapter 8 illustrates, while at the same time restricting migration from refugees and migrants, as Chapter 11 shows. Another target

---

4   Institute of Fiscal Affairs accessed 6.1.19 https://www.ifs.org.uk/publications/13517

5   Nuffield College accessed 29.1.19 https://www.nuffield.ox.ac.uk/news-events/news/new-csi-report-on-ethnic-minority-job-discrimination

for drastic cuts has been local authority spending, with cuts so large that many councils have used up their reserves and several local authorities are on the brink of bankruptcy. And there are still more in the pipeline.

Government performance

The government's performance affects the economy, society and the non-profit sector in a whole range of ways. There used to be a post-war political consensus in the UK about the mixed economy, NHS and the welfare state, until Margaret Thatcher's government changed that and introduced privatisation and competition into public services, which, combined with austerity, has had a debilitating effect. Recent headlines about governmental performance are depressing: 'rail shambles'; 'bed-blocking rises'; 'broken probation service'; 'financial chaos facing councils'; 'NHS ... shocking infrastructure'; '"Chaotic" government reforms are failing in education'; 'social housing decline'; 'deepening crisis in the social care sector'; 'social care disaster looms'; 'hospitals are in a state of "war"'; 'Carillion collapse set to cost taxpayers £148million', and on and on.

The May government was finding it difficult to design and implement viable new policies, particularly around preventive services, because 'nothing is happening except Brexit ... and the civil service, local government and the NHS still operate on a model of crisis management, which costs more than it would to tackle the success of problems'[6].

Privatisation appears to be failing; outsourcing companies are going bankrupt, while the prison crises and failures in court services and disability assessments show how ineffective these measures have been. The new NHS funding, although it is increasing, has been described by Polly Toynbee as too little too late – just 'a sticking plaster budget'. Another commentator has said that it appears that the UK is trying to run a Scandinavian level of social care and health services while charging only US-level taxes (the UK currently has the lowest top rate of tax in the G7). NHS policy seemed to be moving in the right direction, away from competition towards co-operation, as one health think tank pointed out, but privatisation continued to increase in 2018-19.

The May government appeared to respond to the many different problems confronting society by rushing to implement seemingly poorly considered policies and by claiming that it will solve homelessness, young people's mental health and other problems without real prospects of success as no great resources are being allocated. As Charles Fraser points out, there needs to be greater support and specialist housing for different excluded groups,

6   Mara Airoldi Interview Guardian accessed 24.1.19 https://www.theguardian.com/society/2019/jan/16/mara-airoldi-brexit-lost-generation-public-services

such as ex-offenders and homeless people. The government seems to have given up producing any real solutions to social care funding by withdrawing its so-called 'dementia tax', without introducing any new policies, just allocating relatively low levels of funding in the last Budget and initiating some integrated service pilots. It has resorted to introducing untried services, such as the Health Minister Hancock's endorsement of GP at Hand, an untested online diagnosing service, and promoting Alexa[7].

I could even argue that the government appears to be in an ongoing disagreement with itself, not just with the obvious example of Brexit. One hand of the government, the NHS, needs staff from the EU and abroad to staff our hospitals and care homes, while another department issues visa restrictions for medical staff, many of whom are returning to their home countries because of the Brexit effect. The NHS then has to employ more agency staff, all of which leads to the 'worst ever staff and cash crisis', according to *The Guardian*. Likewise, Amber Rudd's response to the Windrush crisis was hampered by her own officials' incompetence, so much so that she had to resign over it. The government cuts youth services drastically, but then funds services targeted at the uniformed services for young people (Girl Guides etc) and those doing community service (National Citizen Service).

It cuts services and staff in prisons and appears surprised when problems result, such as more drug-taking and riots. It cuts the police and tries to ignore the subsequent rise in crime or misunderstands the effects of cuts, as shown in the Audit Office report on police services. It preaches the need for restraint on spending, but continues with expensive prestige projects such as Hinckley Point Nuclear Power Station, HS2 Rail, Trident missile replacement and aircraft carriers ('out of date already', according to one senior army officer), or a Prime Minister's pet projects such as grammar schools and the much criticised National Citizen Service, with its expensive overheads and marketing programme for participants[8].

This government's reorganisations are unsuccessful, such as the unpopular Lansley NHS reforms, while the privatisation of probation services appears to be driven by ideology rather than hard evidence, and in consequence is failing and will be reversed[9]. Part of the problem is that there is too little joined up thinking: the worst example is social care, where the government increases resources moderately for the NHS while at the same time squeezing social care so hard that hospitals are bed-blocked and care companies go bankrupt.

---

7   Pulse Today accessed 24.1.19 www.pulsetoday.co.uk/news/gp-topics/it/new-health-secretary-says-he-is-a-patient-of-babylons-nhs-gp-app/20037070.article

8   CYP accessed 29.1.19 https://www.cypnow.co.uk/cyp/news/1158468/ncs-trust-to-spend-up-to-gbp75m-on-marketing-campaign

9   D Faulkner accessed 22.1.19 https://www.law.ox.ac.uk/centres-institutes/centre-criminology/blog/2018/05/criminal-justice-after-worboys-or-criminal

Education

There has been concern that the UK has been slipping behind Germany in technical education since the 19th century, and one report highlights that there are 600,000 job vacancies in the technology sector in the UK[10], yet the government has cut FE college funding, its University Technical College initiative is disappointing and its cuts could decimate adult learning within two years. Another government reform was the creation of the Apprenticeship Levy, but the result has been fewer apprenticeships than before, with many training providers wound up, while some companies have used these funds for MBAs.

Management and productivity are worse in the UK than in comparable countries. According to research by John van Reenen and others from MIT, this is because of the larger proportion of 'atrociously managed firms'. The researchers state that this is due to a lack of training and the fact that competent managers are undervalued in the UK. Our chapter on non-profit management training shows that we take this seriously. Organisations such as Clore Social Leadership have a good track record for delivering training that encourages trainees to take responsibility for their own learning in order to develop skills and enhance their potential.

Non-profit sector

In spite of the depressing state of the economy, the effects of austerity and the political situation, the non-profit sector is still very strong. One example is the extensive role of volunteers, with the RNLI's 4,700 volunteer lifeboat crew members, the Samaritans' 20,000 volunteers, Cancer Relief's 40,000 volunteers and 580,000 charity trustees. However, it is very heterogeneous indeed; even the different names reveal the differences, whether we call ourselves the third, voluntary, non-governmental, community or non-profit sector. All – well, almost all – organisations pride themselves on their independence and it is difficult to get them to agree policies and strategies.

In fact it would appear that the representative bodies do not represent the sector with as much force as, say, the CBI represents big business, the Federation of Small Businesses (FSB) represents small businesses, or sector organisations, such as the Society of Motor Manufacturers, represent their own sectors, even though the non-profit sector is as large as the car manufacturing sector. The membership is proportionally higher; thus NCVO represents 14,000 out of 390,000 non-profit organisations, much more representative than the FSB which has 126,000 members out of 5,700,000 SMEs. However the NCVO is mentioned only a couple of times in the government's Civil Society Strategy, and then only as the source of some

---

10   Workplace Insight accessed 1.1.19 https://workplaceinsight.net/shortage-of-tech-skills-and-600000-job-vacancies-costing-uk-economy-63-billion-a-year

information. One must wonder if this weakness relates to the government's lobbying restrictions. (The Coalition Government imposed restrictions on lobbying and campaigning by charities, while the current government tied 40 charities into non-disclosure agreements as part of funding contracts.)

Over the past few years, the non-profit sector has been criticised over a range of issues and the reputation of charities has declined. The problems included unfair fundraising, where a new Fundraising Regulator has almost certainly improved practice. Yet small non-profits have been hit very hard by the decline in government grants and the shift to competitive contracting[11]. Also, small non-profits have issues regarding how they have kept up with the switch to more digital communication, with 50% still lacking a website.

Evidence also shows that only 9% of the charity sector is 'non-white', compared to 12% of the private sector and 11% of the public sector[12]. BAME voluntary organisations have been hit even harder by funding problems over recent years, while a number of national charities even have no BAME staff or trustees.

The problems for charities have also included allegations of abuse of vulnerable people, particularly children, which in turn have led to a decline in donations to some charities involved. The big seven disability charities have been criticised for low service user involvement, taking radical steps (e.g. closing homes) without consultation and becoming too involved in government employment schemes[13].

There is clearly a growing divide between small non-profits – with low-profile, high energy, real street credibility, and service user involvement – and the national UK large non-profits, 'with big reserves, highly paid chief executives, and expensive central London HQs'[14].

Civil society

In addition, civil society is much, much larger than just the formally constituted non-profit organisations. According to the NCVO there are between 600,000 to 900,000 unincorporated organisations working in the community, such as sports teams, arts groups and preservation societies, most with no paid staff at all[15]. These are clearly a vital part of civil society.

11 Lloyds Foundation accessed 1.1.19 www.lloydsbankfoundation.org.uk/assets/uploads/too-small-to-fail_Feb-2015.pdf
12 UK Civil Society Almanac (NCVO 2018) accessed 1.1.19 https://data.ncvo.org.uk/almanac18/
13 Steven Dodd accessed 24.1.19 https://core.ac.uk/download/pdf/42137763.pdf
14 Peter Beresford Guardian accessed 6.1.19 https://www.theguardian.com/society/2012/apr/24/tax-relief-row-big-charities-priorities
15 NCVO Almanac 2018 accessed 1.1.19 https://data.ncvo.org.uk/almanac18/

In its strategy the government defines these services as 'individuals and organisations when they act with the primary purpose of creating social value, independent of state control'. One example is the 400,000 people who volunteer to be blood donors, as opposed to be being paid for giving blood, as in many countries. However, civil society is clearly under stress, which the strategy does acknowledge, but skates quickly over. One example is that significantly fewer younger people are donating blood.

The government's Civic Society Strategy makes no mention of key issues such as racial discrimination, nor does it allocate any new resources, though the strategy does push for greater emphasis on social value in commissioning. It promotes the value of youth work, but emphasises the National Citizenship Service, which has been strongly criticised[16]. It stresses digital involvement, although it acknowledges that 'a significant part of the population remains excluded and the latest data shows that the slowest adaptors of basic digital skills are the disabled and older people'[17]. The government has also dropped its 2015 pledge to increase volunteering.

The strategy has been described as 'disappointing' by Rob Wilson, a former government minister. Paul Streets of the Lloyd's Foundation has stated: 'The strategy recognises the need for "new approaches in communities that have not benefited from growth", but it fails to translate that recognition into tangible and targeted action to address the most marginalised people and places'.

Alongside the government strategy, the Rowntree Trust has led an investigation into civil society, 'Civil Futures'[18], with at least 12 other recent investigations by other non-profit networks. Quite rightly, the Rowntree report places a great deal of emphasis on examining racial inequality, which is included in the main report and is also the subject of a separate section. The report also highlights the 'white middle-classness' of the sector. However, I have to say, I feel the Rowntree recommendations seem rather idealistic and unattainable to an old cynic like me, and my worry is that it may just turn out to be a non-profit sector version of the Big Society – in other words, without much effect if local and central government ignore the recommendations.

An example is that sustainability will not be introduced in the UK without the government making key decisions about power supplies or car engines or imposing new taxes on consumables, such as the successful tax on carrier bags (see Green New Deal, below).

16 LGA accessed 1.1.19 https://www.local.gov.uk/about/news/lga-national-citizen-service-funding-should-be-devolved-local-youth-services

17 ONS accessed 6.1.19 https://www.ons.gov.uk/peoplepopulationandcommunity/householdcharacteristics/homeinternetandsocialmediausage/bulletins/internetaccesshouseholdsandindividuals/2017

18 For more information, see Civil Society Futures Open Democracy: civilsocietyfutures.org/ (accessed August 2019).

As Marshall Ganz said, 'Deep reform has rarely come from within government', so enormous efforts are needed. The UK system of government centralises most funding and power within central government. The chapters about St Mungo's and the Windrush campaign show how committed individuals and small organisations can have an enormous effect, even on issues where injustices are deep-rooted and government has officially imposed 'a hostile environment'.

A more practical report was the Barrow Cadbury Report, *Surviving Austerity*, in 2013, which made the following recommendations:

1. Embed the principles of fairness in all decisions that a local authority takes, and use resources to reduce poverty and inequality.
2. Commission services for social, economic and environmental value.
3. Make co-production a standard way of getting things done.
4. Make well-being for all the primary goal of all public services.
5. Develop sustainable local economies.

Economic regeneration

Economic regeneration is needed, but this must reach those parts that other initiatives do not, that is, not just the City of London. A report from Sheffield Hallam University finds 'no evidence that the spectacular growth in employment in London in recent years has been of any direct benefit to the labour market outside southern England'[19]. It also reports that older industrial towns are increasingly becoming dormitories for men and women who work elsewhere on low pay.

One target for regeneration would be the additional training programmes to train the 40,000 new tech jobs that are currently needed, as it is 'forecast that in 20 years 90% of all jobs will require some element of digital skills'[20]. Another measure would be to train up people for the increasing needs in the care industry, as demand continues to rise with an ageing population. A further measure would be a significant increase in building social housing, as recommended by Charles Fraser in his two chapters, and an expansion in Community Land Trusts.

The non-profit sector already plays its part in economic regeneration. Social Enterprise UK claims its research in 2018 shows that social enterprises

19 Sheffield Hallam University accessed 29.1.19 https://www4.shu.ac.uk/mediacentre/economy-older-industrial-towns-essentially-stagnant
20 Good Things Foundation accessed 19.1.19 https://www.goodthingsfoundation.org/bridging-the-digital-divide

contribute £60 billion per annum to the economy, 3% of GDP and three times more than agriculture[21], while NCVO claimed the voluntary sector contributed £17.1 billion in 2016-17.

Sustainable energy

The UK's carbon reduction and energy policies have recently been upset by the collapse of two nuclear power station projects. Thus another option to create employment while meeting green targets would be introducing a Green New Deal, already being pioneered in the US, and covered in Chapter 10 by Kathryn Engelhardt-Cronk. This is also being promoted over here by the UK Green New Deal group, who are pushing for more work on energy sustainability, including insulating the eight million homes with solid walls and installing almost 40 million smart meters. Certain new measures will meet opposition, as in France, so obviously people will need to organise, campaign and lobby to achieve this.

Regional regeneration

Political devolution appears to have benefited Scotland and Wales. Economic regeneration must reach those parts that the UK's main growth points of finance, media and high tech do not reach – that is, the forgotten towns, not just the big cities. Research by Cambridge University underlines how towns in the poorest areas of England have been hit hardest by austerity, while other research shows that *'Globalisation and regeneration has favoured the more dynamic large cities, as has the move from traditional industry to finance and service sectors. This has only exacerbated the already declining old industrial heartlands and has led directly to the feeling of abandonment and anger that an increasing number of their residents feel'*. Local government has been hit hardest by cuts. In addition, the government appears to have given up on regional development in England, abolishing its regeneration body and nine regional development agencies. An alternative is community wealth building, as epitomised by the Preston model, led by the local council, and Alston Moor regeneration, both covered in Chapter 3.

Another aspect of social exclusion, which has worsened with the cuts in adult learning provision, is digital exclusion. 'Currently, 21% of the UK population lacks at least one basic digital skill, leaving the equivalent of 11.3 million adults in the UK digitally exclude' according to a report by the Good Things Foundation. The report goes on to state that 'Providing everyone in the UK with the essential digital skills they need by 2028 will lead to a benefit of £15 for every £1 invested, and a net present value of

---

21   https://www.thirdsector.co.uk/social-enterprises-contribute-60bn-economy-year/social-enterprise/article/1493336

£21.9 billion'[22]. This also provides opportunities for local regeneration if funded properly.

Non-profit role

This book argues that the non-profit sector can play a key role in the regeneration of the UK. This is definitely not just about pumping more funds into large non-profits. One risk is that very large non-profit organisations may lose touch with what they have been set up for, or with their own staff; the recent report on Oxfam highlights this danger[23], as does Jonathan Glennie's reflections on Save the Children[24]. But, as Charles Fraser's chapter on St Mungo's shows, it is possible to create viable structures to consult staff and service users successfully in larger non-profits.

Two other examples, which show the great value of non-profit activity, spring to mind. First, the response to the Grenfell Tower disaster by small non-profit organisations was much faster and more effective than the statutory responses. Second, in 2018, Citizens Advice investigated and then issued a 'super complaint' about loyal customers being overcharged by insurance, mortgage, phone and broadband firms. This led to the government eventually starting to take action, even though the charity is much less well-funded than the Competitions and Markets Authority, which had avoided imposing the necessary measures.

Society is under great stress at this time, with many people feeling without hope and with gloomy economic forecasts making prospects worse. This book highlights a range of endeavours and campaigns in the non-profit sector, although there are crucial areas we did not cover in great detail, such as environmental projects. Like all good non-profit organisations, this is a team effort and, although we have different views on some topics, we all value self-help, community action and social innovation. Currently the organisations, staff and volunteers in this sector are under great stress and are having to develop ways of coping. This book highlights a range of effective actions and strategies from very different organisations and people in the non-profit sector. I believe the contributors demonstrate that the sector has a crucial role to play in civil society and provides a beacon of hope in these difficult times, with its positive and cost-effective solutions.

---

22   Good Things Foundation accessed 19.1.19 https://www.goodthingsfoundation.org/bridging-the-digital-divide

23   BBC accessed 29.1.19 https://www.bbc.co.uk/news/uk-england-oxfordshire-46910085

24   Jonathan Glennie https://www.opendemocracy.net/en/transformation/at-what-cost-reflection-on-crisis-at-save-children-uk/

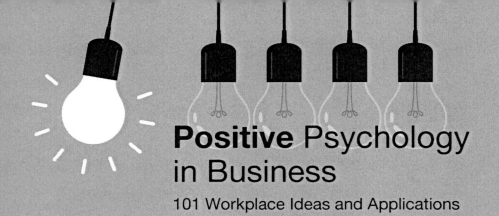

Positive Psychology in Business

101 Workplace Ideas and Applications

*P*ositive Psychology in Business draws together key ideas and techniques for applying positive psychology and strengths-based growth to a wide range of workplace settings and cultures. Mounting evidence demonstrates the returns that come from ensuring that employees feel hopeful about the future, encouraged to be their best selves and appreciated for who they are and what they do, creates a platform for engagement and creativity. Positive psychology places a clear emphasis on recognizing strengths and creating positive feelings, and guidance on how to achieve these two aspects of human life is a running theme in the book.

Each of the practical, to the point chapters addresses an urgent need or a crucial issue of contemporary working life. Sarah Lewis shows how any leader, manager, organisation or employee can apply positive and appreciative concepts such as building social capital, creating a feel-good workplace, encouraging positive deviation, leading authentically, creating conditions for change, having courageous conversations and building happy teams to create effective growth. Hope, gratitude, willpower, forgiveness and kindness are recognized as indispensable qualities in a time of crisis, not added extras to be ditched when the going gets tough.

Whatever the particular business challenge, whether it is improving performance, leading in turbulent times, or even how to downsize, you will find a chapter that offers ideas about how to do it in a positive, appreciative way.

Sarah Lewis,
Appreciating Change

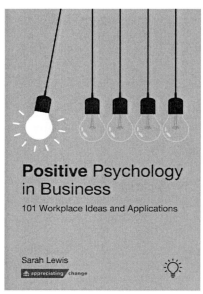

Buy your copy here:
www.pavpub.com/positive-psychology-business
£27.95 | 290pp | Paperback | 9781912755578 | Jun 2019